DATE DUE			

JOHN FOSTER DULLES

A Reappraisal

JOHN FOSTER DULLES

A Reappraisal

BY RICHARD GOOLD-ADAMS

GREENWOOD PRESS, PUBLISHERS
WESTPORT, CONNECTICUT

Library of Congress Cataloging in Publication Data

Goold-Adams, Richard John Morton.
    John Foster Dulles; a reappraisal.

    Reprint of the ed. published by Appleton-Century-
Crofts, New York.
    1. Dulles, John Foster, 1888-1959. 2. United
States--Foreign relations--1953-1961.
    [E835.D85G6 1974]   973.921'092'4 [B]   74-9272
    ISBN 0-8371-7638-7

Originally published in 1962 by Appleton-Century-Crofts, Inc.,
New York

Reprinted with the permission of Hawthorn Books, Inc.

Reprinted in 1974 by Greenwood Press,
a division of Williamhouse-Regency Inc.

Library of Congress Catalog Card Number 74-9272

ISBN 0-8371-8371-7638-7

Printed in the United States of America

Contents

Introduction

THIS is a book about an American by somebody British. Therefore it is understandably open to criticism on national lines.
But as a lifelong friend and admirer of the United States I have
tried to look dispassionately at Mr. Dulles's record from the point
of view of the Western alliance as a whole, to assess his role as the
natural spokesman of that alliance, and to see in particular where
and why things sometimes went wrong between his country and
mine. I believe profoundly in American leadership of the Western
world, and it is in a spirit of frank inquiry that I have felt bound
to say what I think. Certainly none of the many Americans to
whom I owe so much for advice and assistance have ever suggested
that I should do anything else. I am aware, nevertheless, that the
result may possibly be misunderstood, and it is for this reason that
I hope that all those in the United States who may read this American edition of my book will first pause and accept the spirit in
which it is written.

Nothing has been changed from the British edition except for
the insertion of one minor correction of fact and some editing for
style. These pages therefore contain expressions and sentiments
which have not been tailored for any special section of opinion.
What I have done has been to write about Mr. Dulles because I was
genuinely puzzled by him. In Britain, at least, he nearly always had
a bad press, and it was sometimes difficult to get at the truth. Now
I feel that I have done so, and I have tried to adjust some of the
impressions left by the type of comment sometimes made during
his lifetime. The truth is, of course, that Mr. Dulles was such a

challenging figure that almost nothing one could write about him would be likely to meet with the agreement of even six people chosen at random.

Although this book is based on a good deal of published material, its character and many of its judgments have been determined by personal contact with a large number of people who knew Mr. Dulles well, both inside and outside the United States, and by my own memory of him. Those I saw included leading political and military figures who often had to deal with him, diplomats, civil servants, his own staff, journalists, lawyers, personal friends and members of his family. Naturally, some were his admirers and some were among his severest critics. But to all I am extremely grateful for the time and trouble they took in helping me, and for their kindness in bearing with my many questions. I know that they often spoke as freely as they did because they knew they were not going to be quoted or mentioned by name. In particular, I hope that nothing I have written may distress Mr. Dulles's family.

Mr. Dulles's papers are understandably voluminous, and it will probably be several years before his definitive biography is published. But so much material is already available in various forms that the problem is what to omit rather than what to look for. I emphasize this because I do not want anyone to start by thinking that this book is intended to do the work of Mr. Dulles's ultimate biographers. It is what it says—a reappraisal of Mr. Dulles's record so far as we can see it now. Some day, when the actors have all left the stage and the historians alone can read their lines, a different kind of book will emerge. Until then, I think this one can lay fair claim to having a valid contribution to make.

Among the publications to which I would like to make my special acknowledgments are the two books which have preceded mine, *John Foster Dulles* by John Beal (Harper & Brothers, New York) and *Duel at the Brink* by Roscoe Drummond and Gaston Coblentz (Doubleday & Company, Inc., New York); Mr. Dulles's own two works, *War, Peace and Change* and *War or Peace* (The Macmillan Co., New York); *A Testimonial to Grace* by Avery Dulles (Sheed & Ward, New York); *The Spiritual Legacy of John Foster Dulles* edited by Henry P. van Dusen (Westminster Press, Philadelphia); and the privately circulated memorial booklet by

Arthur H. Dean. I am also particularly indebted to *The New York Times, New York Herald Tribune,* Washington *Post, Christian Science Monitor, Life, Harper's, The New Yorker, The Times, The Daily Telegraph, The Guardian, The Sunday Times, The Observer, The Economist, The New Statesman* and *The Spectator.*

—RICHARD GOOLD-ADAMS

JOHN FOSTER DULLES

A Reappraisal

CHAPTER 1

What Kind of Man?

TWO men more dissimilar in character, personality and sense of values than John Foster Dulles and Anthony Eden, would be hard to find. They have been well described as "the Roundhead and the Cavalier," with differences as profound as those between the two elements in the English Civil War. There was much that was Cromwellian about Dulles, and his disdain for Eden as well as Eden's complete distrust of him brought to an end the whole wartime era of Anglo-American partnership, with effects that can be felt to this day. The friction, which began long before the Suez crisis of 1956, was endemic from the moment that Dulles became Secretary of State on January 20, 1953. Indeed, without prejudice to either side in the terrible drama of the internal British crisis over Suez, it is not too much to say that if Dean Acheson had continued to be Secretary of State, instead of John Foster Dulles, the Suez military operation would probably never have happened.

What kind of man was Dulles that this can be said of him, even though he had many of the qualities of greatness and history may in the end concede that he was a great Secretary of State? Dulles was unquestionably cast in a big mold, with a sharper intellect, greater energy, and stronger convictions than ordinary men. He towered above the rest of the Eisenhower Administration, including in many respects the President. If his character had been less complex, without the vital flaws which it certainly contained, he would have been universally recognized as the outstanding American of his time. As it was, he provoked an extraordinary mixture of veneration and hatred during his lifetime; and, since his death, in spite of a surge of emotion in his favor towards the end, his

3

memory had remained contentious and intriguing, a constant challenge to anyone who tries to assess his six unbroken years of power.

The irony of John Foster Dulles was that, while among some people he succeeded in appearing as a man of tremendous principle and courage, to others his main impact was of a devious and tortuous nature which could be neither relied upon nor readily understood. And both impressions were correct. Inside himself Dulles fought a continual battle between principle and what appeared to him as realism, a realism moreover which sprang essentially from his long experience as a lawyer. Thus, while he believed in certain ends and standards with the passionate and unshakeable force of a Presbyterian elder, he also interpreted the ways and means of achieving his objectives with the casuistry and ingenuity of one of the ablest and most outstandingly successful corporation lawyers ever produced by the New York bar. It was a truly formidable combination, but not one that was likely either to endear him even to those who thought he was on their side, or to insure success when he was dealing with human and political problems.

Dulles himself strove very hard to do the right thing. In his earlier days at the State Department he ransacked his conscience again and again in the intensity of his effort not to allow either his pursuit of principle to become naive or his recognition of the need for realism to deny and kill his principles. This struggle inevitably produced a certain lack of confidence which had to be hidden beneath a hard exterior. As time went on his confidence as Secretary of State grew. He came to a working arrangement with himself and he was certainly never rattled by merely external criticism from other people. The final result was a man who eventually mellowed a little and, although nothing was basically different, the more general approval which seemed to reach out towards him in the last year of his life reflected a genuine easing of the inflexible forces driving him on. He was slow to learn that diplomacy is not law. But in the end he half came to do so, and if he had lived till the close of the Eisenhower Administration his place in history would undoubtedly have been clearer. Certainly the ineptitude and folly of Washington's handling of the 1960 summit would have been avoided.

One of the keys to Dulles's public life is to realize how profoundly he was fascinated by the work and failure of President Woodrow Wilson. It was not only that he was determined never to forget the lesson that policies and ideals are useless if you cannot get them accepted. He also knew Woodrow Wilson quite well personally, first when Wilson was president of Princeton and later when he served under him on the American delegation to the Versailles Peace Conference of 1919. And Dulles found in Wilson a kindred spirit for whose motives and beliefs he had the most sincere respect. Wilson, like Dulles, was both deeply religious and at the same time imbued with a desire to build a better world outside America itself. Each in his own way was characteristic of one of the best strains in American life, looking back to the spirit that moved the men who founded the United States, and yet looking forward also to the day when the goodness and wisdom of these original ideals should be as widely accepted among other nations as they have been in the history of America. Dulles was almost as great a reader of the papers of the founding fathers as he was of the Bible.

The exterior of ruthlessness which Dulles presented to the world did not altogether belie what lay within. He scarcely knew the meaning of compromise, and insofar as he understood it he despised it, an attitude of mind which has been much too readily overlooked when considering his relations with Britain. The British so-called "genius for compromise" led Dulles to misunderstand and suspect the behavior of many other people in London besides the unfortunate Anthony Eden. Dulles could be unswerving, hard, dogmatic, opinionated and even cruel, if he believed, as he often did, that the end justified the means. In the exceedingly tough school of American corporation law where Dulles grew up, it is not enough merely to defeat your opponent; he must be crushed and pulverized so that he can never be a threat again. And this training, when coupled to the religious strength of Dulles's convictions, goes some way towards explaining both the inner hardness and the lack of gentleness which Dulles sometimes allowed to show through his character.

What made Dulles's intransigence even more formidable and difficult to live with was his righteousness. As was once said of Mr.

Gladstone, it was not only that he always knew he had a card up his sleeve, but he was also convinced that God had put it there. Dulles believed in God's sovereignty, that there is in fact a moral unity and purpose in the world, and that in spite of the attacks of the wrongdoers we are moving step by step towards the light at the end of the tunnel. And as an elder of the Presbyterian church he knew that he was one of those appointed to show the way. This gave him a sense of mission, a certain fatalism, and an imperviousness to physical danger which carried him unshaken through many a crisis. Unfortunately the obverse of these qualities was that a note of preaching crept into almost all that he said on formal occasions, in both the written and spoken word, and this sometimes so irritated his audience—particularly abroad—that it robbed him of the full effect which he would otherwise have had. Opposition, moreover, only tended to make him more sure of his ground. And when, for instance, unknown people wrote to him, as they did by the thousand, saying how much they admired his determined stand on principle, even though they disagreed with him, this confirmed him in his own views and in the righteousness with which he held them.

One of Dulles's most telling weaknesses was his inhumanity. To some of those who knew him really well this does not ring true. To them he was very good company, generous and loyal. But they were a tiny élite, and his range of close friends was smaller still. To the rest of the world Dulles was an intellectual aristocrat, a man out of touch with the rough and tumble of humanity. His whole background was superior, sheltered, successful, safe. And whereas many men would have found this no insoluble hindrance to understanding others, Dulles's superb intellect made the problem for him virtually insurmountable. He was the last person in the world to suffer fools gladly and all his life he was able to concentrate on something else when compelled, however briefly, to mix with people who bored him.

Although his father's income had always been modest, Dulles was certainly never hungry; then, as soon as he had to earn his own living, he made such a success of it—though at first he drove himself to utter exhaustion in doing so—that he was never in touch with people who knew hunger, poverty, or personal failure. Believing in addition that everyone must make the most of themselves in life and that those who do not have something wrong with them, he never seriously tried to understand the people whose misfortune it is to get left on the bottom rungs of the ladder. Nor did he even read fiction about them. His mind ran to Aristotle or Plato, law or foreign affairs. Once, quite early on at the State Department, Dulles was distressed by the way his speeches never seemed to strike any sparks among the poorer and undeveloped nations, and he asked a friend about it. When the friend frankly explained that his words were cold and lacking in any genuine appreciation of the outlook and problems of these countries because he had never understood any kind of underdog, Dulles accepted the point and asked, "Is it too late to learn?" To his dismay the friend shook his head and truthfully replied, "I am afraid it is."

Dulles was never consciously dishonest. He did not, that is, tell deliberate lies. But he often said things which left an impression of untruth and it was this which, taken together with his habit of thinking out loud and, therefore, of appearing to support a course of action when he was in fact only considering whether it might be worth supporting, made many people regard him as double-faced and untrustworthy. As one British diplomat put it, "Dulles seemed to have a Monday morning policy, another for Tuesday morning and yet another for Tuesday afternoon, so that you never knew where you were with him." Sir Anthony Eden certainly felt this very strongly indeed, and he was constantly puzzled and frustrated by what seemed to him to be Dulles's baffling tortuousness.

The explanation was complex, like Dulles's character, though it was quite consistent with his own attitude to the world and the problems which confronted him. Above all Dulles was a man who, like his mortal foes, the Communists, distinguished between ends and means. Once he was clear what he was trying to do, everything else took on a secondary importance and he worked with great single-mindedness. He was essentially a manipulator of other people, a mastermind pulling here, persuading there, possibly threatening somewhere else. The words he would use in these maneuvers were all subordinated to the central purpose, and if they rang a little false or seemed inconsistent when mutually compared, that was a pity, but it did not matter. In actual fact they never were quite untrue or inaccurate if taken literally and examined under a microscope, although the general innuendo which nine people out of ten read into them might sometimes appear to suggest that they were.

Dulles was thus always a lawyer. That is to say he treated his own words as if they were a part of a legal document, with all the careful loopholes which may be deliberately left in the small print of a contract, the part which the unwise and casual negotiator does not read with sufficient care before signing. Dulles never felt that it was his own task to do his opponent's work for him. This legalistic approach, apart from being used to cover apparent inconsistencies in Dulles's own mind, also helps to explain his rather discomforting procedure in two other ways as well. First, he possessed to an almost superhuman degree the ability to switch his mind off and on at will. He would accordingly treat one problem as one case and another as a completely different one, and the fact that in the world of diplomacy other people might see a close connection between the two could mean almost nothing to Dulles himself, with the result that he sometimes appeared bafflingly inconsistent without necessarily either intending to be so or being aware that he was. Secondly, and of great importance in understanding him, he had a tendency to treat international problems as if they were legal issues in which he was committed solely on behalf of his client. His client was the United States, no more and no less, certainly not the Western alliance and not even the Administration. And once he was clear in his own mind where he thought his client's interest lay, he would set out to look for any evidence which would support him, brushing aside, even seeking to suppress, anything which weakened his case. It was a matter of concentrating on one single-minded purpose and going for it almost regardless of cost.

The brilliance of Dulles lay in fact in his powers as a legal negotiator. When he worked on Wall Street he was more widely respected than liked, and it was not for nothing that he was said to have been the highest-paid corporation lawyer in the United States. Shrewd, tough and unyielding, a typical remark he has left in the memories of colleagues when he was senior partner in the big firm of Sullivan and Cromwell was, on being given a report on how some case was proceeding in which the firm was involved:

"Well, don't go down unless you have to." Don't, that is, lower the figure you are asking, don't reduce your minimum terms, don't whatever you do give way unless you have fought to the limit. As Dulles saw the proposition, if his client was asking, say ten million dollars for the sale of a property but had told him privately that the rock bottom price was eight million dollars, he as his client's legal representative must avoid at all costs letting the other side have any inkling where the minimum lay. It was entirely up to them to find out by meeting him in a battle of wits. And when it came to wits Dulles usually won.

In strict terms of business this is, of course, no more than the normal bargaining which has gone on since the dawn of time. Dulles was extraordinarily successful at it because he combined so many gifts in one person, from the extreme lucidity of both his grasp and his powers of exposition to his enormous knowledge and his unerring memory, from an inspired ability to calculate risks and gamble on them to the run of luck which any outstandingly successful man must possess. And it may well be asked, as Dulles certainly asked it, "Why, if all this is morally right in business, is it morally wrong elsewhere?" Dulles, with his own very high principles, felt quite clear in his own mind that, if people chose to misinterpret his methods and behavior in the general field of life, they only showed that they had wholly misunderstood how any good lawyer would go about serving his client's interests.

There is a good deal to be said for the downrightness of the Dullesian argument. But whether it is really wise to carry these tactics too directly from national to international law, from the courtroom to the diplomatic conference table, is another matter. Dulles sometimes fell down in his dealings with other countries by treating friend and foe too much alike. To him they were all instinctively rivals and opponents of his own clients, America. He made too little allowance for the emotions and sensitivities of those he was working with; he discounted the need for loyalty if there is to be mutual trust; and he tended to work on the basis of fixed images without making adequate allowances either for change or for human idiosyncrasy. Thus, it is with something of a shock that one comes up against the ultimate realization that Britain appeared to be more of an enemy than a friend. In theory Dulles was far too sensible and well steeped in the realities of the international situation not to regard Britain as the most important of America's allies in the cold war—though he also considered that the Federal German Republic played the key role in the West after the United States. But in dealing with the British in practice his whole instinct and approach was to attempt to outsmart them, to suspect them, and to treat them as one of the other corporations in a complicated legal case which his own client must somehow win in the end. For the motives, evolution of thought and inhibitions of the British themselves, Dulles simply did not have any time.

Compared with these rather bleak and forbidding aspects of his character, Dulles had another side which was much more sympathetic and attractive. He was a man with a good sense of fun, rather than a sense of humor. Although no one seems to remember anything notably humorous that he actually said himself, he enjoyed jokes and stories by other people. He could be a delightful companion for those he was fond of, he often had a twinkle in his eye, he was not above pulling anyone's leg, and he was sentimental towards his family. He was courteous and good-mannered to people he met, and thoughtful about those whom he regarded as dependent on him. He also knew how to live. He greatly enjoyed French cuisine and appreciated French culture, speaking French fluently through frequent visits to France, sometimes for long periods, throughout his life. Although Dulles certainly did not rank among the millionaire rich, he earned a good deal of money during his lifetime and certainly from at least the age of thirty onwards he knew nothing but the best. Unlike many of the rich, he learned how to spend his wealth with taste, how to insure that his friends enjoyed the comfortable and generous hospitality he could offer them, and above all how not to lose touch himself with the simplicity of outdoor living or the beauty and challenge of nature.

For much of his life Dulles lived in New York. When he first married, he and Mrs. Dulles moved into an apartment, but once he had begun to establish himself in his law work, they bought a house at 72 East 91st Street. He himself designed the pleasant, though rather complicated, ironwork on the front door and on the little balconies, and there he gave some of the best dinner parties in New York, choosing the wine, the caviar, and the food with the greatest personal care. For weekends he also had a house about forty-five miles out on Long Island, standing among the dogwood trees on a hill overlooking the very pretty inlet with the romantic name of Cold Spring Harbor which runs down from Long Island Sound. It was a large house, but, because he and Mrs. Dulles were willing and able to pay they had a staff of servants who looked after them well. In the summer Mrs. Dulles moved down there from about June onwards, and he commuted each day to Wall Street.

Dulles played tennis until he injured his back, and of an evening after getting down to Cold Spring Harbor he always tried to put in nine holes of golf. The real love of his life, however, was sailing. This he had enjoyed from earliest childhood on the waters of Lake Ontario, when his father had been Presbyterian minister at Watertown in upper New York State. After he grew up he continued to keep a boat of his own in that part of the country, and it was on a sailing expedition in 1929 that he first set foot on Duck Island, which he eventually bought in 1941 and to which he retired for periods of rest and contemplation while he was Secretary of State. In the life of tremendous pressure and constant travel that Dulles lived, Duck Island became his personal sanctuary, totally private and absolutely cut off from the raging twentieth century. He and Mrs. Dulles were almost always quite alone there, except for a lighthouse keeper at one end of the island. They lived literally in a log cabin, without a telephone, without electricity and usually without even a battery radio. Even members of the family were not often welcome, very few friends ever stayed there and all staff, whether domestic, secretarial, or official, were rigidly kept out. Stores were shipped in by arrangement with the lighthouse keeper, but otherwise John Foster and Janet Dulles were on their own. Duck Island was his perfect way of renewing his terms of reference with life. On it he was able to renew those vast springs of nervous and physical energy which carried him ahead of other men.

Dulles was in every sense a big man. He came from a remarkable and dynamic family. He lived almost the whole of his life against a background of top level achievement, both on his own part and by those with whom he worked and associated. He was a Republican American in the sense that he represented power, privilege, and personality in a huge country which believed that it knew what had made it great. He held office at a time when the United States was at the pinnacle of its strength in relation to the rest of the world, when it stood virtually inviolate even from the Soviet Union. At the time that he died in May, 1959, nothing had so affected the entire American nation since the death of Franklin Roosevelt. He threw his formidable gifts into the battle against Communism and, whatever may be the criticism of his tactics or methods, both sides now recognize that in his own right he became a force that no one could ignore.

Two broad questions nevertheless remain, and they should be kept constantly in mind when considering his life and work in detail. For his real place in history will depend on the final answers to them. First, in the conditions ruling at the time, did he or did he not pursue the right policies in dealing with the Communist bloc? Secondly, as spokesman for the leading member of the Western alliance, how far did he succeed or fail in rallying the forces of the free world to accept those policies? In particular, how did America's relations with Britain fare while he was Secretary of State?

CHAPTER 2

The Background of the Early Years

JOHN FOSTER DULLES came from a thoroughly sound background. He was born in Washington on February 25, 1888. His paternal great-great-grandfather, Joseph Dulles, had landed at Charleston, South Carolina, in 1776 and his maternal great-grandfather, Mathew Foster, at New York in 1815, both families being of British descent, the Fosters from County Durham. John Foster was the eldest of five children, two sons and three daughters. His father was the Reverend Allen Macy Dulles, a Presbyterian pastor of Watertown in upper New York State, and his mother, Edith Foster, the daughter of an eminent lawyer, soldier, and diplomat, John Watson Foster, who became Secretary of State under President Benjamin Harrison in 1892, four years after the young John Foster Dulles was born. As if one Secretary of State in the family was not enough, one of his uncles by marriage, his mother's sister's husband, was Robert Lansing, who was appointed to the Department of State during the First World War by President Woodrow Wilson and served from 1915 to 1920. Thus, when Dulles himself assumed this high office in 1953, he was the third member of his family to hold it within sixty years, a record unique in the history of the United States.

Dulles's childhood was spent against a family background of high respectability, good connections and modest finance. As a boy he was influenced to a quite surprising extent by the great traditions of American pioneering, which made him in adult life more of a Westerner and more suspicious of city people than his own New England and cosmopolitan upbringing might suggest. This element in his character was later to accentuate his inherent incompatibility with Sir Anthony Eden. It was encouraged from a very early age, first, by the outdoor life which the family led, sailing, canoeing and fishing on Lake Ontario, and secondly by the way in which Dulles's grandfather, John Watson Foster, the former Secretary of State, took a fancy to his grandchild and saw a great deal of him. John Watson Foster was a good raconteur with an excellent memory, and he used to tell John Foster Dulles endless stories about his early days in Indiana. He remembered very clearly the genuine frontier atmosphere of the log cabin from which he had ranched, hunted, and traded in the years before the Civil War. He had then fought with distinction in the Civil War, rising to the rank of Brigadier General on the Union side. All this made a profound and lasting impression on his grandson, who recalled with feeling the romance of the period when he received an honorary degree at the University of Indiana nearly a century later. In his baccalaureate address on June 12, 1955, Dulles declared:

> My grandfather, whose name I bear, exerted a great influence over my life, and he had ideals and purposes which I have tried to make my own. He was a deeply patriotic American. He belonged to the period which saw this country rapidly developing from a small Atlantic coast group into a nation that spread across the continent. He fought to preserve the Union, and then on diplomatic missions as Secretary of State he helped to spread the influence of this nation throughout the world both in Europe and in Asia.
>
> He deeply revered his forebears, who had been pioneers in settling this part of our nation. He wrote a private booklet ... in which he told for his descendants the story of his own forebears: his grandfather (my great-great-grandfather) on whose grave I laid a wreath today, and his father.
>
> To me that story has symbolized the spirit of our nation. I vividly recall being told of how my great-grandfather, as a young boy of seventeen, had struck out into the West to get away from what seemed to him the overpopulated East. After a foot voyage of exploration, he had fixed upon a forest tract in southern Indiana as a future homestead. He then brought his aged parents—his father was then seventy-nine years old— from the East to settle here and gained a livelihood by hunting and by cutting hickory for hogshead hoops and floating them on a raft down the Ohio and Mississippi Rivers to New Orleans, where hogsheads were needed for molasses. Then he would walk back through the twelve hundred miles of dangerous

trails from New Orleans to his log-cabin home here in Indiana. Finally he became a farmer, a merchant, and then a judge in the growing community he had helped to create.

That spirit of enterprise, that vision, that industry and that rugged independence have been characteristic of our nation.

By the time Mathew Foster had begun trading on the Mississippi in pork and corn (maize), Joseph Dulles, the other great-grandfather was established as a merchant in Philadelphia, where he died in 1818. Although his son and then his grandson, the Reverend Allen Macy Dulles, John's father, remained in the old established Eastern states, they and people like them constituted the essential springboard which made possible the whole thrusting development of the American continent during the nineteenth century. The part played by Allen Macy Dulles in helping to form his eldest son's character was an important one. He frequently accompanied his father-in-law, the patriarchal John Watson Foster, and his son on their fishing expeditions, and while he could not match the range of experience of the older man he was a forceful churchman with a mind very much of his own. He instilled into his whole family from the earliest years a sense of duty and a feeling for righteousness. He had a tremendous love of language and of argument; for the mere fun of it, for instance, he would take the line that the sun rises in the West and then try to get his children to prove him wrong. He was generous to people who were down and out, giving them his coat or allowing them to sleep in the cellar or indeed any part of the house that was not in immediate use. He had great influence on his five children and through him they became self-reliant, adventurous and uninhibited. To outsiders the Dulleses were a formidable and unusual family, just a bit larger than life, full of spirit and character.

John Foster Dulles grew up in Watertown, where his father was minister. He attended the local grammar school and high school, graduating from high school in 1903 at the early age of fifteen. He was a very clever boy but otherwise a normal one, except for being unusually religious as a result of his father's Presbyterian ministry. John Foster, with his three sisters and younger brother, Allen, attended most of the services for which the Reverend Dulles was responsible. They also went to Sunday school and on weekdays were frequently present at prayer and other church meetings as well. They learned long passages of the Bible; John Foster was once supposed to have been able to recite the whole of St. John's gospel by heart. And in the summer they sometimes sang hymns together when walking to and from church. Other special memories of summer were of the cottage at Henderson Harbor on Lake Ontario which was owned by the grandparents, John Watson Foster and his wife. It was twenty miles from Watertown, and members of the family used to go out there either on horseback or in a buggy or by bicycle. Robert Lansing was often there too and John Foster Dulles learned much from him, though it is doubtful whether he ever really liked him. Besides John Watson Foster and to some extent Robert Lansing, the other national figure Dulles knew well in his teens was Woodrow Wilson, who was president of Princeton when he was an undergraduate.

When John Foster's school days came to an end in 1903, he and one of his sisters were taken by his mother to Lausanne in Switzerland for a year to learn French. This was stretching the family budget of about $3,600 a year, but Mr. and Mrs. Dulles ate into their small capital in their determination that their children should gain experience of the world outside the United States. If they had been able to afford more, John Foster would have stayed longer, since he was still very young to go on to a university. At it was, Dulles's father borrowed from the bank on more than one occasion in these years in order to get the family to Europe. They traveled very cheaply on slow boats and lived economically, doing a great deal of bicycling. But as a result John Foster Dulles got to know France and other parts of the continent of Europe unusually well at an early age, and all his adult life he spoke French fluently. Dulles went to Princeton in the fall of 1904 at the age of sixteen. Even though he was old for his age, he was still remarkably young to take this step, and later in life he himself rather regretted that it had come so early.

At Princeton Dulles was a brilliant student. He studied philosophy and began to show his talent for getting a given amount of work done in less time than other people. Tall, active and good-natured, he was also serious and somewhat shy, yet with a mixture of intellectual self-confidence, high spirits and, oddly enough, a

flair for gambling. Good at mathematics, he was apparently ready
and willing to quote odds on almost anything at the drop of a hat.
Some of this may have been engendered by the game of mumblety-
peg which the Dulles children had played at home. As a child John
Foster had loved it. Much of his spare time at the university was
spent playing cards. All his life he enjoyed bridge, when he could
find the time for it, and he was an exceptionally good player. Right
to the end as Secretary of State, he read the bridge column in the
Washington Post over his breakfast.

In 1905 the family moved from Watertown to Auburn, further
west in upper New York State, when the Reverend Allen Dulles was
appointed Professor of Apologetics at the Theological Seminary
there, an appointment which implied the argumentative defense of
Christianity and one for which John Foster's father was eminently
suited. In May, 1907, John Foster himself, at the age of nineteen
and with still a year to go at Princeton, received a most unusual
invitation which he accepted eagerly. This was to accompany his
grandfather, John Watson Foster, to the second Hague Peace Conference (the first having met in 1899) at which this distinguished
American figure was a special counsel to the Chinese delegation,
as a result of his long association with Chinese affairs. The conference, called jointly by President Theodore Roosevelt and Czar
Nicholas II to discuss the general problem of peace, met from June
to October, and the young Dulles managed to become one of the
general secretaries of the conference, partly through his knowledge
of French. It was a dramatic beginning to a lifelong concern with
international affairs and it understandably made a vivid impression
on him. Although Dulles was once supposed to have said in later
life that his not going in to the church, like his father, "nearly
broke my mother's heart," his parents were fully ready to accept his
wishes in the matter and the fact that he did eventually choose
law, as a possible avenue to diplomacy, was greatly influenced by
this adventure at The Hague with his grandfather.

Back in Princeton Dulles entered his final year. He had a knack
with exams and was one of those fortunate people who are quite
unworried by them. Consequently, although he took his time at the
university very seriously, he also never allowed university life to
press too hard on his other interests. During vacations, for instance,

he pursued his love of wind and water, sailing on Lake Ontario in the catboat which his father had given him when he was fifteen. He took with him his younger brother, Allen Dulles—later head of the Central Intelligence Agency (CIA)—and they sometimes went off camping and sailing for several days at a time. John Foster and Allen also introduced skiing into upper New York State. Allen had a Norwegian violin teacher who got them interested in the sport, and, after skiing in Europe, they managed to buy some skis in a shop in New York City and brought them home. As regards Princeton, Dulles was quoted many years later in the *Daily Princetonian* as saying: "The major benefit I got from Princeton was participating in Woodrow Wilson's courses where I gained my interest in public affairs."

On graduation in 1908 his senior thesis, entitled "The Theory of Judgement," won him the Chancellor Green Fellowship which was worth $600 and valid for a year at the Sorbonne. As a result of this striking success the family crossed the Atlantic again that summer and took an apartment in the Boulevard Raspail in Paris, where John Foster, now aged twenty, became an active student in international law. This included the study of philosophy under Henri Bergson, and, full of energy as usual, he made sure that it also involved him to the full in French university life. He is reputed on occasion to have worn his hat stuffed with newspapers in order to take the blows of the truncheons of the Paris police during student riots. More seriously, this period cemented in his mind a regard for French culture that endured for the rest of his life, transcending the normal bias in favor of France with which many Americans used to grow up.

His time at the Sorbonne also settled finally the question of the church or the law, and it was with the law in mind that after leaving Paris Dulles spent six weeks with a Spanish family in Madrid. On returning to the United States he went to Washington and lived at the house of his grandfather, John Watson Foster, in order to pursue his law school studies at George Washington University. He did the course there in two years—1909 to 1911—instead of the normal three, with the result that, although he passed his exams with flying colors, he was refused a law degree on the grounds that he had not completed the required three years' residence. It was to be a quarter of a century before the authorities relented and granted a degree to one of the ablest students ever to pass through the university.

During this period in Washington, John Foster, now in his early twenties, burned the candle at both ends. He spared himself nothing in his studies but also, for virtually the first and last time in his life, embarked upon a gay social whirl. For such an eligible bachelor in the nation's capital this could be had for the asking. He did not, however, go in only for dances and young people's parties. Living as he was at his grandparents' home, he had an open entrée into Washington society of all kinds. He attended his grandmother's famous receptions and made friends of his own generation in the families of those who came to them. Among these was the President, William Howard Taft, with whose son, Robert Taft, John Foster Dulles struck up a lifelong friendship. This was not broken later on either by Senator Taft's bitter disagreement on policy when Dulles was briefly in the Senate in 1949, or by Dulles throwing in his lot with Eisenhower during the early stages of the presidential campaign in 1952.

In 1911 Dulles returned to his father's house at Auburn in order to cram for the law exams which would enable him to qualify for the New York State bar. It was this which led to his engagement to Janet Avery. Her family came from Auburn and he had known her for some time. She and her parents had all visited Paris when he was at the Sorbonne. In spite of his gay life in Washington, he had not forgotten her, and it was a home-town romance which grew into a deep and very happy companionship that sustained him until he died. They were married the following year, 1912, after Dulles had completed his law exams.

Mrs. Dulles had been described at the time that she married as "a girl of much charm, poise, courage, spirit and wit." She devoted her life to him and was of enormous assistance to him when he entered public affairs. Without any strong views of her own, she was nevertheless downright sensible, and clear in her reactions to his. She read in draft form almost every important speech he ever made, providing him with the firsthand reactions of a keen but admiring critic. Perhaps after their children were born she tended to continue to be more of a partner and support to her husband than most mothers of families have time to be. But, if so, it was a natural tendency with a husband whose outstanding gifts nevertheless left him vulnerable in a number of ordinary ways. Although Dulles did drive a car, he was never at home with anything at all mechanical. He never took photographs and was apt to find dialing a telephone number a slight challenge. Mrs. Dulles had the same rather indrawn nature as he had, perhaps without overmuch sense of humor, and she shared his strong convictions about right and wrong. When he became Secretary of State she traveled with him on many of his long journeys, facing their occasional but real dangers with the same imperturbable feeling for destiny that he had. It was a perfect marriage.

After passing his bar exams in 1911, Dulles had to get a job. Without a law degree this turned out to be extraordinarily difficult. At first he went the rounds of the New York law firms without success, and it was not until his ever willing guardian grandfather pulled still further strings that he was given a chance as a law clerk at fifty dollars a month with Sullivan and Cromwell, one of the oldest and most respected law firms on Wall Street. Having taken him on, however, his employers lost no time in making good use of him. William Nelson Cromwell had built up a lucrative business in Latin America in addition to his corporate law at home, and Dulles's foresight in learning the rudiments of Spanish almost at once earned him a business trip to Central America, the first of several. On one of them he caught malaria and nearly died, owing his life to very large doses of quinine which were administered to him. This unfortunately affected his optic nerve and meant not only that he had to wear glasses but also gave his left eye the very slight malformation which was noticeable for the rest of his life. After some months with the firm his salary was doubled and it was on June 26, 1912, that his wedding with Janet Avery took place at Auburn. They spent their honeymoon in the Catskill Mountains and returned to set up their first home in the small apartment in New York, with the aid of a minor but extremely useful legacy which his grandfather started paying him ahead of time. Within three years, however, Dulles was making enough money from his law to render this unnecessary. His enormously successful career had begun.

CHAPTER 3

Through the Two World Wars

IT WAS well over forty years from the moment when Dulles first entered the law firm of Sullivan and Cromwell in 1911 to his swearing in as Secretary of State in January, 1953. This was in fact the main span of his adult life, the time in which most men make whatever mark they are going to make and then retire. Dulles became Secretary of State about a month before he turned sixty-five and, while he had indeed been a world name for at least a decade before that, it is remarkable that virtually the whole of his impact on history should have come at such a late age. What happened during the years between? How was it that this eminent lawyer became a widely accepted expert on international affairs even though he had never been elected to any political office, never held any permanent government post, and never even been a regular writer of any kind?

In answering this question it is convenient to divide Dulles's life into the period of over thirty years before Thomas Dewey invited him to become the official Republican Party spokesman on foreign affairs in 1944, and the period of just under ten years from that moment until his appointment to the Department of State. For most of the earlier period Dulles was a corporation lawyer in New York and, except towards the end, foreign affairs were only a sideline. At the same time much of his legal work was overseas and, while also building up a rich domestic practice, he always had a foot firmly planted in international law, "international" in the sense more of commerce and finance than as between nations. In this way Dulles gained valuable personal experience through travel,

many personal contacts in other countries, and a practical knowledge of the habits of thought and work in foreign capitals.

The process had begun with Latin America, so that shortly before
the United States entered the First World War in 1917 Dulles at
the age of twenty-nine was well qualified to accept a special mission
in Central America as an agent of the State Department. He was
selected for this job by two men who knew him well, President
Woodrow Wilson, whom he had admired since Princeton days, and
his uncle who was now the Secretary of State, Robert Lansing. His
task was to insure that Panama did not allow any German intrigue
to secure the blocking of the Panama Canal, which had been
opened to commercial shipping only three years before; and to
investigate and, if possible, counter known subversive activities
in Nicaragua and Costa Rica. In view of Dulles's handling of the
Suez Canal crisis thirty-nine years later, it is interesting to reflect
how especially knowledgeable he must personally have become in
his younger days about the law and politics of international canals,
even more so since the senior partner of his own law firm, old Mr.
Cromwell, had himself been the original legal adviser to the New
Panama Canal Company and to the Panama Railroad Company.

When the United States did enter the war, poor eyesight prevented Dulles from doing military service. He was accordingly
enrolled for home duties and attached to the general staff, at first
as a captain and later as a major. Major Dulles, with his legal
knowledge, was assigned to the War Trade Board as assistant to
the chairman, Vance McCormick. This body assumed authority
over America's wartime foreign trade, and his work was largely as
a liaison officer with the parallel organization, the War Industries
Board, which mobilized industrial production at home: its head
was Bernard Baruch, who became one of Dulles's lasting friends.
The result of this war service was that in 1919 President Wilson
took Dulles along as an economic counselor with the American
delegation to the Versailles Peace Conference, making him legal
adviser to Bernard Baruch, who represented the United States on
the Commission for Reparations. Still only thirty years old, Dulles
was thus able to witness one of the decisive phases of the first postwar era from the inside.

He himself was also at an age, however, when events had a great effect on him, and he took home three lessons from his experiences. First of all, Dulles helped to draft the clauses in the Versailles Treaty which dealt with reparations, and some years later he was to be drawn in as legal counsel to the underwriters of the Dawes loan in trying to clear up the mess to which those clauses contributed. As a result, he was always subsequently quite clear in his own mind that the nature of a peace settlement is just as important as the war which precedes it, if not more so. The failure of Versailles impressed on him that, since it is useless to win the war if one loses the peace which follows, a harsh peace is one which defeats its own ends. He was to apply this lesson with great determination many years later in 1951 when working on the Japanese Peace Treaty as President Truman's special ambassador.

Secondly, as an American spokesman in Paris in 1919, Dulles was partly instrumental in softening the line his country took, implying that Germany had not surrendered unconditionally and that, even if it had, the Reparations Commission was bound by the spirit of the original armistice agreement. This was directly contrary to the demand of the British for fairly substantial reparations from Germany, and his clash with them and other Allies on this point left a lasting impression, which did no good to Anglo-American relations. It was not to be the last time that Dulles found himself standing up for Germany as against Britain. Thirdly, when the peace conference was over and the Senate Foreign Relations Committee had successfully wrecked President Wilson's attempt to put the United States behind peace in Europe and had ruined his plans for the League of Nations, this too affected Dulles profoundly. He learned a sharp and lasting lesson that in America foreign policy depends for its success on carrying Congress with it.

Soon after Dulles returned to Sullivan and Cromwell from his wartime activities and then his peacemaking, they made him a partner. He was now thirty-two and he constantly represented the interests of his clients abroad, traveling fairly frequently, for instance, to Europe. At the same time, by dint of hard work in New York itself he became one of the highest-paid corporation lawyers on Wall Street. Then in 1927, when he was still only thirty-nine, he had a run of luck which made him senior active partner in the firm. Although the senior partner was still nominally Mr. Cromwell, he had long since ceased to take any active part, and Dulles succeeded to the top post after the deaths of two other leading partners, Alfred Jaretski and Royall Victor, and the retirement of a third, Henry Hill Pierce, following a serious illness. Normally his position would have taken some thirty years to achieve; by good fortune as well as merit he had got there only sixteen years after coming in. The other partners who worked most closely with him were Edward Green, Eustace Seligman and Wilbur Cummings.

The general nature of the work which Dulles was engaged in has been described as "drafting corporate charters, bylaws, preferred stock provisions, underwriting agreements, voting trust agreements, prospectuses for new issues of securities, fiscal agency agreements, indentures, mortgages or loan agreements, escrow arrangements, employment agreements, deeds of trust, wills, and other pleadings, the examinations of witnesses and so on. Perhaps it means more to most people, however, to mention some of the actual cases which he handled. Among the earlier ones was the reorganization of the American Cotton Oil Company with the Gold Dust Corporation, the fight for control of the Remington Typewriter Company, the consolidation of the International Nickel Company, the struggle involving the Metropolitan Trust Company and the Chicago and Eastern Illinois Railroad, and the setting up of the Jones Brothers Tea Company Syndicate. After the stock exchange crash of 1929 Dulles was kept busier than ever as a result of the difficulties many companies got into.

On the foreign side much of his work was for American and European banks. He was also the representative in the United States of various Swedish and Belgian financial and industrial interests. He fought cases for clients in Argentina, Panama, and elsewhere. Over a long period of time he was counsel for various American creditors in respect of German government reparation payments; having originally had a hand in the Dawes loan of 1923 as legal adviser to the underwriters, he personally worked, too, on the formulation of the Young Plan. He had a particularly delicate and long-drawn-out operation in defending the New York Life Insurance Company and the French commercial bank, Credit

Lyonnais, when the Soviet government, which the United States at that time still did not recognize, tried to take over sums deposited with them by former Russian citizens. He acted for the bondholders after the collapse of the Swedish Match Company and the International Match Company following Ivar Kreuger's death. He helped Jean Monnet, whom he had known since Versailles, in working out the Polish Stabilization Plan, which was backed by the Federal Reserve Bank of New York. He did work for the Central Bank of China, for the Bank of Spain and, after the outbreak of the Second World War, for the Bank of Poland in its gold reserve case against the Bank of France.

All this inevitably involved Dulles in an immense amount of traveling during the twenties and thirties, though, even so, it could scarcely be regarded as more than a curtain-raiser to the thousands upon thousands of miles which he covered later as Secretary of State. Sullivan and Cromwell had an office in Paris, and when his ship docked he would often catch the train to the French capital to call in there before, if necessary, going on. Much of his business lay across the Rhine, and there was something about the way he got to know the first postwar Germany which reminded him of his early youth in France, except that this time he had work to do, he was seeing things from above instead of below, and he never had a chance to learn the language well. But Dulles always tended to get on easily with the Germans, and he was among those who admired their efficiency. His first visit after the war had been in April, 1920, during which he drove by car through the Ruhr at a perilous moment when bands of Communists were roaming about and trying to seize control. Berlin, Frankfurt, Cologne, Dresden— they were different only in that he knew them better than some of the other leading cities between Paris and Warsaw, Berlin and Vienna. Eventually he opened another Sullivan and Cromwell office—in pre-Hitler Berlin.

What was noticeable about all this traveling, with its personal contacts and its intimate knowledge of national life, was that at no time did Dulles get to know Britain as well as he did France and Germany. His business did not take him there in the same way. He seldom had clients in London, though he had plenty of legal contacts which he maintained through the city solicitors, Linklater and Paines. He was quite fond of London itself, usually staying at Claridges', and he and Mrs. Dulles occasionally went motoring through the English countryside. He liked Cornwall, and they stopped sometimes at Newquay. But by and large, if it was a matter of choice for a holiday, he avoided Britain because he could not stand the food. Thus for a variety of reasons it came about that, in spite of a number of English friends and the traditional respect of American lawyers for their heritage of English law, Dulles never quite understood the British as he did the French and the Germans. And this was a pity both for him and for them, for him because it later made him agonizingly disliked in Britain, and for them because it meant that his lack of sympathy struck an almost mortal blow at the kind of Western alliance that they believed in.

Dulles was always an adventurous man, inclined to scorn physical danger and constitutionally well able to put up with discomfort and fatigue. From the earliest days he made great use of the airplane. He is believed to have first flown when he went up on a cheap sightseeing trip over Paris in the early nineteen-twenties. Then, as soon as commercial airlines began to establish themselves in the United States, he used them fairly extensively. He flew across the Pacific the year before the Second World War broke out when, in 1938, the conquest of long distances over water by air was still in its relative infancy—as he and Mrs. Dulles found when two of their four engines cut out and they very nearly failed to make Wake Island. This side of Dulles's character reflected the pioneer spirit with which he had become imbued as a boy. Like many people who find themselves stretched taut by success in the highly competitive complexities of modern life, Dulles felt a strong need to be able to get away from it all. Golf and tennis, both of which he played, were not enough, and for much of his life he exorcised this need by sailing, later retiring to the primitive remoteness of his famous hideaway on Lake Ontario, Duck Island.

Dulles owned three boats during the course of his adult life. In the early nineteen-twenties the first was the small catboat with which he had grown up and which enabled him to make trips of thirty or forty miles, exploring the eastern end of Lake Ontario. The next, a bigger catboat called the *Duck,* made it possible for him and the family to undertake longer trips, though she still had no cabin and they slept in her only by tying up at night in some sheltered spot. It was on a trip in the *Duck* in 1929, however, when John Foster and his brother, Allen, and their two wives, were away in the boat for over a week that he first set his heart on acquiring what later came to be known as Duck Island. Negotiations there and then with the Canadian owner fell through, because the latter was finding the island far too profitable as a jumping-off ground for smuggling liquor into prohibition-ridden United States territory. Dulles was offered the island in 1933 after prohibition was repealed, but felt that he could not then afford it in view of the depression. The sale finally took place in 1941, when the Canadian owner died and when Dulles himself decided to give up the third and last of his sailing boats, because by then wartime conditions had rendered impossible the kind of major sailing expeditions which he had grown to love.

This third boat had the Indian name of *Menemsha*, with the accent on the second syllable, and she featured prominently in Dulles's life. He bought her in 1933, owning her for eight very happy years during which he sailed her nearly twenty thousand miles. She was a forty-foot gaff-rigged yawl, built in 1916, with an auxiliary engine. Dulles was a bold and able sailor, intrepid but not foolhardy. In the *Menemsha* he and his family and, sometimes, close friends, explored the Great Lakes, then, not satisfied with these inland waters, went down the river past the Thousand Islands and beyond Montreal and Quebec to the Gulf of St. Lawrence and eventually the open sea.

Once, and once only, after sailing the *Menemsha* south from Labrador round the beautiful coast of Nova Scotia, he took her on down to watch the race for the America's Cup, and eventually dropped anchor off the little wooden wharves of Cold Spring Harbor, under the windows of his own house upon the hill. But she made the return journey up the Hudson and by inland waterway. Base was always Lake Ontario, and in cruising to such places as the Gaspé Peninsula, Prince Edward Island, and the Bay of Fundy Dulles needed to plan his trips very carefully. Navigation sometimes called for a high order of seamanship and there were inevitable mishaps. One occurred in 1935 when the *Menemsha* hit a rock at night through a slight error in chart reading; although she was

lucky not to sink, a good deal of internal damage was done by
the force of the impact. Another, on the same trip, was when Dulles
badly hurt his back pulling at the anchor. Several years later he
had to be operated on for a slipped disc, and although this was
put down to a tennis injury the damage, as is often the case, may
have started a long time before.

Dulles worked very hard, normally arriving at his office early and
not leaving before seven, with half an hour or at the most three-
quarters for lunch. Thorough and painstaking, he believed in
careful work rather than sudden inspiration. He was not good at
delegating—as his later record at the State Department showed.
He handled conferences with skill, often reserving his own major
intervention until towards the end when one can have the most
effect. After a conference was over, he would at once dictate his
own notes and then get on with the next job. His appointments
were apt to be tightly compressed and he expected the schedule to
be kept. In squeezing so much into twenty-four hours he set a high
standard, which he believed should be followed by his senior
colleagues as well as his junior ones. To this day new members of
the firm, on looking up his old cases, are apt to be struck by his
"exquisite work."

One of the things which countless people who worked with
Dulles remember about him was his inseparability from yellow
ruled pads of paper, measuring 8½ by 14 inches, which are commonly used in law offices. He always carried one in his briefcase
and would have it either on his desk or on a table near him whenever he was working. At home he filled it with notes and lists of
things to do, and his staff got to dread it when he had been away
for a while. These yellow pads used to go up to Duck Island with
him and come back very full. After Dulles had moved to the State
Department in Washington the government stopped supplying this
particular type of legal-size pad, but he continued to obtain them
from his old law firm in New York where Arthur Dean, his successor as senior partner, insured his supply.

Dulles showed few outward traces of the streamlined mental
effort which was normally being made within. In conversation,
however, he would sometimes lean back in his chair and pull
slightly on a lock of hair behind his head. At conferences he did a

lot of doodling. He liked using a pencil but spent a great deal of time sharpening it, and sometimes even carved designs on it with his knife. Over a drink he very frequently stirred the whisky with his forefinger. For most of his life he was a pipe smoker, but in the nineteen-forties he gave this up entirely and after that did not smoke at all. Dulles appreciated the elegant sophistication and the enormously expensive simplicity of the Sullivan and Cromwell offices up on the nineteenth and twentieth floors of the Bank of New York Building at 48 Wall Street. Down below, the familiar scenes around him, the massive dark columns of the First National City Bank which faced him whenever he stepped into the street, the subway entrance on the corner, the sight of Trinity Church at the end of Wall Street dwarfed in the canyons of the skyscrapers, the memorial on the steps of the old city hall recalling that it was here that George Washington had taken the oath as the first President of the United States in April, 1789, all these gave him a sense of certainty, confidence and continuity, a feeling for American power and the knowledge that he had a part in it.

Towards the end of the nineteen-thirties, however, in the two or three years immediately before the Second World War broke out in 1939, a change began to take place in Dulles's mind. He became restless and disturbed by what was happening in the world. Now in his late forties, there were no more heights to scale in his own legal career, while abroad the mushrooming tragedy of Hitler's Nazism troubled him increasingly. Unlike many Americans, he knew from personal experience what Nazi Germany was up to. Not only was he constantly over in Berlin himself, but he had many Jewish clients there, and distinguished Jews were among his own partners in Sullivan and Cromwell. He had met Hitler only once, some time before, when he and Mrs. Dulles were invited to a concert by Dr. Schacht, at that time head of the Reichsbank. But the position rapidly became intolerable, and Dulles closed his firm's office in Berlin in 1936.

The outcome of all this was that his thoughts turned increasingly to the deeply religious background against which he had been brought up, and to a desire to play some more positive role in international affairs himself. So it was that he attended two conferences in 1937, one in Paris and the other in Oxford. The first was a meeting of intellectuals under the auspices of the League of Nations, which Dulles found in retrospect curiously sterile compared with the second, a meeting of the Oxford Council of Churches. This latter conference set him thinking about the scope for moral action in the world, if Christians were to live up to their principles. As a result, Dulles began actively supporting the work of the churches in their search for peace, by attending a considerable number of conferences and study groups and making public speeches on this theme.

With the same idea in mind he went out to the Far East in 1938 in order to learn at first hand about the long-smoldering war between China and Japan. With Mrs. Dulles he went first by ship to Tokyo, where he talked to leading Japanese ministers and officials, and then to Shanghai and Hong Kong, from where he made a dangerous flight to the seat of the Chinese government at Hankow. After a week in which he saw a good deal of Chiang Kai-shek, he formed a favorable view of the Chinese government and set off for home across the Pacific by air, rightly convinced that there was an alarming danger of war between Japan and the United States. It was on the way in mid-Pacific, quite some time before their flying-boat was due at Wake Island, that he and Mrs. Dulles were dismayed to hear first one of the engines cut out and then another. The plane limped on, slowly losing height, and they only just made it. Once there, they were stuck for a week, until spare parts could be got out to them and major repairs effected. Dulles's reaction was fully in character. He sat down to write a book, partly in longhand and partly by dictation to his wife.

This first book, published in 1939, contained thoughts which his mind had been playing on ever since he had attended the Versailles Peace Conference twenty years before. It was called *War, Peace and Change,* and its theme was that no one can expect to achieve peace without intense effort. Peace must be worked and fought for just as hard as victory in war. Peace requires clear thinking, strategic planning, a willingness for sacrifice, and the dynamism of a true faith. At the same time, if the causes of war are examined, it is clear that war will never be avoided unless alternative methods are provided for bringing about change peacefully. Change, Dulles declares, is inevitable, whether "satisfied"

nations like it or not. And this is why a definite system is vital, such
as that envisaged under Article 19 in the Covenant of the League
of Nations. *War, Peace and Change* makes heavy involved reading.
It is geometric in pattern, idealistic, legalistic, and somewhat tauto-
logical. In real life, a friend commented, "you can't run the world
this way." But it is vintage Dulles. It is more him than his second
book with the confusingly similar title, *War or Peace,* which was
published in 1950 and far more widely read, partly because he was
better known by then, and partly because the writing itself was
competently edited.

When war came in 1939 (though the United States was not to
come in for another two years) Dulles became adviser and legal
counsel to the British, Dutch and Belgian purchasing missions in
the United States. He also pressed ahead even harder with his work
for the churches, taking a leading part in creating a body called
the Commission for a Just and Durable Peace. This consisted of
over a hundred representatives from all the Protestant communities
making up the Federal Council of Churches, and thus directly
represented about twenty-five million people. Some critics have
since asserted that Dulles went in for the Commission for what he
could get out of it, in the sense that its success would be his success
and that this would put his name prominently before the American
public as a pundit on world affairs. This is certainly unfair. For
several years he had felt very deeply about the religious and moral
aspects of peace, and his work for the churches bears the stamp of
completely genuine conviction. He was a patient and skillful
chairman, admired and loved even by many of those who disagreed
sharply with him on points of detail. At the same time, it is an
undoubted fact that as a result of this work he *did* become much
more widely known, with the result that its significance for his own
career was considerable. His efforts for the churches in the international field did in fact single him out as a prominent candidate
for high political office.

Perhaps the best known achievement of the Commission for a
Just and Durable Peace sprang from its publication in 1941 of the
Six Pillars of Peace, criticizing the Atlantic Charter just signed by
President Roosevelt and Mr. Churchill as not going far enough.
This booklet called for some form of continuing collaboration by

all those nations in the world which were interested in peace; some form of international agreement covering the economic and financial actions of one state as it affected another; a definite organization which could promote the revision of international treaties in order to meet changing conditions; the gaining of autonomy by subject peoples; the control of armaments; and recognition of the right of all peoples everywhere to intellectual and religious liberty. This declaration received wide publicity, and the favorable response which it obtained not only in the United States but also in other English-speaking countries such as Britain, Canada, Australia, and New Zealand influenced President Roosevelt in taking a more positive view than he had done hitherto about setting up some kind of international organization after the war. When Churchill had raised this with him he had been somewhat lukewarm, remembering the lesson of President Wilson's setbacks at Versailles. But with the moral support of the public reaction to the initiative taken by the churches the President instructed his Secretary of State, Cordell Hull, to draw up the proposals which eventually led to the conference at Dumbarton Oaks in 1944, and then later to the drafting of the United Nations Charter at San Francisco in 1945.

During the war years Dulles's other activities, apart from continuing with his legal work, included helping to establish the National War Fund, which financed special wartime charities. He also made his first Atlantic flight, under service conditions, to visit Britain in 1942 at the invitation of the Archbishop of Canterbury. There he attended a conference on the spiritual basis of peace, making a considerable impression with his plea that members of the church must "get down into the gutter of international politics and fight for your principles." In addition to all this Dulles continued with his many directorships. Among other companies, he was at various times a director of the Bank of New York, the American Banknote Company, the American Agricultural Chemical Company, the North American Company, the Edison Company of Detroit, the International Nickel Company of Canada, and of Babcock and Wilcox. He gradually became a member of a number of other bodies too, notably as Chairman of the Board of Trustees of the Rockefeller Foundation, and of the Carnegie Endowment for International Peace.

By now, however, the magic year of 1944 was approaching, the year in which he took his final plunge into the muddy waters of politics by accepting the invitation from Governor Thomas E. Dewey, the Republican candidate in the presidential election of that year, to be the Party's chief spokesman on foreign affairs. For Dulles it was a momentous step, marking the beginning of his direct association with government and his eventual transfer from the financial canyons of New York to the political merry-go-round of Washington.

CHAPTER 4

He Speaks for the Opposition

THE first contact between Dulles and Dewey had taken place in rather surprising circumstances in 1937, seven years before Dewey invited Dulles to be his foreign affairs spokesman when he ran for the Presidency in 1944. On this first occasion it had been the other way around and Dulles who had done the inviting. Impressed by Dewey's growing reputation, he asked him if he would join Sullivan and Cromwell as a courtroom lawyer. For Dewey at the time this was a handsome offer. He was still a young man, in spite of the considerable reputation he had just achieved as a prosecutor in a special inquiry into New York rackets, and he would very much have liked to join Sullivan and Cromwell. He therefore accepted in principle, but subject to a certain delay until the special inquiry was finally over. Before this happened, however, he was strongly urged to run for the office of district attorney and, having got Dulles to release him from his commitment, did so, being elected handsomely. From there he later went on to become Governor of New York State, and twice the Republican candidate for the White House.

Although, therefore, Dewey did not join Dulles's law firm, the two of them continued to keep in close touch, and as Dewey's political stature grew he consulted Dulles extensively. This began formally in 1939 when Dewey was just defeated by Wendell Willkie at the Republican Convention in Philadelphia and Franklin Roosevelt was elected for his third term. It flowered into Dulles's national status as opposition spokesman on foreign affairs, when Dewey was defeated by Roosevelt's victory for his unique fourth term in 1944 and then again in 1948 by Truman's success in getting back against the predictions of virtually every opinion poll in the country. Dulles himself played an increasingly prominent part in national politics. Thus in 1944 he criticized the Roosevelt policy at the Dumbarton Oaks Conference, as being too concerned with the possible role of the great powers in organizing the world after the war and paying too little attention to the rights and wishes of the smaller countries. This is of some interest in view of the later charges against Dulles himself as Secretary of State that he impatiently rode roughshod over his allies, despised the neutrals and would willingly have discussed only directly with Russia.

As the Second World War entered its last year in 1945, Dulles's name acquired a particular prominence for sponsoring "bipartisanship," or the concept that foreign policy should not become a major issue between the government and the opposition. This again is particularly interesting in the light of the fury with which Dulles himself was later denounced by many of the Democrats for his contentious policy as Secretary of State. The point at this earlier stage, however, was that he felt keenly about the need to develop a united American view on the problems of postwar organization, while President Roosevelt and the Democrats were worried, to quote Cordell Hull, that "the word 'bipartisan' might concede the Republicans an equal status in a project that was now presumed to be politically profitable." In any event, Dulles became the active proponent of bipartisanship and in due course, at the suggestion of Hamilton Fish Armstrong, was nominated in 1945 by the new Secretary of State, Edward R. Stettinius, to serve as an adviser to the United States delegation at the San Francisco Conference which drew up the United Nations Charter.

This proved to be the beginning of a long series of international meetings at which Dulles was present, as a Republican spokesman, at a time when the Administration was still Democratic under the leadership of President Truman. In this way he became an American delegate at the United Nations General Assembly sessions in 1946, 1947, 1948, and 1950. He was also present at the important series of postwar four-power meetings known as the Council of Foreign Ministers. Dulles went first to London in 1945 as adviser to the Secretary of State, James R. Byrnes; then to the Moscow and London sessions of 1947 with the new Secretary of State, General

George C. Marshall; and finally under yet another Secretary of State, Dean Acheson, to the last and by now totally abortive session in Paris in 1949.

The main feature of these meetings of the Council of Foreign Ministers, opening with the one in London in September, 1945, and closing with the session in Paris in 1949 after the Berlin blockade had led to the Allied airlift, was that, whereas they began in the immediate postwar euphoria of American and Western readiness to give and take in dealing with the Soviet Union, they ended in the new atmosphere of the cold war. As this transition took place, it became Dulles's view that there existed the same type of national emergency which had confronted the United States in wartime. And it was for this reason that he attached increasing importance to bipartisanship, claiming with much justification that it had, for instance, been his presence as a Republican spokesman in the American delegations at the meetings of the Council of Foreign Ministers that had enabled American policy to be switched relatively easily from the Roosevelt-Yalta approach to the epoch-making signature of the North Atlantic Treaty in 1949. Dulles's views of this period were clearly set out in his second book, *War or Peace,* published in 1950. He wrote:

> Bipartisanship is not easy . . . to produce. It . . . seems to cut across two fundamental American principles. One is that the President, and the President alone, has the responsibility for the current conduct of foreign affairs. The other is that, under a two-party system, it is the duty of the opposition party to be a watchdog rather than a teammate. Because bipartisanship in foreign policy thus cuts across our basic constitutional and traditional political views, it ought to be used only sparingly when the needs and perils are so great that exceptional measures are demanded. . . . Winning a war is important. But winning peace is equally important. Also, the winning of a "cold" war is as important as the winning of a "hot" war. In each case our liberty, our free institutions, are at stake. . . .
>
> The fact that I was at London with Secretary Byrnes as a Republican and with powerful Republican backing enabled me to play an important part in the momentous decision to end the policy of seeking to get agreement with the Russians by "appeasing" their aggressive ambitions. Since then the policy of "appeasement" has become generally unpopular. But that particular mood had not clearly developed by September,

1945. Without my presence, Secretary Byrnes could not have known that he could come home with what, superficially, was a total failure without being subjected to criticism by the opposition. Because I was there, he knew that to make concessions would involve Republican attack, while not to make them would encourage Republican support. I made it clear that that was my own view, and that I believed it would also be the view of Dewey, Vandenberg, and other Republicans when I reported the circumstances to them. Thus the Secretary of State was able to make a momentous and clear cut decision with confidence that it would have bipartisan backing.

Then Dulles speaks about the importance of bipartisanship when there is a possibility of a change of Administration at home during a crisis abroad. This was in fact the precise position in 1948, when the blockade of Berlin was instituted by the Russians during an American presidential election year. Dulles wrote:

Perhaps because 1948 was a presidential election year, when internal division and consequent paralysis could be expected, the Soviet Union stepped up its pressures in Europe. In March, 1948, General Clay advised the Chief of Staff that he had given up his position that war was impossible, and felt that we could no longer preclude its possibility. Shortly thereafter the Soviet forces in Eastern Germany began gradually to cut the Western access to Berlin by railroad, canal and road. Thereby, as we have seen, Soviet leaders attempted to compel the Western Allies to retreat from that advance base. The blockade got into full operation about the time that that presidential campaign was getting under way. It was countered by the airlift. But the airlift was vulnerable to Soviet interference. The big question in the minds of friendly governments and peoples in Europe—and no doubt also in the minds of the Russians, although they were less communicative—was whether the uncertainties and division of a presidential campaign would prevent our nation from acting strongly abroad. I was at that time (July, 1948) called into confidential conferences with the State Department on measures that might be taken to counter the blockade. Thus informed of the facts, including the military estimate of the situation, I was in a position to advise Governor Dewey, the Republican candidate. . . . If at that time the Republican leadership had given the slightest sign of weakening, the result might have been disastrous. But there was no such weakening.

Dulles certainly took himself seriously. But he was right to do so in the sense that during the summer and autumn of 1948 he was regarded as the future Secretary of State, since Dewey was confidently expected to beat Truman. His reaction, incidentally, when Dewey failed to get in was such as to suggest that his own ambition was indeed to be Secretary of State, and that he was very disappointed at not getting in on this occasion. This is interesting in view of his undoubted hesitations at the eleventh hour when Eisenhower did finally offer it to him in 1952, and of the fact that it is nowadays denied that the Secretaryship was the cast-iron lifetime's ambition which he is popularly supposed to have made it.

The reason why Dulles did not form part of the American delegation to the United Nations General Assembly of 1949 was that the Assembly coincided with a curious but significant episode in his career. It met during the brief period of four months for which he was a member of the United States Senate. These four months constituted the first and last occasion on which he ever held an elected political office. Senator Dulles, however, never was elected. What had happened was that one of the senators for New York, Senator Robert F. Wagner, resigned through illness, and Dewey, as Governor of the state, used his constitutional power to nominate a successor until the next election. He nominated Dulles, who was sworn in on July 8, 1949. When the midterm election arrived in the autumn Dulles found himself opposed by a powerful Democratic figure, Herbert Lehman, a former Governor of New York, who was very well known and had a wide following. Dulles lost the election by quite a margin, though the Republicans claimed, not without justice, that he had done better than might have been expected.

For Dulles the campaign itself was a strange experience. Although his long training as a lawyer had taught him a good deal about the rough and tumble of human affairs, he had never himself undergone the mud-slinging, the false issues, the bitter personal innuendoes of politics. He was never one for half measures, however, and accordingly he pitched in with the rest, with the result that there has been a sharp controversy about his campaign ever since. His critics assert that he attempted to use two weapons which are not generally regarded as permissible. He is said to have indulged in anti-Semitism, and to have accused Lehman of being soft on Communism.

Lehman, of course, as a Jew had a large ready-made backing,

particularly in New York City. It seems unlikely, therefore, that Dulles would have been so stupid as to get himself out on such a limb so unnecessarily, quite apart from any other considerations— including the fact that his own law firm was one of the only leading ones on Wall Street with Jews among the partners; and the strong Republican denials of any anti-Semitism in the campaign do seem to be borne out by the lack of adequate specific evidence to support the hostile charges. Lehman, moreover, had a reputation for always claiming that his political opponents were being anti-Semitic, on the calculation that he gained more than he lost by having the issue raised. On the question of Lehman's lack of a firm line on Communism, however, Dulles's friends do not repudiate what is attributed to him. They point out that Lehman led the UNRRA mission (United Nations Relief and Rehabilitation Agency) in the Ukraine after the war and came back deeply impressed by all that needed to be done to help the Russians get on their feet again. Like other well-meaning people, they say, Lehman thus went too far in his sympathy. This, nonetheless, would hardly be called pro-Communism.

On the other side of the fence, this election also dredged up one particular aspect of Dulles's own personal life which was a painful surprise to him. He was accused of having patched up for the purposes of the election a complete family break between himself and his youngest son, Avery, and of having had a photograph taken of them together to prove their reconciliation. This was nonsense, though it was certainly a case of there not being smoke without any fire at all. The facts were that Avery Dulles had been converted to Roman Catholicism while an undergraduate at Harvard just before the war, and had even gone to the limit with his new faith, becoming a priest and joining the Jesuits in 1946. Naturally this had been a pain and grief to both his father and his mother, whose Presbyterianism was basic to their whole lives. But Foster Dulles certainly never split with Avery, and so no reconciliation was necessary.

Dulles had three children, John, Lillias and Avery. But it was in the nature of both Mrs. Dulles and of himself to be a little remote from their family, and, given Avery's inheritance of qualities by no means unlike those of his father, it was not surprising that in the circumstances he should have gone through a profound religious experience when he went to college. In the family he had, moreover, been just a bit the odd man out. Lillias was probably Dulles's favorite of his three children, and John Mrs. Dulles's. But when Avery became a Catholic both his parents were very upset, not so much because of the Catholicism, but because they suddenly came to feel with an agony of acuteness that they had failed as parents. Avery Dulles himself has described his own conversion in a little book of compelling sincerity called *A Testimonial to Grace,* published in 1946. He wrote it when he took the further step into the Society of Jesus and after his wartime service in the Navy, when, as he says, "thanks to a period of relative leisure at sea . . . I had an opportunity to reflect somewhat carefully on the processes by which my ideas had evolved." Reading it, one cannot help feeling that, with the grace of God in a different form, it might almost have been written by his father.

Avery had always seemed to be the clever one of the family. But, in spite of Dulles's somewhat surprisingly Victorian temporary hesitation about a college education for his daughter, Lillias and John have both shown that they possess the Dulles brains and character. Lillias is married and lives in New York. John Dulles, the eldest son, has been heard of far less than his younger brother, because he is a mining engineer and has chosen a life which takes him far away from the center of attention. He also has had, however, a not altogether usual story. Always a person of ability and particular charm, he nonetheless did not do so well at school or college, because he was not interested. When he first went out to work he had two or three different jobs in succession, one in a New York bank which he hated. Then, one day he found himself employed by a mining company as a nontechnician out in the field. He suddenly became bitten with the work, realized he could not get very far without professional qualifications, went to the University of Arizona and took the mining engineers' course in just half the usual time, and passed the grade brilliantly. He has since been in charge of important operations in Brazil, and has shown that he too is a son of his father.

John Foster Dulles did not earn very high marks in the Senate, though it was hardly his fault. Like many other parliamentary institutions, the United States Senate has a number of jealously guarded traditions. One is that new members do not make a lot of noise when they first come in and, although by 1949 Dulles was a distinguished American figure in his own right, he was a new boy as far as the other senators were concerned. Unfortunately, it so happened that within four days of his appointment the North Atlantic Treaty came up for ratification, and this was quite obviously a subject on which he both felt strongly and had many qualifications to speak at some length. He accordingly leaped into the debate. But he was never fully forgiven for doing so. One scathing attack against him was particularly hard to bear, since it came from his old friend, Senator Robert Taft. Taft, however, was a semi-isolationist and his anger sprang in part from his political views. Dulles did indeed have an unfortunate manner, both in speaking and writing, in the sense that only too often he gave an impression of being superior. His style improved a bit towards the end of his Secretaryship, as he grew mellower with age, but the fact that he was nearly always better informed and more intelligent than most of his audience only made the sense of irritation worse.

One of the incidental results of Dulles's term as a senator was that on July 8, 1949, the day of his appointment, he resigned from his position as an active partner in Sullivan and Cromwell. Although he remained as an outside consultant and adviser until December 31, 1952, when he resigned finally and completely from the firm shortly before becoming Secretary of State, this day in 1949 marked the effective end of a great legal career which had begun before the First World War. When Dulles failed to get elected for the Senate he decided not to rush into anything else immediately, and for almost the first time in his life he was rather at loose ends for a few weeks.

Early in this period the Dulleses had the Eisenhowers to dinner, Eisenhower at that time being president of Columbia University. They had known each other for a few years, though by no means as intimately as they were to do later on. After dinner, Eisenhower reflected a moment and said to Dulles, "You know, Foster, what you ought to do now is to write a book."

Dulles thought it over that night, and the following morning a table was cleared upstairs, several girls were taken on to type, and he began dictating. Inside a month he had finished. He had no interest in the tiresome details of polishing up the text for the printers, checking, altering, adding and cutting. All that was seen to by others, with Mrs. Dulles ably supervising the entire operation. As far as Dulles was concerned he had written his second book, *War or Peace,* and it was published the same year, 1950. A day or two after he had finished this tour de force the Eisenhowers had the Dulleses to dinner. After dinner, Eisenhower reflected a moment and observed, "Foster, you know, I still think you ought to write that book."

"Well," Dulles took great satisfaction in replying, "as a matter of fact I have."

War or Peace was a historical survey of developments since the end of the Second World War, together with a succinct statement of Dulles's anti-Communist faith and a blunt warning about the need to fight Communism with all the resources available. "War is probable," Dulles opens by declaring, "unless by positive and well-directed efforts we fend it off." He says later:

> There is no illusion greater or more dangerous than that Soviet intentions can be deflected by persuasion.... Power is the key to success in dealing with the Soviet leadership. Power, of course, includes not merely military power, but economic power and the intangibles, such as moral judgment and world opinion, which determine what men do and the intensity with which they do it.

Then, in order to rub the lesson home, he compares the cold war with the shooting war so recently over:

> In the dark days of 1942 we were not thinking about "peace" in terms of some settlement that might temporarily allow us to go on existing as an oasis in a totalitarian desert. We were not thinking about how to save our necks, but how to save freedom. We need more of that spirit today. If we had it there would be far more chance of getting real peace. Security is the by-product, not of fear, but of great endeavor and great faith.

Although Dulles never attached the same importance to this second book as he did to his first, it acted as a fairly reliable vehicle for his thoughts and it enjoyed a considerable sale. Written into it were some lively comments about personalities and events. Dulles used his own experiences, for instance, to illustrate vividly the skill of the adversary:

> During ... the 1945 London Council of Foreign Ministers, Mr. Molotov conducted himself with an adroitness which has been seldom equalled in diplomacy. ... His words, even when uttered in a language that is not understood, strike with the force of bullets from a machine gun. ...

Molotov, Dulles reported, noticing that Secretary Byrnes spoke a great deal without notes, repeatedly sought to draw him out,

> hoping that ... he might somewhere in the course of an extended talk utter some words or phrases that could be seized upon as fitting into the Soviet program. After Mr. Byrnes had spoken, Mr. Molotov would frequently say that he was perplexed because Mr. Byrnes had seemed to state his position in slightly different ways. What precisely was it that he proposed? Would not Mr. Byrnes be good enough to restate the case so as to clarify it?

Towards Bevin, Dulles wrote, Molotov adopted a different technique:

> Mr. Bevin was bluff and hearty, easily angered and quickly repentant of his anger. Mr. Molotov treated him as a banderillero treats a bull, planting darts that would arouse him to an outburst—from which he rapidly reacted in a manner implying a tendency to make concessions.

Then there were the French:

> Mr. Molotov's objective with M. Bidault was to provoke him to leave the conference. To that end, he played upon the sensitiveness which is natural to the French character, and which was particularly marked at that time. For the first time since the surrender of 1940, France was sitting as an equal at the table of the great. French feelings were still raw from the indignity of exclusion from the inner conferences of San Francisco and total exclusion at Potsdam. So, Mr. Molotov tried to outrage French honor by petty slights. He would, for example, ask Mr. Bevin and Mr. Byrnes for a postponement by an hour of the time of the meeting and then would not tell M. Bidault.

Finally there was Molotov's method for dealing with the fourth party at the Council of Foreign Ministers, the Chinese. Dulles described Mr. Wang, the Chinese Foreign Minister as:

... stolid and shrewd. He spoke rarely and could not be provoked. The Molotov technique was to ignore him. When Mr.
Wang did speak, Mr. Molotov paid no attention whatever and
proceeded as though nothing were being said.

Dulles summed up by saying that this:

remarkable performance ... did not, however, get the results
that Mr. Molotov wanted. The professional artistry of Mr.
Molotov had to succumb to the sincerity of his colleagues.

In the course of the book Dulles made a number of observations
about countries and events, which did not stand the test of time.
Two only perhaps should be quoted against his own later record
at the State Department. On Communist China, he said that if it
proved "its ability to govern China without serious domestic resistance, then it, too, should be admitted to the United Nations." For
well-known political reasons he was in practice unable to live up
to this view. And on the rearmament of Germany, he was cautious
in declaring: "We cannot risk a German national army. We might
risk having Germans individually as part of a European army,
along with French and Belgians, under non-German command and
stationed anywhere in Western Europe, preferably not in Germany." But here too he was to change his mind, though only after
making dramatic efforts in 1953 and 1954 to push the European
army through.

There was, however, one passage which reflected a view about
Britain that nothing he ever did quite expunged. It was, of course,
written while a Labour Government was still in power in London,
and no Republican could at that time see any good in socialism.
Dulles commented:

Never has the world made material, social and indeed moral
progress equal to that during the century of British dominance
between the Napoleonic wars and the First World War.
Through that dominance, England thrived. ... This ship of
state called "England" was manned by officers and crew who
were hard-working, courageous, resourceful, inventive, and
venturesome. They had set full sail in a turbulent sea. Now,
however, all is changed. The captain and crew often act as
though they were in charge of a derelict drifting to no discernible haven, with no dependable means of propulsion and
only limited supplies of food and water. Under such circum-

stances "socialism" is natural. When men, women, and children are adrift they usually divide the food and water on an equal basis. That is what is happening in England.

One of the outstanding achievements of Dulles's entire career was his handling of the Japanese Peace Treaty negotiations. These began in 1950, the year his book came out, and lasted for over twelve months into 1951. But before considering them as a whole it may be noted at this point that his dealings with Britain on the subject were marred by an incident which did lasting and imponderable damage to Anglo-American relations. It arose through his misunderstanding with the Foreign Secretary in the Labour Government, Herbert Morrison (now Lord Morrison), from which sprang in part Sir Anthony Eden's endemic distrust of Dulles and the aggravation of Dulles's reciprocal hostility to Eden. The misunderstanding concerned the question of which China, if either, should sign the treaty. Dulles was determined not to let Communist China have anything to do with it. Morrison took the standard British Foreign Office view that the only realistic signature would be that of Mao Tse-tung's representative. And the issue was brought to a head during Dulles's visit to London at quite a late stage in the negotiations during the spring of 1951 by the problem of which China, if either, the Japanese themselves would recognize.

After discussion with Morrison, Dulles amended the draft treaty to give minor concessions in terms of Japanese trading rights, in return for what he regarded as British acceptance of the compromise proposal that neither China should sign, but that the Japanese should be empowered to decide which China they would recognize, if either, *after* they had obtained their sovereignty. This was regarded in London outside government circles as a considerable concession on Dulles's part. Herbert Morrison, however, whose lack of grasp during his brief tenure of office as Foreign Secretary did permanent damage to his political career, genuinely felt that he had seen his agreement with Dulles in a different light. Writing in his memoirs, Morrison has said that he and Dulles informally agreed that Japan should not be required to recognize either China. Dulles asked him not to make any public announcement about this for the time being, and Morrison says he agreed. According to Morrison, the next he heard of it was that a United States Senate subcommittee had gone to Japan and that "there were in due course issued details of a decision by Japan to recognize the Formosan government. I may be forgiven if I resolved there and then not fully to trust Dulles again."

Japan did in fact recognize Chiang Kai-shek, and it is difficult to see how any other course was really open to Tokyo, given the close relationship which the peace treaty created between Japan and the United States, when it was signed a little later in the year. At the same time Dulles is now known to have put considerable pressure on the Japanese government and to have given Morrison at least a legitimate cause for complaint by keeping him in the dark about what was going on. Although the Japanese would presumably have recognized Formosa anyway, what Dulles felt he needed was an advance assurance to this effect in order to help him get the treaty past the Senate. He got it in the form of a special letter from the Japanese Prime Minister, Mr. Kishi, at the end of the year.

To go back to the beginning, however, Dulles was given the unique assignment of negotiating the Japanese Peace Treaty by President Truman as a rather last hope, after three years of interminable departmental discussion had got virtually nowhere. It was also a result of Dulles's own efforts at bipartisanship in foreign policy. In March of 1950, with the help of Senator Vandenberg, he had got himself appointed as one of two special consultants to the State Department with responsibility for the liaison between the Democratic Administration and the Republican party. After a few weeks in this post Dulles had persuaded the Secretary of State, Dean Acheson, to let him go to Tokyo as a first step towards trying to reassess the possibilities of signing a peace treaty with Japan. When Acheson agreed, Dulles flew to Tokyo on the first of three visits he was to pay there during the course of the negotiations; and it was the lucid report he made on his return which some months later led to his being put in charge of the whole operation, with the rank of roving ambassador.

In 1950, as Dulles reported the position, both General Douglas MacArthur, the Supreme Commander of the occupation forces in Japan, and the chairman of the Joint Chiefs of Staff, General Omar Bradley, were personally quite prepared to agree that the Japanese, having behaved very well under five years of occupation, would from now on begin to agitate for their sovereignty with increasing vigor. If they were to be converted from a conquered people into allies in the cold war, it was essential that their relationship with the United States should be put on a basis politically acceptable to them. Japan was one of the key prizes in the cold war and it would be the height of folly to fumble and drop it. Yet, as with the other similar prize, Germany, it was out of the question that the Russians would let Japan go without a stern fight. For years Moscow had vetoed and blocked every move to reach an agreed solution in both Germany and Austria, and hence, if anything was to be achieved in Japan, it must be done over the heads of the Russians. At the same time Moscow ought to be given every opportunity of joining in, if some sudden brainstorm made the Soviet leaders decide to co-operate. This was Dulles's view.

That summer, however, before any course of action had been decided upon, the Communists launched their attack on South Korea. The gravity of the sudden crisis inevitably held up any further practical discussions of the Japanese treaty for several weeks, until it was realized that the new situation had made the need for a treaty even more urgent than ever, since almost all the American occupation troops in Japan had been thrown into the Korean battle, and this vital base was usable at all only because the Japanese themselves wanted it to be so used. Hitherto the general service view at the Pentagon in Washington had been against ending the Occupation and giving the Japanese their head; in the regular cast-iron mold of the military mind it seemed better to run the show with troops than to hand a country over to civilian administration. Now that there were no troops, however, the experts in the Pentagon changed their mind, and it was on September 8, 1950, that Dulles was given a free hand to explore and exploit every means of bringing about a peace treaty with Japan.

He decided at once that a formal conference of the interested powers must at all costs be avoided until the last possible moment. Soviet stone-walling would thus be prevented until it might be ineffective, as in fact proved to be the case. Handling the matter through diplomatic channels would also sidestep the intractable problem of the two Chinas, which presented an acute difficulty in two senses, one that China had of course been the oldest belligerent of all against Japan, and the other that in signing a treaty the Japanese would have to recognize one or the other of these two governments as the régime with which they were making peace. In two months, that is by November, 1950, Dulles had made sufficient progress to circulate a seven-point draft proposal to all the interested governments, including the Russians, but excluding the Chinese Communists (whom America did not in any case recognize —though it must be remembered that at this stage they had only just achieved full power over the whole of the Chinese mainland). But before his proposals could be seriously considered the negotiations were again interrupted, this time by the full-scale intervention of the Chinese Communist government in the Korean war through the dispatch of its so-called volunteers across the Yalu River; these succeeded in sending the American and allied United Nations forces reeling back to the 38th parallel.

By January, 1951, further progress with the treaty negotiations was again possible. This now turned on two fundamental issues, the defense of Japan and Japanese reparations. On the former, the Japanese, who had undertaken in their postwar constitution not to build up national forces again except for internal security duties, now found themselves with frightening evidence only just across the water of the very real danger in which they themselves stood. Ever since the defeat of Czarist Russia in the Russo-Japanese war of 1905, the Russians had feared and resented Japanese power in the Northern Pacific. Having seen the defeat of Japan in the Second World War, the Soviet Communist government, just as its Czarist predecessors would have done in similar circumstances, feared the rise of a new Japan allied to the modern power of the United States and would do anything it could to prevent this happening. The Japanese for their part were predominantly anti-Communist and, particularly after coming to terms with the West through the intimacy of the Americans' Occupation era, had no wish whatever to become victims of Communist aggression. At that time at any rate, they were accordingly most genuine in welcoming a treaty which would give them an American security guarantee, together with an American garrison.

There was, however, the other side of the coin. Countries which the Japanese had occupied or threatened during the Second World War, notably the Philippines, Australia, and New Zealand, naturally demanded guarantees against any future resurgence of Japanese power and ambitions. To meet these various needs, Dulles proposed that the long arm of an American security guarantee should be stretched over Japan and Japan's former victims alike. And this is what in essence the Japanese Peace Treaty insured. The Philippines secured a unilateral American guarantee, and the positions of Australia and New Zealand were covered by the separate ANZUS Treaty (Australia-New Zealand-and-United States) which was Dulles's idea and which he played a major part in bringing about.

The question of reparations was nearly as difficult. Much damage had resulted, for instance, from the Japanese invasion of the Philippines, and there was a natural feeling that, even where specific damage had not been done, Japan should make some form of payment as compensation for its years of occupation and exploitation. This applied particularly to the case of Indonesia, which had at last achieved its independence at the beginning of 1950, and which stood in considerable need of technical assistance as an undeveloped area since the departure of the Dutch. Dulles, however, was absolutely adamant that the Japanese economy should not be made to carry more than the traffic would bear. It was at this moment in his life that he saw again very vividly the disastrous experiences of Germany after the First World War and was inflexibly resolved that he would have no part in re-creating such a situation with regard to Japan after the Second. And he was naturally reinforced in this resolve by his passionate devotion to the cause of anti-Communism, being determined that the valuable prize of Japan should not go to the Communists through any Western folly in making it impossible for the Japanese to earn their living. Dulles's often-quoted words were:

> You can have two kinds of peace. One is a Carthaginian peace, which is cruel, ruthless, inflexible and must be enforced with military strength for a long time. It is a peace that can tolerate no infractions whatever. The other is a peace based on the belief that human nature is capable of regeneration;

that, if it fails at times, it is capable of better ways of life. This kind of peace is one of magnanimity based on power. There is no halfway between these two kinds of peace. You must have one or the other. We want the kind of peace that has a good chance of making Japan and the United States close associates in the future. It cannot be done without the free will of the conquered. It must be a peace of reconciliation.

In arguing with those who pressed for reparations, Dulles went on to say:

> If you use the lash, if you exact reparations, if you constrict Japanese economic opportunity, if you act as jailer and master of slave labor, if you drive Japanese shipping off the seas and shut down her textile mills, you will create a peace that can only lead to bitter animosity and in the end drive Japan into the orbit of Russia.

In the end Dulles got his way on all these points, though negotiations were again held up by yet another crisis, this time the storm over President Truman's sacking of General MacArthur. However, by March, 1951, the actual draft of the treaty was circulated, and it was following this step that Dulles flew to London for his unfortunate encounter with Herbert Morrison. After that, between June and December, the closing stages of the treaty negotiations were characterized by Soviet protests. For months the Russians had lain rather low, merely being quietly un-co-operative. Now at last they reacted. They took the offensive by rejecting everything Dulles had done so far and proposing to start afresh with a four-power conference instead. But Dulles was ready for them and rejected this typical obstructiveness in his best legal manner—so much so that his draft Note to Moscow is quoted as having drawn the comment from Dean Acheson, the Secretary of State: "This is a jewel. It's one of Sullivan and Cromwell's $25,000 briefs." To the Soviet claim that the Potsdam Agreement had laid it down that the four nations, America, Russia, Britain and China should draw up a treaty for Japan, Dulles retorted that the war with Japan was still in progress at the time of Potsdam and the Soviet Union "was then neutral in that war."

By the end of the summer, however, the moment had indeed arrived for a conference, not to start fresh negotiations from scratch, but to confirm and sign the draft treaty already negotiated. The Japanese Peace Conference was accordingly held at San Francisco from September 4 to 8, 1951, and fifty-two countries attended, including Russia. Yugoslavia, India, and Burma refused their invitations. Japan was represented by its Prime Minister, Shigeru Yoshida. In spite of the earlier Soviet rejection of the whole Dulles concept, the Russians came—with the more or less open intention of wrecking the conference. For the United States, Dulles and Acheson worked as a team, Acheson taking the chair at the conference and Dulles leading the American delegation. In that delegation, it is interesting to note, was President Kennedy's future Secrtary of State, the then Assistant Secretary for Far Eastern Affairs, Dean Rusk.

The plan of campaign was gloriously neat and wholly Dulles's. It worked like a charm and turned Gromyko, the Soviet delegate, apoplectic with fury. In the invitation to the conference Dulles had been careful to put it that the purpose was to discuss the treaty as already drafted. After the conference had been opened by a speech from President Truman, therefore, and the Russians began raising questions of substance, Acheson said that these would have to wait until the rules of procedure had been adopted, a view which was carried by majority vote of the other delegates. Gromyko perforce had to accept. Then, when the rules of procedure had been passed, he got up to raise the important questions he said arose out of the treaty. Acheson interrupted him to point out that under the rules of procedure, which the conference had just passed, no new questions could any longer be introduced, only matters of detail already included in the draft treaty. When this was also supported by the majority of the other delegates, Gromyko was again compelled to accept—though he staged a furious five-minute walkout and held a press conference afterwards, declaring the treaty an "aggressive" pact aimed at Russia and China. Russia never signed the treaty.

Thus, the Russians' attempt to block the Japanese Peace Treaty —as they have always blocked a German one—failed. The treaty itself was very moderate in tone and exacted virtually no reparations from Japan, apart from the employment of Japanese labor to repair certain war damage; but Japan did surrender sovereignty over Korea, Formosa, the Kuriles, South Sakhalin, and several other islands. On the eve of the conference on September 1, Dulles signed the mutual security pact, known as ANZUS, which he had negotiated with Australia and New Zealand when he had been in Canberra and Wellington in April. And on the last day, September 8, a U.S.-Japan bilateral defense pact was also signed, in which the Japanese agreed to American forces being "in and around" Japan indefinitely, in return for a U.S. security guarantee. Thus, Dulles rounded off his brilliant series of negotiations without ever holding anything but a virtually formal conference at the very last moment. It was a tour de force for which his own special gifts as a negotiator were ideally suited, and, in spite of all that he did later on, the Japanese Peace Treaty remains one of the most lasting accomplishments of his public career.

Some months later, when the treaty had been ratified by the United States Senate, Dulles resigned from his position as a Special Consultant to the State Department. He did so in order to make himself free to take a leading part in the forthcoming presidential campaign of 1952, the campaign which saw President Eisenhower elected to the White House, and John Foster Dulles himself installed in due course as Secretary of State.

CHAPTER 5

The First Few Weeks

D ULLES was not General Eisenhower's inevitable choice as Secretary of State. In the early stages before the 1952 presidential campaign got properly under way, several other possible names were mentioned, such as Henry Cabot Lodge and John McCloy. But he did have a very high claim. If a Republican president had been elected in either of the two previous elections, Dulles would have been virtually certain to get the job, and the qualifications which had commended him to Thomas Dewey made him the most suitable candidate still. As for Dulles himself, it is an extremely interesting question how far he made the office of Secretary of State a long-standing ambition. The popular myth is that he aimed at it nearly all his life. But those who knew him best deny absolutely that this was so, and the truth probably lies somewhere in between.

Dulles probably wanted to be Secretary of State more than he ever admitted. He wanted it, however, on his own terms, and since he knew that those terms would be hard to meet he did not regard his attainment of this objective as either easy or so very likely. In the main these conditions, which were swept aside in spite of Dulles's genuine efforts when it came to the point, laid down that the Secretary of State should be relieved of almost all his departmental and administrative responsibilities, so that he could concentrate on high policy and long-range thinking. Apart from these reservations, Dulles was obviously attracted by the appointment or he would never have accepted the post of Dewey's foreign affairs spokesman. And it seems that he wisely went to a certain amount of trouble at the various postwar international conferences he attended as the Republican observer not to queer his own pitch by taking any line which might be used against him later on.

Dulles was in any case never one for leaving matters entirely to chance. When it became evident early in 1952 that General Eisenhower, still at that time the Supreme Commander of the Allied Forces in Europe, was willing to run for President and that, if he did so, he would almost certainly win the Republican nomination and then go on to win the election, Dulles made his way to Paris. Having known each other for some time, though not at all intimately, the future President had suggested they should meet—without any commitment. The two men talked at considerable length and came to an understanding with one another. Dulles was appalled at Eisenhower's naïveté about American politics, he felt he could work with him, and Eisenhower found in Dulles the kind of man to whom he believed he could give his trust.

Another man who might have won the Republican nomination for President in 1952 was Robert Taft, who had widespread support in certain sections of the party. Dulles's long personal friendship with him made the position a little delicate, particularly since the Taft faction had more or less promised Dulles the State Department if they won. But Dulles neither approved fully of Taft's semi-isolationist views about American foreign policy nor believed that Eisenhower could be beaten. Accordingly, he told Taft privately that he was for Eisenhower some time before he declared himself publicly, and it is to Taft's credit that after Eisenhower had duly entered the White House Taft did not hold Dulles's action against him. Nor indeed did he allow his own deep disappointment at not becoming President to color his thoughts towards the man who did, even though for him the Presidency certainly had been his lifetime's ambition. President Eisenhower, for his part, always hoped, as he approached his Inauguration Day, that Taft and Dulles between them would be the twin pillars on which his Administration would rest.

Eisenhower, uninterested in party politics, never really pictured the Presidency as so very much the center of party patronage. Although he understood and respected the vast powers accruing to the President of the United States, he preferred to regard the office as above party like a constitutional monarchy, and seeing himself in this position he planned to have Senator Taft as a kind of prime minister. Taft's standing in the Republican party would enable him to be a highly effective leader in Congress as well as a home affairs minister. The whole foreign side meanwhile would be looked after by Dulles. It was when this concept was destroyed by Taft's illness and unhappy death soon after Eisenhower became President that he turned instead to Sherman Adams as the link between the White House and the Republican Party. Although Dulles and Sherman Adams did in fact work together for several years as President Eisenhower's two chief lieutenants, the position was never as satisfactory as it would have been if Taft had lived, because Taft was a superlative politician as well as being a popular figure in the Republican party.

Robert Taft somewhat complicated the situation shortly before he died by passing his own mantle on to Senator William F. Knowland, who became the Republican leader in the Senate. Apart from sharing some of his views on foreign policy, however, Knowland was an entirely different figure from Taft. He had a bee in his bonnet about Communist China, and, compared with Taft's forthcoming personality, gave an impression of inflexible obstinacy. Consequently there never was and never could be the kind of contact between him and the White House which Eisenhower had originally planned for Taft. Nor indeed could there be much confidence between Knowland and Dulles. Dulles for his part always tried to work along with Knowland, but, for the first year or so, this was particularly difficult, since Knowland seemed to have fallen under the spell of that fatal figure of the era, Senator McCarthy, and he was therefore more of a critic than a supporter of the Administration. President Eisenhower, in fact, found it easier to deal with Congress in his second term when, ironically enough, there was a Democratic rather than Republican majority.

On the eve of the Presidential election in November, 1952, Dulles and his wife had flown to Duck Island to recover from the election campaign, and it was there on his battery radio that he heard the news of Eisenhower's election. Some days later, on his return to New York from Duck Island he was formally offered the post of Secretary of State by the President-elect. When the moment came Dulles is reputed to have had an eleventh-hour hesitation about accepting, and it seems that he did try to insist on not being weighed down with the responsibility of the administration of the State Department as well. Although Eisenhower neither accepted nor rejected Dulles's conditions, beyond intimating that he must naturally carry out his job to the best of his ability, Dulles did in fact accept on the spot and in due course was sworn in on January 21, 1953, the day after President Eisenhower's first Inauguration.

Dulles's reputed last-minute doubts have some interest in view of the intense criticism, both at the time and since, of his failure to stand up for members of his Department under the attacks of Senator McCarthy; to many people this was really the most sickening thing that Dulles ever did. The Eisenhower Administration so completely outlived the McCarthy era that one sometimes too easily forgets that McCarthy was at the height of his influence when the President took office. During this sordid chapter in American history many innocent people, both inside and outside government service, walked in daily fear that some chance twist of one of the pieces of so-called evidence produced at the endless McCarthy hearings would launch a vicious witch hunt against them with accusations of Communist associations or Communist leanings. Even those elected or appointed to some of the highest offices in the country were justifiably afraid, not of the truth but of the false innuendos and lies which might at any moment be manufactured out of the truth.

The President, with his immense popularity, was untouchable. So indeed was Dulles personally in the sense that almost the whole of his public life had been devoted to a passionate anti-Communist crusade. But their own inviolability increased, if anything, their moral obligation to help others under them. Dulles, however, did not see matters in this light and it was he who was to no small extent responsible for inspiring Eisenhower to take the line of giving McCarthy enough rope to hang himself. In the end Mc-Carthy did, but it took a painfully long time. Dulles seems to have been prompted to support the President in this stand-off line by three factors—his absolute determination, particularly right at the start, not to make Acheson's mistake of running foul of public opinion, his own religiously anti-Communist philosophy, and his rather Jesuitical personal tendencies. Meanwhile, unfortunately, several members of the State Department came under a vicious frontal attack by the McCarthyites, and Dulles incurred undying hatred from certain elements of liberal and intellectual opinion for doing nothing to save them.

This behavior rapidly aggravated à disastrous impression which he had in any case managed to create on his very first day in office. It arose from a personal statement which he issued to each of the many thousands of State Department employees. Designed to raise morale by giving everyone a sense of purpose, it had precisely the opposite effect. In its own way it was an early example of Dulles's unfortunate gift for wanting to do the right thing but only too often doing it in the wrong way. He came to grief mainly because he included the injudicious use of a phrase which had become publicly associated with McCarthy. The relevant passage ran:

> We are frontline defenders of the vital interests of the United States which are being attacked by a political warfare which is as hostile in its purpose and as dangerous in its capabilities as an open war. . . . The peril is of a kind which places a special responsibility on each and every member of the Department of State and the Foreign Service. It requires of us competence, discipline and positive loyalty to the policies that our President and the Congress may prescribe.

The offending words were "positive loyalty." The fear went round that, unless members of the State Department showed the kind of thought-controlled "loyalty" which the distortions of the McCarthy hearings demanded, they would risk being hounded out of their livelihood. Dulles had shown himself unable to see things from the other person's point of view.

All this, of course, was just the kind of administrative problem which he had hoped to avoid. In trying to do so, Dulles did as a matter of fact make matters even more difficult for himself than they might otherwise have been. When he first assumed office he arranged with the President for the appointment of two Under Secretaries of State, instead of the normal one. General Walter Bedell Smith was given the ordinary political post, while a second one, created to handle administration, went to a former President of the Quaker Oats Company, Don Lourie. Lourie was inadvertently instrumental in letting Dulles in for a great deal of extra difficulty, by appointing as State Department security officer Robert McLeod. Whereas Lourie had rather innocently supposed that his appointment might pacify and appease the inquisitors, the effect was the precise opposite. McLeod had access to the personnel security files and a great deal else besides, with the result that he assisted rather than hindered the McCarthyite onslaught against the State Department, and to this day Dulles is remembered for having allowed this to happen.

Dulles was undoubtedly in a very difficult position. He was new to the job. He hated getting involved in personal details. And he was determined to put his relationship with Eisenhower first, to do nothing to offend Congress or mass opinion, and to keep the road clear for the planning and execution of broad national policies for which, as he rightly saw it, he had been put in charge of his country's foreign affairs. On the other hand, the atmosphere at the top was one that percolated right down through the whole Department of State, and Dulles became responsible not only for the immediate personal tragedies of a number of individual cases, but also for a mood of frustration and a feeling of insecurity which affected many of the junior staff for years afterwards. His critics are not unjustified in asserting, for instance, that ambassadorships tended to go to those most ready to toe the line, and that Dulles's whole method of developing a personal diplomacy, of using a small brain trust, and of not keeping the Department fully informed about his own thoughts and actions were calamitous for morale. Certainly, by the time that Christian Herter succeeded Dulles as Secretary of State the confused position in the Department had become a liability to American foreign policy, and steps to do something about it were accepted as urgent.

The more notorious cases of McCarthyite clamor against senior State Department officials in 1953 have become very well known. Those of John P. Davies and John Carter Vincent were already well-advanced by the time Dulles arrived, though it was up to him as Secretary of State to give the final ruling about their future careers, following the investigations which had been conducted about their loyalty. In these and other similar leading cases Dulles did not stand up for the accused, and they were either dismissed or had to resign. His argument was specific: where a man had incurred public suspicion that even some of the charges against him might be true, he had already lost his usefulness as a member of the Department, whether he eventually managed to clear himself or not. Obviously there was a certain logic in such a view, but it did nothing either to soften the blow to the man concerned or to moderate the feelings of those who regarded Dulles as monstrously inhuman. And a good many did.

Three cases of a special kind were those of Paul Nitze, George Kennan and Charles Bohlen, all of whom were later to receive high appointments in President Kennedy's Administration. Nitze, who was to be Assistant Secretary of Defense under Kennedy, had been head of the policy planning staff when he became a target for McCarthyite criticism. Dulles himself wanted to keep him, but Nitze felt that the practical support he received from the top was inadequate, and he resigned. George Kennan, who had been the American Ambassador to Russia and was later appointed Ambassador to Yugoslavia by President Kennedy, parted company with Dulles on analogous though somewhat different grounds; he and Dulles disagreed about the nature of the pressure which the United States should put on the Soviet Union, Dulles standing for a more obviously tough line, and in due course Kennan was retired from the Foreign Service. Perhaps the most intrinsically important case was that of Charles Bohlen, because it involved the whole principle of the Administration's freedom of choice in its own senior appointments, because it finally curbed McLeod's more extravagant activities, and because it marked a turning point in Dulles's own willingness to fight for what he believed in, even when it was unpopular.

When the Eisenhower Administration's appointment of Charles Bohlen as the new Ambassador in Moscow came up for confirmation by the Senate in the normal way in March, 1953, it was bitingly attacked by the McCarthyites because of Bohlen's record. Soon after entering the American Foreign Service in 1929, he had made himself a specialist on Soviet Affairs. He was the chief American interpreter at both the Yalta and Potsdam Conferences, with the understandable result that he defended the Roosevelt policy. He was also closely associated with the Truman Democratic Admin-

istration. All this was anathema to the McCarthy chorus, and
Senator McCarthy himself declared that the findings of the Federal
Bureau of Investigation showed Bohlen to be a poor security risk.
For many people the Bohlen case came to be regarded as the acid
test of whether the State Department was to be able to run its own
affairs or not. In this case, Dulles did stand up for Bohlen, the
Senate Foreign Relations Committee did unanimously approve the
nomination, and an important round was won.

All through this troubled early period Dulles relied very heavily
on his relations with the President. He certainly cared greatly about
Congressional opinion, and his healthy respect for Congress was
enhanced by his own brief and rather unhappy time in the Senate.
But from the very start he never allowed himself to forget for an
instant that in the last resort the only thing that really mattered to
him was Eisenhower's confidence. Dulles made absolutely certain
from beginning to end that his own line to the White House, both
metaphorically and literally, was open. In the tough days of the
McCarthy era, while he himself was still new to the job, it must
also at times have seemed like a lifeline.

Dulles's personal relations with President Eisenhower were unusually close, sincere and important. In one sense they were those
of a good lawyer to a very old family friend who is also his client.
As Secretary of State he saw himself, on the one hand, briefing
the President and, on the other, speaking for the President to the
outside world. Admittedly, the lawyer-client relationship is an
equally good analogy to explain Dulles's attitude to American
policy as a whole. Indeed, he suffered from one of the usual con-
genital weaknesses of the many lawyers who become foreign ministers all over the world, in that he sometimes seemed to speak to
a brief without giving the impression that he took full responsibility for what it contained. His personal friendship with Eisenhower, however, certainly went deeper than a merely professional
or ministerial one. Naturally, during the first few months after they
had both assumed office they were feeling their way, and it was not
until they had come to know and trust each other thoroughly that
their relationship broadened into the extremely close and cordial
understanding which it later became. But Eisenhower has been

quoted as saying after Dulles's death that "Foster and I worked, as nearly as can be imagined, as one person."

Dulles was above all absolutely loyal to the President in everything he said and did. This loyalty, even if it sprang from a shrewd understanding of the Constitution, developed into a two-way affair. And Dulles on his side went to very great trouble to see that nothing spoiled it. He always cleared everything with the President first. No major speech, no major move, no major contact with a foreign statesman was made without the White House knowing about it first. Dulles carefully kept Eisenhower informed of every world development that he thought the President ought to be aware of. He was scrupulous in preparing his own summaries of the situation, and he never failed to outline his own opinion or his own suggestion for dealing with it. Churchill once condemned a paper submitted to him with the comment: "It is written at such length as to insure that no one of any consequence will ever read it." To an almost incredible degree Eisenhower developed this necessary prerogative of men in very high places by refusing to touch anything that was not extremely brief. Dulles understood this thoroughly and it suited his own lucid analytical style very well. The result was that the President came to see the world through Dulles's own spectacles.

The question has frequently been asked how much of American foreign policy in these circumstances was Dulles's and how much Eisenhower's. The answer is that, while Dulles was always the prime mover, he meticulously respected Eisenhower's authority in making the final decision. He was far too well aware of the troubles which had beset previous Secretaries of State, among them his own uncle, Robert Lansing, when they had ignored the simple precept that the President is the Chief Executive. In practice, during the earlier years of Eisenhower's Presidency, that is before his first heart attack in 1955, Eisenhower often influenced Dulles's own judgment, and Dulles would defer to the President's views after they had both discussed a problem between them. Later, although Dulles always acted in line with his categoric determination not to take any step in which he did not carry the President with him, the relative decline in Eisenhower's mental and physical resilience meant that his own influence on the actual decision became less and Dulles's domination of the situation in Washington became more complete. Eisenhower for his part gradually came to place utter faith in the loyalty of Dulles, and Dulles never once let the President down.

The fact that the two men were quite unequal in intellectual capacity was not allowed to detract from this relationship. Although Dulles knew that he could run rings round the President intellectually, he enormously respected the popular image of Eisenhower. He had a feeling for the realities of power both inside the American government and in the international field. Hence he came to see himself as something of a bridge, indeed the only bridge, between the political power represented by the President's overwhelming popularity and the strict military power of the Strategic Air Command (SAC) of General Curtis LeMay. He thus aimed at being the controlling genius who could manipulate the strength of these two forces in combination. Dulles himself, however, was not a military expert and never pretended to be. In some ways it would have been easier for him if he had been able to take a more Churchillian attitude to this vital interaction between the military and political sides of the problem. In practice, although he personally carried a good deal of weight with the Chiefs of Staff, partly because of his closeness to the President and partly because of his own record in international affairs, the State Department's general influence on the Pentagon was less under Dulles than it had been under Acheson.

The world which Dulles and President Eisenhower found around them when they assumed office was dominated by two major uncertainties—one in Europe and the other in the Far East. In Europe the problem of how to rearm the Germans had not been solved, although more than two years had passed since the decision to do so had been taken in principle; the United States itself still stood committed to supporting the proposal for a European army in order to avoid the establishment of a German national force. In the Far East the Korean War was still smoldering, although the interminable truce talks had already dragged on for a year and a half.

The focus of America's own interest in that winter of 1952–53 was the Far East rather than Europe. Between the President's election in November and his Inauguration in January, he had made an unprecedented journey as President-elect to visit Korea from December 3 to 5, in order to see for himself what could be done to honor his election promise to bring the war to an end. The United States was faced with the dilemma that, if the Communists were to be induced to let the truce talks reach a successful conclusion, they must be made to prefer peace to war, and this could only be done by threatening to widen the war. After Eisenhower's tour of the battlefront, he flew to Guam in mid-Pacific, where he went on board the U.S.S. *Helena*. At Wake Island he was joined by Dulles and Charles Wilson, the Secretary of Defense, together with General Bradley, chairman of the Joint Chiefs of Staff, and Admiral Radford, Commander-in-Chief, Pacific. Together they agreed in principle that the prospect of greater military effort must indeed be made to look convincing. Thus, they took the ugly and difficult provisional decision to step up operations, if need be, regardless of the risk that this might lead to the use of nuclear weapons with unlimited consequences, and regardless of the possible attitudes of their allies in the United Nations command. It was a grave move, but in the end it paid off. It was in some ways as clear a piece of brinkmanship as anything for which Dulles was primarily responsible later on.

When the Eisenhower-Dulles team assumed office and faced this Far Eastern problem, relations between Washington and London were under something of a strain. While the Americans were critical of the British for not pulling their weight in the Korean War, the British, like America's other European allies, felt that, harsh as the Korean challenge might be, it was in Europe that the new President ought most urgently to make a fresh start. In the United States, the successive Labour Foreign Secretaries, Ernest Bevin and Herbert Morrison, had been widely censured for quite some time, in the press and on the air, for prolonging the Korean struggle by failing to give the American military effort adequate backing. And although some of this criticism had abated after Sir Winston Churchill's Conservative government had been returned to power in October, 1951, there remained an underlying sense of doubt in both Washington and London whether enough really was being done to work together against the Communist effort in the Far East.

America's challenge to its allies, as well as to the Communists, was thrown down right at the start, and it set up an immediate emotional reaction all over Europe. It was the so-called unleashing of Chiang Kai-shek. Emphasizing the positive rather than negative aspects of United States policy, Dulles prompted President Eisenhower to announce in his first Message to Congress that the American Seventh Fleet would no longer be used to prevent any possible operations by Chiang Kai-shek's Chinese Nationalist forces in Formosa against the mainland of Communist China. This cancelled an order made in June, 1950, by President Truman to the effect that the U.S. Seventh Fleet was responsible for patrolling the Formosa Straits and preventing any major action by either side.

In practice the new Eisenhower statement remained no more than a matter of words. Chiang Kai-shek's army of 350,000 men, his small and at that time obsolete air force, and his minute run-down navy were quite incapable of delivering any serious blow against Communist China. This was not, however, how the President's Message was regarded either inside America itself or in Communist China or in Britain and Europe. Many Americans hailed it as a bold new initiative in the Far Eastern deadlock. I traveled from coast to coast in the United States during February of 1953, and among most Republicans I found a sadly misplaced sense of elation and anticipation. Against all the evidence of the real facts they seemed to believe that the Chinese Nationalists could now land on the coast of China, rally mass support, and win back the kingdom they had lost. They had in fact fallen victim to Nationalist propaganda and to their own wishful thinking. They had also certainly not thought out what might be the consequences if such a Nationalist attack failed—or indeed if it really succeeded and Russia came to Communist China's rescue.

If Americans could take the unleashing of Chiang Kai-shek seriously, so, it seemed, could Peking. The possibility that the new Washington Administration might after all be in earnest about presenting a fresh threat on another flank to the south of Korea seemed to make the Communists a little less truculent in pressing their demand, which had been holding up the truce talks for nearly a year, that the Chinese prisoners of war in United Nations hands should be forced to return to Communist territory, regardless of the declared refusal of the vast majority to do so. This doubt having been sown by the President's Message, the second prong of the

American psychological offensive was skillfully driven home later on by Dulles himself when he visited Delhi in May. Although Mr. Nehru is since reported to have denied that he personally knew anything about it, there seems little doubt that Indian officials to whom Dulles talked passed on through the Indian ambassador in Peking exactly what Dulles hoped they would. This was the impression which he had tried to create that, while the Americans genuinely wanted a truce in Korea, their patience was exhausted and they were making detailed plans to implement the provisional decision taken on board the U.S.S. *Helena* for carrying the Korean War across the Yalu into Manchuria. The result was that Peking suddenly dropped its demand over the prisoners and the truce deadlock was broken.

A very nasty last-minute hitch then occurred, however, when, without warning, the South Korean President, Syngman Rhee, released all the prisoners held by South Korea, anticipating that this would make the Communists accuse the Americans of bad faith, thus restoring the deadlock and probably provoking a renewal of full-scale war. But this did not happen. Not only did Dulles act with great determination in using American troops to round up the released prisoners—who had in any case nowhere to go—but the Communists stuck to their new view that a truce was now urgent. Within two months, therefore, by July 27, 1953, it was signed. The biggest limited war in modern times was over, and President Eisenhower's election pledge to bring peace in Korea had been redeemed—thanks to Dulles.

In Britain, on the other hand, the President's original suggestion amounting, as the press had put it, to "unleashing Chiang Kai-shek," was generally regarded with dismay, as adding yet another alarming uncertainty to the worrying instability which already existed all through the Far East. Quite apart from Labour criticism, Anthony Eden, the British Foreign Secretary, expressed this for the Conservative government when he said in the House of Commons that he feared that the decision would have "unfortunate political repercussions without compensating military advantages." There were of course genuine grounds for America's allies to fear that, if the Chinese Nationalists were unwise or deliberately provocative enough to attempt anything approaching a major operation, they might rapidly get into such difficulties that they would need rescuing by American ships and planes. If that happened, not only might this drain away military resources urgently needed for the Korean War, but it could, and indeed probably would, involve the United States in a direct and wider war with Communist China, the very thing which the allies feared and argued about ad nauseam when threatened with all-out action by General MacArthur. At the end of that road, they felt, lay either a very dangerous deflection of American power from the effective support of the Atlantic alliance in Western Europe, or even the final tragedy of a nuclear war involving a struggle to the death with the Soviet Union. Although admittedly in those days the United States still possessed a big potential nuclear superiority over Russia, few people outside the Pentagon seriously envisaged putting it to the test.

To some extent the whole American maneuver had indeed been bluff, a word for which one might substitute "brinkmanship"— though it was not brinkmanship in the popular Dullesian sense that the United States might deliberately resort to nuclear weapons. Nevertheless Dulles was quite downright about it at the time. In private he made clear his basic philosophy that there could be no success against the power of the Communists without taking risks. To him the Korean maneuver had been a relatively small risk, with the real possibility that it might have an immediate effect, as indeed it did. History has already justified him for extracting the United States from an intolerable situation. What Dulles did not appreciate sufficiently, however, was the extent to which his action would seriously reinforce the many doubts about American leadership and American objectives among America's allies. While he recognized that this danger existed—it was part of the risk —he brushed it aside too lightly and subjected the whole Western alliance to a strain for which it was by no means prepared. Already in fact Dulles was setting the pattern by which his whole record must be judged—that he gained his point with the Communists but lost the soul of his allies.

Once he had dealt with Korea, however, Dulles did turn his mind to Europe. There his NATO allies were convinced that a solution to the problem of German rearmament was quite as urgent in its own ways as the Korean truce. The Eisenhower-Dulles team had assumed control in Washington at a moment when Western Europe was in the grip of a paralyzing neurosis about the European Defense Community (EDC). This scheme had originated nearly two years before, in July, 1951, when it started life as the Pleven Plan. In the name of France, M. René Pleven had hastily thrust it forward as a means of side-stepping the Anglo-American decision to rearm Western Germany, following the Communist rearmament of Eastern Germany. Instead of creating any national German forces, the idea was to incorporate German military units in an integrated international force, which became generally known as the European army. No satisfactory technical details were ever given, however, to show how it would work. Under Dulles's guidance, the new Administration in Washington carried American policy straight on from where its predecessors had left off and backed EDC to the hilt. Thus in President Eisenhower's Inaugural Address he specifically asked for progress on the deadlock, urging that the "enlightened and inspired leaders of the Western nations try with renewed vigor to make the unity of their peoples a reality." And Dulles himself was to put it a good deal more strongly than merely asking.

For any British government EDC was bound to present a special problem, since it raised in a practical form the whole challenge of Britain's relations with its Continental neighbors. For Sir Winston Churchill, then in his last period as Prime Minister, the dilemma understandably seemed particularly acute. On the one hand, a year after the war, when he was in opposition, he himself had spoken strongly in his famous Zurich speech of September 19, 1946, in favor of closer contact between Britain and the rest of Western Europe, a speech which many Continentals had by no means forgotten; and had he not also even proposed a political union between Britain and France in the dark days of June, 1940? On the other hand, Churchill yearned with a passionate nostalgia for the atmosphere of exceptional Anglo-American political comradeship, which he managed to create with President Roosevelt during the war, and he had great hopes of re-establishing something of the same kind, if not with President Truman, then at any rate with President Eisenhower.

Now back in power, Churchill and Eden had rejected British

participation in EDC in the belief that it would weaken the London-Washington axis, and in the hope that members of the United States government would come to attach the same sort of value to that axis as the two British ministers did themselves. When they first returned to Downing Street in the winter of 1951–52, Truman and Acheson still had a year to run in Washington, and the Conservative leaders were somewhat disappointed to find that the Democratic Administration did not appear to respond with any noticeable extra warmth to their taking the place of Clement Attlee's Labour government.

Relations between Acheson and Bevin had indeed been most cordial and, although Eden's association with Acheson was a honeymoon compared with his subsequent clash with Dulles, from the American point of view there was nothing to get excited about in having Eden rather than Bevin; Morrison's brief tenure of office had hardly counted. From the British side, however, it did seem natural to expect that, once Eisenhower had settled in, he would pursue not only a more forward European policy, but also one of particular friendliness to Britain. There, memories of his wartime co-operation with the Churchill government were still fresh, and, even more, so was the excellent impression he had just left as Supreme Commander of the NATO forces on the Continent. Thus, while President Eisenhower's Inaugural appeal for Western European unity did not fall on entirely deaf ears in London, it came nowhere near to inducing a positive response. Although quite a number of people in Britain always have felt that their country ought to have done far more for European unity, and have recognized throughout that EDC was eventually killed as much by the British attitude as by the French, this was neither the government view nor that of the bulk of British public opinion at the time.

Nothing President Eisenhower said could accordingly shake the fundamental attitude that, since both the proposed European Defense Community and the already existent Coal-Steel Pool were widely thought to be the forerunners of an eventual federal European system, Britain could have no part in them. Admittedly London felt that it should work very closely with both organizations, particularly since any military defense of the continent of Western Europe would be gravely weakened if it were not backed by support from the British Isles. But none of this ranked as the top priority in Britain itself. That was still regarded as the Anglo-American alliance.

The tragedy of this attitude was that the British had put themselves in a false position, since their views about the Anglo-American link were not reflected in Washington, least of all after Dulles came to power. Two very important factors which affected Dulles's attitude to Britain are frequently forgotten. The first was that he never went through the experience of that peculiarly close wartime partnership with the British which many other Americans did. British observers of the American scene are sometimes too apt to classify Americans as either pro-British or anti-British. In reality a large mass of Americans are not necessarily either for or against Britain; they do not think much about the British, except when special circumstances force them to do so. The most powerful and remarkable of any such circumstances in history were the closing years of the Second World War. Hundreds of thousands of Americans, from those at the top to the most unsophisticated GI, lived, worked, and thought alongside the British for days and months on end, united both spiritually and physically in a common struggle which they could not afford to lose, and in which, in spite of the presence of other Allies, they were the dominant Western partners. Dulles entirely missed this experience, and it is a great pity that he did. He was occupied throughout the war in work based on the United States; moreover, this was somewhat outside the scope of government, since he had already begun to associate himself closely with the Republican opposition, fighting the 1944 Presidential campaign as Dewey's foreign affairs adviser. It would have been better for the whole vast alliance, of which he was to be the guiding spirit in the nineteen-fifties against another and far more powerful enemy than Nazi Germany, if he had taken some part in the intimate teamwork of the nineteen-forties.

The other factor which had an unfortunate effect on Dulles's attitude both towards the British and to the Western alliance as a whole was that he himself came to high office only after the superiority of America's own power had become indisputable. He never held great responsibilities, that is, in the conditions prevailing during the nineteen-thirties or even in the early years of the war, when, in spite of the obvious latent strength of the United States, Americans appeared neither willing nor ready to take over the active leadership of the Western world. Although Dulles had studied international relations for nearly half a century, through the Council on Foreign Relations and by many other means, he had never really gone through the emotional experience of sharing in the actual development of America's role. In another man this might not have mattered so much. But it was unfortunate that someone as intellectually self-confident, and indeed vain, as Dulles undoubtedly tended to be, should have found himself so suddenly in charge at the very peak of his country's power, accentuated by a flying economic start in the ravaged postwar world and by an overwhelming nuclear lead at that point in the arms race. All this helped to breed a superiority complex which Dulles sometimes needed to fight harder than he did, if he was to succeed in keeping it in its place.

Within a week of assuming office Dulles made the first of his many broadcasts as Secretary of State. In it he outlined his own approach to the leading aspects of American foreign policy. It was not altogether a bad speech and the worst interpretations put upon it at the time were hardly justified. But, although parts of it were designed more for domestic than for foreign consumption, it provoked both irritation and some degree of alarm in Britain as well as on the continent of Western Europe. Dulles's main move was to attempt to exert his influence over those who were still jibbing at the European army. He threatened that:

> If France, Germany and England should go their separate ways, then certainly it would be necessary to give a little rethinking to America's own foreign policy in relation to Western Europe.

His "little rethinking" at the outset of his official career was to blossom by the end of the year into the much more famous threat of an "agonizing reappraisal." But neither achieved its object, since in spite of the dismay of the Europeans they saw that America could not afford to abandon Europe, however disingenuous Dulles's threats might be.

He made several mistakes in taking the line he did. It was no use pretending, as he tried to do, that American economic aid had been given on the understanding that greater political unity would necessarily follow. The generosity of General Marshall's famous offer in 1947 was fully appreciated in Western Europe, though no one could quite have defined where America's own interest ended and generosity began. Indeed that is probably best left undefined. But the basic facts were that the United States needed to help rebuild the war-shattered economies of the Western European countries, whether individually or collectively, in order to resist Communism; and, for the same reason in a military sense, it was vital for Americans to defend the frontiers of the free world, whether they were those of half a dozen countries or of a single federal union. It was for this that the North Atlantic Treaty had been signed, and it was also for this, though not this alone, that the European Recovery Program had come into being.

As regards the British, the idea of frightening them into a closer union with continental Europe, by threatening a possible American withdrawal, was a bad psychological mistake. It had the precise opposite effect. Far from making them more likely to sink their sovereignty in that of their neighbors, the possibility of doing so without the Americans behind them simply made the British even more cautious than they had been before. Instead of going forward towards Europe, they drew back towards the tie with America. Equally, on the continent of Europe the image of a less active and more neutral America simply made many national leaders less, rather than more, willing to take political risks. If America was going to be neutral, then instead of committing themselves to an untried scheme like the European army, they recoiled into their outdated nationalist shells. Some, on the Left, began wondering whether it might not be better after all to seek ways and means of coming to terms with the Communists. This was the last thing that Dulles wanted, but he was to take a long time to learn that it was the kind of development which his rough tactics encouraged.

Dulles also made pronouncements about the Far East and Middle East. He recognized that the Soviet Union's ambition to control Japan was at the root of its aggressive policy in both Korea and Indo-China, since Russia's prewar fears of Japan were being revived by the new Japanese association with the United States. He did not, however, seek to draw any special conclusion from this view; and, in spite of the farsightedness of his own liberal peace treaty with Japan, it was to be another seven years before serious riots in Tokyo, shortly after his death, forced President Eisenhower to call off a state visit and compelled Washington to take a fresh look at the long-term requirements of American-Japanese relations.

On the Middle East, Dulles bracketed the British and Americans together as being the object of hatred stirred up by the Communists, adding that, if the oil of the area were to pass into the hands of potential enemies, this would mean a big shift in the balance of world economic power. At that time Communist infiltration into Middle East countries was relatively mild, and it was gratifying, if not surprising, to find an American Secretary of State linking British and American interests in the Middle East so closely. In reality the weakness of the Western position among the Arab countries lay in the divergence of British and American policy for handling a crumbling situation. In spite of a good deal of help when the crisis came, American pressure in Persia had weakened the original British bargaining position over Abadan. Washington's traditional anticolonialism, particularly as expressed by some of its professional representatives on the spot, had helped to break up the existing pattern of Middle East power without substituting anything worthwhile for it. And, however much Dulles and Eisenhower may have just begun to see that the inevitable British retreat was leaving a vacuum, they did nothing effective to fill it. If they had, the tragedy of the Suez crisis three years later might have been avoided.

Three days after his broadcast Dulles left on his first official visit to Europe, taking with him Harold Stassen, at that time head of the Mutual Security Agency, which was responsible for the distribution of the astronomic sums of American aid being poured into Europe, already totaling since the war nearly thirty billion dollars. On these many flights that Dulles made, a certain routine developed which enabled him to get a good deal of work done in the air, and he personally reveled in the luxury of not being available on the telephone. The aircraft was usually one of the several Constellations, later Super-Constellations, operated for VIP's by the Military Air Transport Service (MATS); occasionally the President's personal aircraft was used. Each of these aircraft was fitted up with good sleeping berths for ten and comfortable lounge accommodation. They were rented from MATS at definite fixed rates by the State Department or any other government agency, complete with crew including two stewards.

At that period, with gasoline-driven engines, departure from Washington for a flight to Europe, for instance, would be at about 4 P.M. For two or three hours after take-off Dulles, having changed into more informal clothes, would be at work with his secretary, dictating notes perhaps for a speech the following day, until they touched down at Gander to refuel. After leaving Gander he would probably come through to the main cabin for a drink and then supper with the rest of the party; this would probably consist of Mrs. Dulles, at least one personal assistant, perhaps an Assistant Under Secretary, and officials from the State Department concerned with the special problems he was expecting to deal with. After supper Dulles might play a rubber or two of bridge before going to bed. He almost invariably slept soundly on the aircraft and rose fresh the following morning for his arrival.

He never bothered at all about any difficulties that might arise over the flight, concerning either the functioning of the aircraft itself or the weather. His only technical interest was sometimes in the navigation. Things did, of course, occasionally go wrong, but never disastrously. On one occasion, engine failure over the Atlantic forced them down at the Azores, where it was found that immediate repairs were impossible. They would have been stuck except for the stray chance that another MATS plane happened to land soon after them, with an officially sponsored troupe of showgirls on their way to the U.S. forces in Germany. Dulles and his party commandeered their plane, and left the troupe on the Azores, to the delight of the locally-based American personnel at the airfield. On another occasion, when trying to land at Taipei, the capital of Formosa, in extremely bad weather the pilot made five runs at the airfield before he managed to get down, to the great alarm of most of his passengers, some of whom were very rattled indeed. Dulles went on dictating throughout and appeared quite unaware that anything special had happened at all. His general attitude was that aircraft were a great deal better than they used to be when he first started flying on commercial airlines, and anyway he was in the hands of God.

This first official trip to Europe at the beginning of February, 1953, took less than a fortnight, in which Dulles and Stassen visited London, Paris, Bonn, Rome, The Hague, Brussels, and Luxembourg, where the Coal-Steel Pool had its headquarters. Dulles was well aware that he had antagonized the Europeans in the few days he had been in power and he did what he could to reassure them. Yet he found it personally rather painful that so many people in Europe had not only greeted his original appointment with so much uneasiness, but were now also finding only too much justification for their distrust in his opening pronouncements as Secretary of State. Many of them he had himself known for many years, and some he had worked with in the recent past, both at the United Nations and previously in connection with the meetings of the Council of Foreign Ministers after the war. It was a measure of his own lack of political sensitivity, however, that these misunderstandings should have arisen at all, since they had begun with the hyperbole he had used in his Presidential campaign speeches. He had expected people to take what he said as so much electioneering —just as he partly did himself. Inevitably, however, his condemnation of the "containment" policy, so carefully worked out between the Truman Administration and its European allies during the previous difficult years, and his much-vaunted substitution for it of a dynamic attitude to "liberation," were bound to cause uneasiness in an area as sensitive to the cold war as Western Europe.

The fact was that the first weeks of a new Administration in Washington were almost bound to be difficult ones for the Western alliance. All the allies on both sides of the Atlantic had gone through a worrying and testing time in the years that were just over. In spite of the North Atlantic Treaty and the gradual buildup of military strength under NATO, there was still an anxious feeling that war might be only just around the corner; indeed the future judgment of history may well be that this was one of the most dangerous periods of the whole cold war. Moreover, European politicians had grown accustomed to the methods and reactions of President Truman and Dean Acheson. Working with them, an enormous amount had been done to strengthen the dikes against the Communist flood. And it was no more than inevitable that the leaders of Western Europe should flinch a little at facing these problems all over again with President Eisenhower and John Foster Dulles. The President they knew and trusted. Dulles they also knew, but did not trust. As a result, the new Washington Administration had much more difficulty in working its passage than it might have done, if the President had chosen a less contentious figure as his Secretary of State.

CHAPTER 6

After Stalin

STALIN died on March 5, 1953, only seven weeks after Eisenhower became President. Although the world could not know for some time just what difference this would make to Soviet policy, it was obvious at once that major changes in the Kremlin were bound to follow this long-awaited event. Looking back from the nineteen-sixties, however, there seems to be a clearer break the following year, 1954, between the problems of Stalin's own time and those which arose during the rest of the nineteen-fifties. There is a certain cohesion, that is to say, in the period from 1947 to 1954. This marked a term of consolidation by the Western powers against the Communist pressure. It was the era of containment, even though containment as an official American policy was no longer admitted after the Administrations changed in 1953. But the crucial fact about this period was that it was, in effect, also the last in which American atomic superiority went unchallenged. During the succeeding period, that is from 1954 to the collapse of the summit meeting in Paris in 1960, the Soviet challenge in the nuclear and then the missile field was growing year by year. And although there was probably a greater inherent stability in the nuclear balance of terror at that stage, in which the main delivery system was the bomber, the very fact that Russia was reaching a theoretical position of nuclear parity with the United States made the old pre-1954 days of American superiority look in retrospect rather safer and more secure than they felt at the time. Where the truth lies in all this is very hard to judge. But one important point about the growth of the Soviet challenge was that, once it had begun to grow,

76

a new danger appeared in the possibility of overconfidence in the Kremlin.

This was the broad background against which the problems of the spring and early summer of 1953 must be judged. Oddly enough, the first of the high-level callers in Washington was actually there when the news of Stalin's death came through. He was the man with whom Dulles was to quarrel as deeply as with anyone, the British Foreign Secretary, Anthony Eden, accompanied on this occasion by R. A. Butler, at that time Chancellor of the Exchequer. Their conversations in Washington took place between March 4 and 7, 1953, being followed towards the end of the month by Dulles's talks with the French Prime Minister, M. Mayer, and the French Foreign Minister, M. Bidault, together with M. Bourges-Maunoury, the Finance Minister, and M. Letourneau, the Minister for the Associated States, that is Indo-China. After the British and French came the Germans on April 7, when Dr. Adenauer duly made the first of his several trips to see Dulles and President Eisenhower in Washington.

This particular visit by Eden and Butler was widely regarded as more of a success than had seemed likely only a few weeks before, although Eden was disappointed in not getting any active American support for various economic proposals to encourage world trade which had been discussed at the recent Commonwealth Economic Conference. This relative success was partly due to the stimulation provided by the great change in Moscow, and partly to the fact that both sides were being rather careful in this their first formal contact, since neither wanted to be responsible for anything that might widen the distance between London and Washington at this important opening stage in the life of the Eisenhower Administration. Dulles and Eden announced at the end of their talks that they had in fact reached agreement on the key issue of EDC, saying that, while its ratification was urgently necessary, Britain's attitude was appreciated in Washington. Dulles did not in fact blame the British for the failure of EDC quite as much as many others did. Together they also confirmed the previous understanding that, even in an emergency, American air bases in Britain would not be used without a joint decision by the two governments. On the Far East, although of course they reserved

their positions on the recognition of Communist China, Eden gave
Dulles the satisfaction of telling him that the British had decided
to introduce a new system of licensing vessels, which would prevent
strategic material being transported to China in British ships, and
would insure that no ships of the Soviet bloc, or of any other
nationality carrying strategic cargoes for China, would be bunkered
in a British port.

Lastly, but of considerable importance, there was a full exchange
of views about the Middle East, which became in fact the main
focus of the discussions. There were two important aspects of the
Middle East problem at that moment: the Anglo-Iranian oil dispute arising out of Dr. Mossadegh's nationalization of the Anglo-
Iranian Oil Company, and the equally long-drawn-out Anglo-
Egyptian negotiations on the British military withdrawal from the
Suez Canal Zone base. One of the main British objects in these
Washington talks was to co-ordinate tactics with the new Administration on the joint handling of both issues. On the whole Dulles
and Eden reached a form of understanding on each of them,
though, while it worked out quite well during the next few months
over Iran, it did not do so over Egypt.

How far, then, did the apparent sense of general agreement
reflect the underlying truths? Put at their simplest, these included
on the British side the still latent emotions which had been aroused
all over Europe by the image of aggressiveness that Dulles had
created during the electoral campaign; and on the American side
criticism of Britain's refusal to join EDC, disapproval of British
policy in the Middle East, and disappointment at the size of
Britain's effort in Korea. But there was much more even than that
to the obstacles which both Eden and Dulles inevitably encountered
in trying to reach an understanding with one another. Apart from
any immediate questions of international politics, there were two
permanent and imponderable factors which hung over Anglo-
American relations like the dark threat of monsoon rain. One, the
least difficult, was the discrepancy in power. Not only was there
great difference in the relative power of each of the two countries,
but both were going through a period of major adjustment. While
the British were having to adjust themselves to a still declining
status in the world, the Americans suddenly had to face almost

overwhelming responsibilities of leadership, knowing at the same time that their vast superiority of power was neither lasting nor such that the power could ever be freely exercised. The other factor was the difference in temperament, character, and personality of the two chief spokesmen, John Foster Dulles and Anthony Eden.

At the beginning of 1953 Dulles was by no means alone in Washington in being highly conscious of the strength of the United States. The whole Administration felt the same. These, after all, were still the days in which the broad acres of North America seemed so distant from the enemy that they were virtually invulnerable to direct attack. On the other hand, this invulnerability was far indeed from promoting any disposition to war. What these new men in Washington looked for, in dealing with the Communist problem, was the scope for initiative and action. What precisely that action was to be, they did not really know. All they were sure about, all that Dulles himself was sure about was that they were determined to prove to the world, as well as to themselves, that they could prosecute the cold war harder and more effectively than the Democrats had done. For Dulles the days of bipartisanship in foreign policy were definitely over.

For the British at this juncture, as for all Europeans, there was danger in the unpredictability of the Americans. If the Americans looked like being overkeen to push their Western allies into courses from which the latter instinctively shrank, the British and other Europeans were equally overcautious in the restraints they instinctively felt they wanted to place on the new Administration. The danger to the alliance as a whole was thus that constant quibbling from across the Atlantic would increase American impatience, with the chain reaction that the Europeans would become even more cautious and have less and less respect for the leadership in Washington. If that danger had developed, it might have pushed Dulles and his advisers into acting without consulting their allies even more than they sometimes did anyway. As regards the British, while Dulles's own attitude was highly complex, in day-to-day matters he usually took the line that, although he rejected the British view that there was something exclusive about an Anglo-American alliance, they were to all intents and purposes the first of his allies. And certainly, in these initial Dulles-Eden conversations, the

Anglo-American wrangle over Chinese policy, doubts about Western European integration, disputes in the Middle East, and misunderstandings on liberation were all cut down to a size which could be dealt with.

In these early days Dulles and Eden each personally repressed their mutual antipathy to one another, though the seeds of divergence had already been sown at the time of Dulles's handling of the Japanese Peace Treaty negotiations more than a year before, when they had had extensive talks with one another. Sir Anthony Eden specifically denies today the reports that he ever "put pressure" on General Eisenhower not to appoint Dulles as Secretary of State, because he would never be able to work with Dulles and because such an appointment would inevitably impair Anglo-American relations. "You don't," he has expressed it, "put pressure on the President of the United States." Nevertheless, Eden could scarcely conceal even at that time his instinctive reaction that Dulles was personally unsatisfactory to deal with and, compared with Dean Acheson, exasperating and unreliable. Acheson for his part did not think quite as much of Eden as Eden thought of Acheson, though compared with what Dulles's views of Eden later became, Acheson's opinion was positively golden. While both these Americans found Eden rather baffling, to Dulles he seemed just the kind of Englishman many Americans dislike most. This was not, therefore, a promising start to their several years of contact and, although the views of neither of them had yet by any means crystallized, they both went out of their way at the beginning to cover their common distrust with a superficial gloss of friendliness. By the time of Suez, however, Eden thought Dulles a liar and Dulles regarded Eden as an arrogant fool.

It was in fact impossible that Dulles and Eden should ever really understand one another. Dulles was essentially intellectual in his approach, appraising, legalistic, logical, weighing the pros and cons —all too often out loud. Eden as a politician was intuitive, quick-tempered, rather apt to use his great experience emotionally, and not very open to argument. To this day Eden finds Dulles an enigma, and Dulles certainly died without coming to terms with the image of Eden. When they were together they were often on such different wave lengths that it sometimes seemed to their staffs a pity that they could not have stuck to the conduct of their business through intermediaries in the good old-fashioned way. Dulles's relationship with Eden, indeed, afforded standing proof that personal and direct diplomacy is not always the best.

One of the most lasting memories many world leaders will always have of Dulles is of his awkward bulk descending from or climbing into an aircraft, and it is the type of memory which President Kennedy decreed from the start would not be repeated under his Administration. United States ambassadors are now used more as ambassadors used to be used, their reports are read, and they themselves deliver America's views to foreign governments. Under Dulles all this was set aside. He believed that in the modern age of swift transport and immediate communications a whole range of fresh achievement had been made possible by face-to-face contact. It was in some ways the hallmark of his diplomacy, the main symbol by which his impact on the world might be judged. But he failed with Eden, and it was a failure with such ugly consequences that it will always stand as a special monument to the weakness of his method. For Eden and Dulles could talk together by the hour and never understand each other at all.

Dulles was very given to longish monologues which helped to clear his own mind, and he expected others to follow his reasoning as closely as he enjoyed following it himself. Eden, on the other hand, could not stand anything so academic and often found it impossible to listen. At the end of such a talk when Dulles would ask for Eden's view, Eden would seem to brush off much that Dulles might just have said and would give an answer that appeared to Dulles too inconsequential to be taken seriously. In spite of this Dulles always tried to appreciate Eden's point of view, and he sometimes failed only because the fundamental assumptions from which each of them started were so different. Basically these were that Dulles sought to exercise a certain authority in the world, since he felt he had a right to do so—because of his strong moral views, his wide study of affairs, and the great power of the United States. For Eden, by contrast, while America's pre-eminence was obvious, this did not mean that its allies were to be treated as dependent inferiors, and he found the self-righteousness of the

American attitude, as expressed by Dulles, both hypocritical and intolerable.

All these factors did not, of course, operate at once, and, even when they did, they were held more carefully in check at some periods than others. Naturally they were all blown up to fabulous proportions by the Suez crisis of 1956; but that came as a ghastly final chapter to the Dulles-Eden relationship and, while the basic tendencies were always present, they were never as strong at the beginning as they were at the end. Indeed, at this opening stage in 1953 what was probably the high-water mark of Dulles's and Eden's association with one another was still to come, namely the decisive period of allied co-operation at the Berlin Conference with the Russians in January, 1954. Meanwhile, as has already been suggested, Dulles and Eden did reach a relative and amicable identity of view at this first official meeting in March, 1953, on the problem of Iranian oil, to which the British attached the greatest possible importance.

Various accusations have been made from time to time about the role which Washington played in this Iranian dispute. In general they have been exaggerated and have done more harm to Anglo-American relations than they need have done. The Iranian oil crisis began for Britain with the oil nationalization decree of May 1, 1951, immediately after Dr. Mossadegh became Prime Minister of Iran, and well before either Eden or Dulles had taken office. But for over two years throughout the premiership of Mossadegh, that is until his final overthrow in August, 1953, the position went steadily from bad to worse, in spite of a number of joint Anglo-American efforts to solve the problem during the course of 1952, when Eden and Acheson worked closely together on it. Eden has deliberately put himself clearly on record in his memoirs as being grateful throughout to the State Department, first under Acheson and then under Dulles, and particularly to Loy Henderson, who was appointed as American ambassador in Teheran in the middle of 1952. Some people in Britain had doubts about Henderson, but Eden, it appears, was not among them.

Anglo-American relations nevertheless always ran somewhat unevenly in this dispute, since London and Washington never saw their own vital interests in quite the same light. In London, there

were two key points that mattered. First, the actual oil which was
extracted, refined, and shipped to Britain by the Anglo-Iranian Oil
Company, was a major factor in the British economy; hence its
loss created a balance of payments problem, with the ultimate risk
that alternative purchases might have to be made in hard currency
dollars instead of in sterling. Secondly, not only was it an important
matter of principle that countries should not be able to seize foreign
holdings without proper compensation, but events in Iran could
set a disastrous example to other countries in the Middle East.

On the American side, while these factors were naturally recognized, particularly the second one, three others outweighed them
by the time that Dulles assumed office as Secretary of State. First,
and this was the fundamental point which always prevented any
absolute Anglo-American agreement in the dispute, Washington
always tended to take the view that Mossadegh was the last barrier
in Persia to the Communists; if the ground were cut from under
his feet on the oil issue, they would move in. Secondly, there was
the oil lobby in Washington and the straight commercial rivalry
between the American oil companies and the British, which, while
somewhat inhibited by recognition of the general need to stand
together against exorbitant nationalist claims for royalties, meant
that the American companies saw no reason why they should not
profit from the difficulties of their British rivals in this particular
instance; and certainly they did not want the American government
to lean over backwards simply to get the British out of a jam.
Lastly, a factor of some importance after the Eisenhower Administration had taken over was Dulles's deep-rooted inhibition about
any course of action which appeared to run counter to his own
deeply ingrained anticolonialism.

When the Anglo-Iranian Oil Company was expropriated by the
Iranian nationalization law of May, 1951, the British government
backed the company in demanding arbitration under the 1933
Anglo-Persian Agreement. It was, incidentally, of some interest
that this prewar agreement was negotiated by the then British
Foreign Secretary, Sir John Simon, since he was a man in some ways
not altogether unlike Dulles. A brilliant lawyer, he was inclined
to look at foreign affairs through the same kind of legalistic spectacles which Dulles himself used. The main difference between them

was that Simon could never make up his mind; at least, his indecision was more genuine than Dulles's unfortunate facility for
apparently saying one thing and, to judge by later statements,
meaning another. Although Sir John Simon's character thus bears
comparison with that of Dulles, the nearest to the American
Secretary of State in British Foreign Secretaries of modern times
would probably by a cross between Sir John Simon and Lord John
Russell in the nineteenth century.

The history of the Anglo-Iranian oil dispute when Dulles and
Eden came to discuss it in March, 1953, had been exceedingly
irritating. At the ouset, after backing the company, the British
government took the dispute to the International Court of Justice
at The Hague, asking that the President of the Court appoint an
arbitrator. Finally, in July, 1952, the Court decided that it had no
jurisdiction, although it had in the meanwhile proposed various
interim steps which were all rejected by the Iranians. Anglo-
American co-operation in the dispute had begun when President
Truman sent Averell Harriman to Teheran to exercise America's
good offices. All this, however, was useless, the British staff of the
oil company was expelled from Iran, and London next took the
dispute to the UN Security Council. The Security Council eventually adjourned discussion of the issue by passing the buck; it
decided to do nothing until the Hague Court gave a ruling—which
it never did.

During 1952 Acheson and President Truman gave the British
considerable support, but not enough to prevent Mossadegh receiving wide public approval in Iran for his brusque rejection of
a joint message from President Truman and Sir Winston Churchill
in August of that year. Far from being impressed, the Iranians
thought they could play the United States off against Britain in the
belief that Washington's support was not genuine. The final
episode under the Truman Administration had been a joint British
and American proposal, in which the Iranians were once again
asked to submit the mass of claims and counterclaims between
themselves and the British to impartial arbitration. As an induce-
ment they were to receive in return a substantial measure of
American economic aid. In itself this was a generous offer by the
United States. But, with Mossadegh stronger than ever in Teheran,

its impact was weakened by the fact that the State Department was known to be more worried by the prospect of failing to reach any kind of agreement at all with Iran than by the possibility of getting a bad one.

This broadly was the situation when Dulles and Eden discussed it, though there had been certain fresh British amendments to the proposals during February. Dulles was inclined not to press the matter any harder for the moment, and to suspend negotiations if the Iranians would not come to an early agreement. He was particularly worried at the possibility of Mossadegh breaking off diplomatic relations with America, as he had long ago done with Britain, if Washington appeared to go too far out on the British limb. And there indeed the matter was perforce to rest until five months later, when, on August 19, 1953, the situation was transformed by the revolution in Teheran which deposed Mossadegh once and for all, restored the position of the Shah, and brought General Zahedi into power as Prime Minister. It was still to be several months before the final oil agreement was signed, but from then on the going was easier. Eden, for his part, was away from the Foreign Office for six months from April after his first operation.

By April Dulles himself was beginning to get into his stride. He had survived severe criticism at home and he had begun to get the measure of his allies abroad. During April he flew across the Atlantic again to attend a ministerial meeting of the Atlantic Council in Paris, at which NATO ministers of foreign affairs, defense, economics and finance were present. Once again he seized the opportunity to do all in his power to support the creation of the European Defense Community, declaring that he knew of no alternative. Once again he did it by hinting that, if no means could be found for bringing a German defense contribution into NATO, the United States would have to review its entire NATO program. Once again, however, neither his entreaties nor his threats were to prove of any avail. But this time, although the European leaders could not help being somewhat influenced by the American attitude, his words did not cause as much of a stir as they had done earlier because everyone knew roughly what he would say.

During April and May the hopes of a truce in Korea had begun to grow, encouraged not only by a slightly better atmosphere across

the negotiating table at Panmunjom, but also by the wider calculation that the death of Stalin at the beginning of March must inevitably have meant a complete review of their commitments by the
Soviet leaders in the Kremlin, still led at that time by Stalin's
immediate legatee, Malenkov. It was now nearly two years since
the electric morning of June 23, 1951, when Mr. Malik, the Soviet
delegate to the United Nations, in a broadcast under UN auspices
had let drop the first exciting hint that Russia might be willing to
discuss a possible cease-fire in Korea, "providing for the mutual
withdrawal of forces from the 38th parallel." And in the many
weary months of abortive negotiation which had followed, the
United Nations allies had held together remarkably well. Now,
however, as tension somewhat eased, the drop in Communist pressure began to reveal like an ebb tide some of the rocks of allied
disagreement on Far Eastern policy, hitherto kept more or less
under water by the swell of war. It would be an exaggeration to
say that the modest success of the Dulles-Eden conversations in
March was thereby undone, but there was certainly a tendency in
Washington to look around for scapegoats, and an obvious one
was Britain. As a result, a good many things were said which would
have been better left unsaid.

Dulles, whose confidence had grown with his somewhat improving stature, used this rather more fluid situation to send up a
characteristically challenging trial balloon. In the middle of April,
just before departing on his first retreat to Duck Island since
becoming Secretary of State, he threw out a number of ideas about
a possible Far Eastern settlement at a press conference. These
caused consternation among some of the less responsible right-
wing elements in the Republican party. Included in the calculated
indiscretions which drew the wrath of the China lobby was the idea
that, when it came to a political settlement after a military truce,
Korea might well be divided at the narrow waist which was about
one hundred miles north of the existing fighting line. Although this
proposal implied a considerable Communist withdrawal and would
include over three-quarters of the total Korean population in
President Syngman Rhee's Republic of South Korea, many Republicans at that time regarded it as a disgraceful abandonment of the

accepted, basic American aim of a united Korea free from Communist domination.

Dulles also suggested that, once a military truce had been
negotiated in Korea itself, the subsequent political negotiations
might include other Far Eastern questions as well, notably the
struggle in Indo-China and even the position of Formosa. On this
latter point, he deliberately allowed himself to be understood to
have given thought to a possible United Nations trusteeship for
Formosa; but, owing to the violence of the general uproar, this was
promptly denied from the White House, and it was made clear
that the new Administration had no intention of going so far as
to withdraw its positive support for General Chiang Kai-shek's
claim to be the legitimate government of China. What Dulles was
up to, of course, was a deliberate testing of the Republican party
attitude on some of the hoary old problems which the Administration had inherited from the Democrats. And although the explosive
reaction compelled him to cut his balloon adrift, at least for the
moment, he chuckled in private at the success of the test. Unfortunately, from the point of view of actual policy the result was
barren. Dulles had too much respect for the political power of the
die-hards to be willing to pursue his ideas any further.

Both the President and the Secretary of State were in fact search-
ing hard for ways in which they could express their determination
that the new Administration should, at one and the same time, put
pressure on the Russians to negotiate and yet also make it clear
that America's own position was less rigid than might be supposed.
Thus, while President Eisenhower made speeches in which he
discreetly challenged Malenkov to disavow something of the brutal
and even deceitful bluntness of the Stalin era, it was left to Dulles
to be more specifically tough in the cut and thrust of international
debate. The President, for instance, was heard making carefully
phrased statements urging the Communists to come to an "honor-
able armistice" in Korea, to sign the long-delayed Austrian peace
treaty, and to release the German prisoners of war whom they had
held for eight years since the end of the World War. Then the very
next week Dulles could be seen doggedly rejecting point by point
the latest Communist "peace plan" in Korea. It was a difficult situation for the Secretary of State, but one which events had almost

inevitably forced upon him and from which he gradually emerged with relative profit.

Perhaps the main danger to the Western alliance, since many people at least in Britain had become suspicious and critical of American stubbornness in the truce talks, sprang from the fact that the immediate handling of these negotiations was virtually in American hands alone. Washington naturally tended to overplay American interests and to let the pressures of domestic politics outweigh the views of its allies. Both were characteristic of Dulles himself. The difficulty, however, was that for America and its allies to discuss their differences too strongly or too publicly was to play into Communist hands. Moreover, as the British Prime Minister, Sir Winston Churchill, pointed out, it was not as if there were any real barrier to the conclusion of a military armistice. The negotiations at Panmunjom, he rightly said, "no longer involve a difference of principle," and "if at any time there is a wish among the Communists to reach an agreement as between rational human beings the matter could be almost instantly settled."

On May 9 Dulles turned thankfully from the frustrations of Korea and flew off on another of his fact-finding tours, like the first one he had made to Western Europe just after assuming office. Again accompanied by Harold Stassen, the Director of the Mutual Security Program, this one was to the Middle East, India, and Pakistan, and it lasted for three weeks, bringing him back to Washington on May 29. Before leaving the capital, Dulles made a statement that he would not be taking any part in the negotiations then going on between Britain and Egypt for the withdrawal of British forces from the Suez Canal Zone. What he said was no more than a restatement of the position that had emerged during, and immediately after, the talks which Eden had had with him and President Eisenhower two months earlier in Washington in March. But his denial was not at the wish of the British and, although the State Department at that time favored a British withdrawal, it did not want to see the big military installations, which the British had built up, fall into hands hostile to the West. Dulles could accordingly have afforded to be rather more positive about the need for a settlement, as indeed he was after he reached Cairo. British and American interests are by no means always the same.

But, when they are, it is a disservice to the common Western cause
not to admit the fact. Dulles's first public reaction to the problem
of Egypt was thus an unpleasant warning of the troubles his
evasiveness was to cause later on.

During the previous eighteen months, that is since October,
1951, when Nahas Pasha had denounced the Anglo-Egyptian
Treaty of 1936, Britain and Egypt had been in contact off and on,
sometimes cordially but more often acrimoniously, in an attempt
to reach agreement on the status of the British military base in the
Suez Canal Zone and on the progress of the Sudan towards independence; hitherto the Sudan had technically been under an Anglo-
Egyptian condominium. This period had been characterized, first,
by the steady deterioration of relations on the spot between the
British army and the Egyptians; secondly, by the collapse of the
Egyptian so-called democratic regime, following the seizure of
power by the young army officers under the apparent leadership
of General Naguib but the real direction of Colonel Nasser in
July, 1952, and the abdication of King Farouk; and, thirdly, by an
abortive attempt to create some form of Middle East Defense
Organization on the flank of NATO.

The issue of the Sudan had been greatly simplified when King
Farouk abdicated, since the Egyptians could then no longer claim
that the head of their state should be recognized as king of both
countries; and by the spring of 1953 the Sudan was in fact well on
the road to genuine independence. On the question of the base,
the British had in principle taken the fundamental decision to
evacuate the Suez Canal Zone, soon after "Black Friday" in Cairo,
January 25, 1952, when the Egyptian mob had ransacked and
burnt some £3 million worth of British property and killed a number of British subjects. But what remained was the exceedingly
thorny problem of getting Egyptian agreement to terms for the
reactivation of this very considerable military establishment in the
event of a general war in the Middle East. And it was here that
American interests were involved. Directly rebuffed by the Egyptians a few months before on the straight issue of a Middle East
Defense Organization, Washington was concerned that this valuable asset of the Suez Canal Zone base should not be thrown away,
even though the Administration believed that there could be no

stability in the area until the British and Egyptians reached agreement on the pace and timing of the proposed British withdrawal.

Unfortunately the mood in Cairo was such that no practical progress was possible unless the Americans and British acted in concert. And while a broad Anglo-American understanding about the objectives seemed to have been agreed upon during the March conversations between Dulles and Eden, Dulles had always personally remained lukewarm about pushing the matter at all actively. The result had been that, promoted by the American ambassador in Cairo, Mr. Caffery, the Naguib-Nasser government had told the Americans that it would not accept Washington as a party to any negotiations about the Suez Canal Zone, however general any proposed package deal might be. Thus, although a satisfactory outcome to these negotiations was a direct American interest as well as a British one, Dulles refused to see this in a positive light, and in doing so undoubtedly weakened the general Western position in the Middle East, with evil consequences almost as much for the United States as for Britain. It is almost certain that, if he had insisted on some form of American participation, the Egyptians would have found it difficult to exclude him. As things were, the Egyptians, like the Iranians, gained the impression that they could play London and Washington off against one another. In a sense they were quite right.

This was the situation when Dulles reached Cairo in May, 1953. To do him justice, he did then administer something of a momentary shock to opinion inside the Egyptian regime. While talking to General Naguib, he made it quite plain that America wanted an Egyptian settlement with the British which would be satisfactory to both parties, and one moreover that would retain the effectiveness of the elaborate military installations created over so many years by the British, including the extensive tank repair workshops. After the talks he issued a statement declaring that, while he favored a solution of the Canal Zone problem "consistent with full Egyptian sovereignty, and with a phased withdrawal of troops," the defense and well-being of the Middle East were of great concern to the United States, and the Canal base "should remain in good working order and be available for immediate use on behalf of the free world in the event of future hostilities."

In the event, Dulles's visit to Cairo did not change any basic feature of the situation, and the efforts which the British had been making both before and after his visit to get the talks going again with Egypt were unsuccessful. It was to be another eighteen months before an agreement on the base was finally achieved on October 19, 1954. Although Dulles's much plainer speaking in May, 1953, had come as a rather nasty surprise in Cairo, the Egyptian regime did not modify its politically satisfying anti-British stand. What no one outside could know at the time was that it was already suffering internally from Colonel Nasser's growing need to get rid of General Naguib, if his young officers' revolution was to be completed. For the British themselves, therefore, Dulles's visit left the position just as tense and insecure as it had been before he came.

It seems quite odd today to look back and recall that as recently as 1955, there was still a British force of nearly eighty thousand men on the Suez Canal. This was an army much too strong to be defeated in any open attack by the Egyptians. But, as is well known, the working of the base depended on Egyptian labor, and the military effectiveness of the force was critically undermined by the subversive and semiguerrilla attacks which the Egyptians were making on it. Britain was faced with the unpleasant alternative of either hanging on through a period of guerrilla warfare, which could do nothing but great political harm, as well as being extremely unpleasant for the troops on the spot, or withdrawing lock, stock, and barrel.

All through Dulles's time in Washington, even long before the Suez crisis of 1956, the full extent of Britain's difficulties was never generally appreciated in the American capital. The British and Americans were in fact always divided in their fundamental reactions to the political changes then going on in the Middle East. There were, of course, also many critics of official government policy in Britain itself, and the fact that the Suez crisis finally brought the whole of this era to a sudden end can be read as proof that the British government's domestic critics were right. Yet it is something of an open question whether they would have proved so right if the British had received full American support during this period, and if they had been seen by the Arabs to receive this support. Thus, while the common Anglo-American objective of preventing Communist infiltration was often readily agreed to in conferences between Dulles and Eden, the methods for achieving it virtually never were.

Throughout these years the British were unwilling to abandon any part of their own increasingly hard-pressed position, unless it could be shown that such a handover would promote, rather than reduce, the general sense of military security and stability. Dulles, by contrast, was merely expressing the point of view of progressive opinion in all western countries, including the United States, when he always insisted that the first essential was to win the good will of the local people, as well as of their governments. There are sensible arguments on both sides and the right answer is really a matter of judgment and degree. What is good will, for instance? Sometimes it is in practice no more than respect, and that depends on power. What is military security? At some times and in some places it does depend on the attitudes of local government rather than their people, since the view of the people will depend on the line taken by their governments. But how far that would have been generally true in the Middle East of 1953 is an open question. Obviously, where the forces of nationalism were beating against the old men in some of the Arab governments, the latter could not have seriously influenced opinion in a matter concerning relations with the West. But who could say that, if Nasser had thought it expedient to play along with a solidly united Anglo-American approach, the Egyptian people would not have accepted his lead? It seems virtually certain that they would have done so. The problem was to reach an agreement with Nasser personally, but in 1953 Dulles did not yet see it in quite such individual terms, and no concerted attempt was ever made.

After Egypt, Dulles went on to visit India and Pakistan. In both Delhi and Karachi he listened and talked. But there was no problem demanding or capable of an early solution, and neither Dulles, whose views condemning neutralism were well known, nor his hosts materially modified their respective positions. Dulles found the experience useful, even though some four years were still to pass before he effectively changed his mind about neutralism. It was during his visit to Delhi on this occasion that he skillfully dropped the hints in Indian ears about plans to step up the war in Korea which, when relayed to Peking, undoubtedly contributed to breaking the deadlock at the Korean truce talks.

Just over a fortnight after he got back to Washington, however, something far more dramatic took place which cruelly revealed the hollowness of a different aspect of his current political philosophy. This was the rioting in East Berlin on June 16 and 17, which spread the next day to Halle, Jena, Leipzig, Görlitz and Magdeburg in the Soviet-occupied zone of Germany. Here, within five months of his coming to power, was the ideal opportunity, so it might have been argued, for the new Administration to put into operation its policy of liberation for the peoples of Eastern Europe. Here was the first spark which, if Dulles's words in the election campaign meant anything, he must fan and feed till Soviet rule was "awed" back into its own borders. For twenty-four hours the world watched and waited. What would America do? What could America do—without war? Though no one knew it at the time, this was the curtain-raiser to Hungary three years later. How would Dulles react? How did he react this time in 1953, and later in 1956?

The riots in East Berlin began as entirely spontaneous demonstrations by East German workers against the raising of their norms of work, a step which meant that they had to do more work for the same pay and implied in effect a lowering of their wages. This step appears to have been taken by the East German authorities on their own initiative and without reference to Moscow, since they were opposed to a number of minor concessions, which had been announced in the previous few days by the Soviet occupying power, as something of a sweetener before the arrival of the new Soviet High Commissioner for East Germany, Vladimir Semeonov. This was the first but by no means the last occasion on which the East Germans were to act quite independently of their Soviet masters.

The general importance of both the changes lay in the fact that among people all over the Communist empire a slight sense of relaxation had been felt since the death of Stalin in March, and with it had inevitably come fresh hope, a burgeoning restlessness, and an exciting impression that Moscow itself was feeling its way without the old ruthless certainty. There was also all that the new Administration in Washington had apparently been saying about the possibility of help from the West. So the East Berliners rose.

Soviet tanks came out in the streets and the Germans fought them with fists and stones. A number of people were killed. It was the bravest expression of hope and despair the world had seen since the war.

Dulles was far too experienced not to know instantly what this challenge meant. He knew, even if others wanted to forget, that East Germany was the keystone to the Soviet arch over Eastern Europe. It was, as it has remained since, at one and the same time the permanent basis of Russia's bid to insure that Germany should not be reunited except under Communism; an important weather-vane for every other Communist regime in Eastern Europe, warning them that, if Ulbricht's government collapsed, they might in the end collapse too; an economic factor of irreplaceable value as a manufacturing center for the rest of the satellite area, as well as a useful source of supply for the Soviet Union itself; and, by no means least, the military key to the whole Soviet threat to Western Europe and NATO. The Russians could not conceivably contemplate the possibility of the overthrow of the East German Communist regime under Ulbricht without reacting drastically and dangerously. All this Dulles knew very well indeed. When, accordingly, the news came to Washington that riots and disorders were spreading in the Soviet Zone of Germany, his bluff was called. There would be no serious American reaction, because there could be none.

Dulles did not even have a plan. He and the other Western allies protested to the Russians, and the United States offered fifteen million dollars worth of free food to Eastern Germany. Molotov refused the offer, following this up later with a protest through Semeonov to the latter's opposite number in Germany, the American High Commissioner, Dr. James B. Conant, declaring that the offer was deliberately provocative. The only effective action America could and did take was to distribute extra food to the increased tide of East Berliners, who came over into West Berlin to get it. And when the Russians stopped the issue of railway tickets in reply, even this pathetic episode came to an end. Silence once more descended on Eastern Germany.

On the credit side of the balance sheet, however, two items deserve a place. One was that, after these circumstances in Eastern

Germany had been put down, no one in the rest of Eastern Europe could expect the West to come to their aid, if they revolted against their Communist masters. And in so far as false hopes had sometimes been encouraged by the recent tone of American broadcasts, this was a sad but salutary lesson. Even the Hungarians three years later did not seriously rely on America coming to their aid. The other credit item was a direct corollary of this, namely that in the capitals of Western Europe, where Dulles's inaction had been greeted with relief, there was a slight increase of confidence in the stability of his intentions, and his influence slowly rose. On the debit side, nevertheless, was the fact that the West had once more come face to face with its inability to do anything practical to eject Soviet rule from Eastern Europe. There, moreover, not only had that rule been once more clamped down as firmly as ever, but much of the hope had inevitably evaporated that the post-Stalin changes in Moscow would mean any revolutionary easing of the conditions of life in the satellite empire. As for Dulles himself, this hour of reckoning for his exaggerated electoral claims did not exactly add to his stature inside the United States.

A month after the East German riots an armistice was signed in Korea on July 27, 1953. This was at last that end to the war which Eisenhower had promised in his electoral campaign. It was, however, only a strictly military truce, providing for a solution to the bitterly contested dispute over the return of prisoners, for a control being placed on the future entry, re-equipment and rotation of troops in Korea, and for various supervisory commissions. All that was said about a political settlement was that, within three months of the signing of the armistice, a political peace conference should be held. To this day, no political settlement of the Korean problem has been achieved. But the armistice has endured, and it says much for the recognition of realities by both sides that, in spite of temptations, this futile and frustrating war has never been restarted. If fighting began again, it would certainly be on a different basis.

For the Americans the Korean war was an incident without precedent in their history. One of the strengths, as well as the weaknesses, of traditional American processes of thought has always been the implicit assumption that every problem has a solution. The only difficulty is to find it; but that it exists is certain. In reality many problems have no solution, except with a generous admixture of time, and that is an element which American tradition is very unwilling to allow for. In the Korean War the Americans were forced not only to fight a cruelly unsatisfactory campaign, but also to acknowledge at the end of it that nothing as cut and dried as a "solution" could be found.

At that moment of postwar history the United States still possessed a vast potential nuclear superiority over the Soviet Union and, in the bombers of the U.S. Strategic Air Command (SAC), a delivery system which the Kremlin was not to equal for another five years, if then. In addition, a new Administration had just been elected, full of determination either to end the war on terms acceptable to the nation, or, as everyone presumed, to prosecute the war to final victory—whatever that might mean and whatever it might cost. Yet in spite of these factors of superiority, and in spite of a high rate of American casualties in the field, the United States had been brought to a standstill. To millions of Americans this was almost as puzzling as it was frustrating. Never before in history, particularly in the modern period of their immense power, had Americans been forced to accept this kind of situation. It was therefore understandable that the nation should have been restless, frustrated, and shocked by the course of events.

Inevitably this mood made it difficult even for the truce to sweep away overnight every trace of the sense of distrust and irritation towards their allies which had been induced in some Americans by the long months of fighting and waiting. By contrast, for most people in Britain the Korean War always seemed a long way away— as indeed it was. Admittedly, an unprecedented step, for anything but world war, had been taken in building up a British Commonwealth division as part of the United Nations force under American command. Into this division had gone some of the best troops and commanders that Britain possessed; the stand of the Gloucestershire Regiment in the battle of Solma-ri in 1951 will never be forgotten in the annals of military warfare. But the fact remains that, when the shooting stopped, Britain's own casualties, in killed, missing, and wounded, amounted to 4,106 compared with total American casualties of 141,705, of whom 22,628 were killed in action and 13,597 were missing. Even making due allowance for the combination of facts that America's population is more than three times as large as Britain's, that the United States looks on the Pacific much as Britain looks on the Atlantic, and that the actual decision to intervene in Korea was taken by President Truman, it would nevertheless have been surprising if many Americans had not felt that they had been called upon to bear an excessive share of the burden in this peculiarly harsh campaign.

For Dulles personally the truce started almost as many new problems as it settled old ones. Not the least of them was that the ineffable Syngman Rhee, autocratic President of South Korea, immediately began an attempt to hold his great ally up to ransom with the threat that, if no satisfactory progress towards a *political* settlement had been made within ninety days, South Korea would restart the war. This would have been catastrophic in its wider implications for the allies as a whole, since the Russians would have been justifiably convinced of the West's bad faith, the fighting would almost certainly have spilled over this time into Manchuria, and the danger of a global war would have come very close indeed. Dulles knew that the threat was no empty one; Syngman Rhee, whose country had already suffered appalling damage, felt he had little more to lose and thus, like Chiang Kai-shek, possessed something of a vested interest in widening the struggle. Within a week of the armistice, therefore, Dulles was aboard his aircraft once again and on his way to Korea. At work in the cabin in pullover and slacks as was his custom, he wrestled with the exceedingly awkward situation which he knew he would find waiting for him when he landed at Seoul, the war-swept capital of South Korea. Coming after Berlin, this was the second practical crisis he had faced since becoming Secretary of State, but it was much the gravest one.

Dulles and President Syngman Rhee ended by taking only four days to draw up and sign a draft mutual defense treaty between the United States and the Republic of South Korea. For Dulles this was a very considerable success. Under the terms of the treaty he managed to get Syngman Rhee to agree to settle international disputes by peaceful means and, in particular, to refrain from the threat or use of force in any manner inconsistent with United Nations purposes, or with a member's obligation towards the United Nations. On the specific issue of the proposed peace con-

ference, both parties agreed that, if the unification of Korea could
not be achieved within the proposed ninety days, each government
would be free to withdraw from it, but would consult with the
other on what to do next. For Syngman Rhee this was a major
concession.

In return Dulles did in effect give him the positive American
guarantee of security which South Korea had long wanted. Each
party, that is to say, recognized that an armed attack in the Pacific
area on either of them would be dangerous to its own peace and
safety, and they each undertook to "act to meet the common danger in accordance with . . . (their) constitutional processes." Admittedly, the United States could hardly have let the Communists
overrun South Korea, after all that had happened, treaty or no
treaty. Nor was Dulles committing the United States to do more
than "consult" and to "act . . . in accordance with" its constitutional
processes; and what he said had, of course, still to be ratified by
the U.S. Senate. But this treaty did go further than any other
signed by the United States up to that time, in the sense that it
pledged America to intervene directly on the mainland of Eastern
Asia. There was, as it happened, bound to be a delay of several
months before the treaty could come up before the Senate for
ratification, and, since the most dangerous risk of South Korean
intransigency almost certainly lay in the period immediately ahead,
it could be argued that pending, say, January, 1954, there was a
loophole in America's guarantee. But this cut both ways. If Syngman Rhee was ever going to get the guarantee which he badly
wanted, it also behooved him meanwhile to interpret his joint
statement with Dulles in the spirit in which the Secretary of State
had meant it to be taken.

Both in Britain and on the continent of Europe there was a good
deal of sympathy for Dulles in the predicament in which he had
been placed. At the same time, in Britain at least, it was also felt
that the Americans would have to reconcile themselves to getting
into this kind of difficulty from time to time, if they continued to
rely on headstrong right-wing leaders as their allies. Although this
criticism came mainly from the Labour Party and from the left-
wing press, it was by no means confined to them. Even among
Conservative supporters of the Churchill-Eden government there

was a certain disquiet about the people Dulles sometimes felt bound to accept as allies.

America's support of Syngman Rhee inevitably led on to much public discussion in Britain about the role of the smaller countries in the cold war, some of them being clearly determined to maintain their neutrality, but others, although openly anti-Communist, not being necessarily at all pro-Western. In London, as in several other West European capitals, it was widely felt that Dulles's attitude in these first two or three years of office was to narrow. He was well known for his impatience with neutralism, and, while he was later to change his ground in this respect, he constantly seemed from across the Atlantic to be too willing to sacrifice the genuine democratic ideal of the Western alliance for a short-term marriage of convenience with any anti-Communist regime which came along, no matter how dictatorial and patently undemocratic its domestic policy might be. Admittedly, there was little choice in the case of South Korea. A terrible war had turned that unfortunate little country upside down and inside out. Moreover, South Korea had become a vital symbol of resistance to Communist aggression, while being utterly dependent on American military support and American economic aid. And since at that time there genuinely was only one major political figure on the national scene, Syngman Rhee, if there was to be any coherent government at all it was virtually inconceivable that it should not be a government dominated by Syngman Rhee. South Korea was therefore a special case. But it was the case which hit the headlines and did more than any other to draw attention to the cul-de-sac into which Dulles's attitude towards neutralism was driving American foreign policy.

CHAPTER 7

Talking with the New Russia

BY THE summer of 1953, particularly after the truce in Korea, a good many people in the Western alliance began to feel that the time had come to put the new situation in Moscow to the test. Stalin had now been dead for several months, and in varying degrees in different countries public opinion was pressing for an entirely fresh attempt to reduce the dangers of the cold war by negotiation. With this in mind suggestions were made in the Western press that a conference of the three heads of government, President Eisenhower, Sir Winston Churchill and whoever happened to be French Prime Minister at the time, should be held as a first step, possibly at Bermuda in July. Unfortunately, Sir Winston Churchill had suffered a stroke in April, the full extent of which had been effectively kept from the general public, and July would have been too early for him to attend. The official alternative was therefore put forward that the three Western foreign ministers should meet first. Here again, however, the British were in difficulties since Anthony Eden, too, was still prevented from attending by the prolonged illness after his operation.

Some form of direct consultation was nevertheless felt to be so imperative and urgent that the British were pressed to nominate someone else. The choice naturally fell on the acting Foreign Secretary, the Marquess of Salisbury. Lord Salisbury had sat in the House of Commons earlier in his career and had been an Under Secretary in the nineteen-thirties. Consequently he had long been regarded as eligible for the post of Foreign Secretary in his own right, but he had been generally regarded as barred from such a highly political appointment because he was a member of the

House of Lords. Ironically, although this issue was taken so seriously in the early nineteen-fifties, nearly a decade later in the early nineteen-sixties a different British Prime Minister, Harold Macmillan, felt able to flout public opinion to the extent of appointing another peer, the Earl of Home, as Foreign Secretary, whose qualifications at the moment of appointment in 1960 were by no means as good as those of the Marquess of Salisbury in 1955.

When the three Western representatives did meet in Washington early in July—simultaneously with the intriguing news of the arrest of Beria in Russia—Dulles found Lord Salisbury a much more agreeable person to deal with than Eden, and he got on with him as well as he ever got on with any British spokesman. In particular, Salisbury shared Dulles's hard-boiled attitude to the much overrated prospect of successful negotiations with the Russians. Admittedly, Eden from his sickbed was very cautious about them too; on the British side it was Churchill who most wanted to have a try. But Salisbury was more skillful than Eden in impressing Dulles with his sincerity and with Britain's sympathy as an ally.

As for French views, Bidault was quite specific in putting it to Dulles that some attempt must be made to solve the German problem by negotiation with the new post-Stalin Russia, if the French Assembly were ever to be persuaded to accept the plan for a European army—an argument which Bidault well knew would be likely to remove any of Dulles's lingering doubts about proposing a four-power conference with the Russians at all. What clinched it with Dulles, however, was a cable from Adenauer actually insisting that definite Western proposals for talks with the Russians about German reunification would be a great help to him in the forthcoming German general election on September 6. The Chancellor could then demonstrate that, however much he might personally share Dulles's complete cynicism, he had no obstacle to the opening of negotiations. Dulles's answer was his notorious message that he regarded Adenauer's re-election as vital to the West, a move which was rightly condemned most bitterly by the German Social Democrats and others as a quite unwarrantable interference in the internal affairs of another country. Dulles was still in the first flush of his enthusiasm for his own influence, and it is doubtful whether he would have made such a move in later years. But Adenauer did win and Dulles's interference probably did help him a bit. So the gambado came off.

At their Washington meeting, which ended on July 14, the three Western Foreign Ministers did not confine their discussions to Germany. They discussed the Austrian peace treaty, the future of Western European consolidation under the projected EDC treaty, the winding up of the Korean War, and the latest developments in Indo-China. On Europe, they declared that EDC forces would never be used for aggression, and that other free countries might later become members of the European Community, if they wished. On Indo-China, Dulles said that the French declaration of July 3 giving full independence to the Associated States of Indo-China marked a very significant change in the situation. As he was later to tell the American Federation of Labor at St. Louis on September 24, it transformed the war in Indo-China in American eyes from being a struggle between Communism and colonialism to being a war of independence, and this made it far easier for the United States to contribute with a clear conscience towards a victory for the anti-Communist forces. Henceforward, in fact, the Americans made an increasingly substantial contribution towards the Indo-Chinese campaign, thus turning it the following year into almost as crucial an aspect of the East-West struggle as Korea had been. But, whereas Korea ended by being a stalemate in favor of the Western powers, they were lucky to get out of Indo-China without losing more than they did.

The period from the July, 1953, meeting in Washington to the Berlin Conference which opened on January 25, 1954, was one of great diplomatic activity. In preparation for this proposed first meeting with Stalin's successors, many speeches were made, plans drawn up, committees formed. There was a meeting after all of the heads of the three Western governments in December at Bermuda, when, accompanied by their foreign ministers, they reviewed the position only a few weeks before the Conference opened. Personally, Dulles carefully allowed himself to be associated in public with expressions of willingness to negotiate with the Soviet Union, on terms that could appeal to any reasonable-minded person in the Kremlin. In planning for the four-power Berlin Conference at all, he was in a sense compromising with his own views in order to help his allies. A skeptic he might remain, but he was determined to prove that he would not allow mere skepticism to prevent progress, if progress were possible. It is important to recognize the realities about his attitude at that stage, in view of the many accusations which have since been made that Dulles, as American Secretary of State at the peak of America's power, missed what was perhaps the only and most vital opportunity of negotiating a settlement with the Russians.

Dulles indeed spoke with greater confidence in the second half of 1953 than he had in the first, and his words carried more authority. His allies were less concerned to look for trouble in what he said, and he had begun to modify some of the roughnesses of thought which had been apparent earlier in the year. On his side, throughout these formative months, Dulles was always more conscious than he sometimes seemed of the problem of dealing satisfactorily with America's allies. Thus, in a speech at Boston on August 26 to the American Bar Association, he said that the only answer to the "coerced unity of the Soviet-dominated world" was "voluntary association of free nations for their common defense," and that it was therefore essential for the United States to win friends and allies. Another example of his thinking was his press statement on December 1, when he took up Senator McCarthy's sarcastic and idiotic comment that, in dealing with America's allies, the State Department "sent them perfumed notes instead of using threats and intimidation to compel them to our bidding." Dulles felt bound to come down flatly with the view that other nations should naturally be treated as sovereign equals, whether large or small, strong, or weak. The trouble was that he did not always act up to these principles.

Although his allies were the main cause of the efforts made in 1953 to prepare for talks with the Russians, once Dulles felt himself committed to this course he handled the situation with ability, and the abortive but important Berlin Conference of January, 1954, was one of his most distinguished performances. His tactics with his allies as well as with the Russians were masterful, and some of those who were present in the conference room still relish their memories of his polite but firm handling of Molotov personally. Behind all this, however, the fundamental charge remains, which is perhaps one of the most persistent leveled at the Eisenhower-Dulles regime, that in this period the West missed an unrepeated opportunity of reaching some kind of abiding settlement with Russia. In so far as this accusation is not merely wishful thinking, it rests on a combination of two factors, one on each side of the Iron Curtain. On the Western side, while American nuclear superiority was still absolute, the build-up of the strength of the allied ground forces in Europe had totally changed the picture, compared with that which existed before NATO was formed; Churchill, indeed, had put it with his characteristic simplicity that "We arm to parley." On the Soviet side, with Stalin's death the coming of the new regime represented the chance of a complete break from the evil past.

Those who say that Dulles and Eisenhower missed the boat must naturally be assumed to believe that there was at least a boat to catch. They must at least consider that, if Dulles and others had pursued different policies on the Western side, the possibility of an agreement with the Communist bloc in those circumstances was a real one. But was it? Rebuttal of the charge depends as much on taking the view that no such opportunity ever really existed, as on criticizing the American Secretary of State for what he actually did. As regards the Soviet side, during the months following Stalin's death it was easy enough to hope that the change of attitude, apparently adopted by the Kremlin, represented a fundamental shift both in the Communist view of the world problem and in the Communist will to reach agreement with the West. But knowing, as we now do, that Malenkov's regime was only a quite temporary stage in the evolution of the Soviet government, even after this relatively short passage of time it already appears almost inconceivable that he or anyone else in the Kremlin at that moment could have come to a settlement with the West. As was really shown by the shooting of Beria, the Soviet regime was going through a period of immense uncertainty, and it was in no mood or condition to launch into heretical concessions to the West, which even Khrushchev in his heyday was later to find it difficult to get the diehard wing of the Communist dogmatists to swallow.

That was one side of the proglem of negotiating with Russia. The other was naturally the fact that some basis for negotiation had to be found. And it had to be found, one must remember, in an atmosphere in Washington which, in its own way, was hardly more conducive to negotiating than that in Moscow. All through 1953 Dulles and Eisenhower had to contend with the full virulence of McCarthyism, and it was not until towards the end of the year that Dulles was in a position even to take the initiatives that he did. Nor did anyone ever put forward a plan for a settlement that was convincing on its own merits, though several quite different varieties of scheme were in fact suggested.

When, for instance, Dulles spoke on October 6 about the possibility of giving certain security guarantees to the Soviet Union, this was the result of a great deal of independent thought on his own part and some consultation by the State Department with London, Bonn, and Paris. Then there was Churchill's suggestion of May 11, made in another of those speeches which rang round the world, that there might possibly be some kind of Locarno-type treaty between East and West; by this the British Prime Minister implied a nonaggression pact between two or more countries, which would be guaranteed by certain others. During the sharp debate which took place after Sir Winston had spoken, several variations of this scheme were discussed. Again, in Germany Dr. Adenauer mentioned a possibility that, once the European Defense Community had been set up, it might collectively sign a treaty with Russia, America, and Britain, involving a number of mutual nonaggression guarantees whereby each signatory would pledge itself to come to the assistance of any other which might be under attack. In America, talk in general ran more towards the idea of five, instead of perhaps only three, signatories to something like the original Churchill plan. These would be the four Western powers, America, Britain, France, and Western Germany, together with the Soviet Union.

Whatever form such a treaty took, however, all these suggestions came up against certain technical obstacles, which in the end boiled down to the question of territorial guarantees, that is to say, to a line drawn on a map. If the security either of the West or of Russia were to be guaranteed, at what point could aggression be said to have taken place? At some point troops crossing a line on a map would have to be regarded as taking part in an aggressive act. But

the problem of defining aggression has always raised multiple
difficulties, which have in fact defied solution ever since the idea
of definition was first put forward in the interwar years. Would
such a line, for instance, be drawn on the present boundary between Eastern and Western Germany? Might it be drawn in such
a way that a demilitarized zone would exist between the two sides,
or would there necessarily be no such zone? If there were one,
should Western Germany be included in it? Or, if not the whole
of Western Germany, should a part of it be included? And if part
or all of Western Germany should be included, how much Communist territory should also come in? This was later to be the
specific problem ventilated under the general title of "Disengagement," when the particular variation known as the Gaitskell Plan
proposed that not only Eastern Germany but also Poland and
possibly Czechoslovakia should be included as well; if so much
Communist territory was to come in, however, there was the question of how much sacrifice the West should make in return. All
these problems were posed by the early ideas of a nonaggression
pact. And it is quite clear now, looking back on the period 1953–54,
that thinking on the subject was not nearly mature enough at that
time to come anywhere near providing any satisfactory answer to
such complicated questions.

All that can be said with any certainty is that Dulles went about
as far as was possible in the American atmosphere of the time in
encouraging the discussion of these various ideas, once he had
decided that something must be done to probe Soviet thought and
Soviet intentions. The Administration was in fact in a very difficult
position. Lambasted by McCarthy and the Republican old guard
at home, they were almost universally criticized abroad for the
apparent inflexibility of American policy. Adlai Stevenson, the
defeated Democratic presidential candidate of the previous year,
had returned from a foreign tour considerably shaken, as he put it,
by the loss of confidence in Washington's leadership which he
found among America's allies. It is in this light that Dulles's observations about the possibility of a nonaggression pact or security
guarantees for Russia should be judged. They represented a fairly
bold attempt to present a different American face to the world,
and to throw down at least a possible bone that would draw the

Russians to a meeting. They were not, and should not be judged as being, the solemn and decisive beginning of East-West negotiations which would change the face of history.

When Eisenhower and Dulles went to Bermuda for their four-day meeting with Churchill and Eden, Laniel, and Bidault, in the first week of December, 1953, they rightly had no great hopes of the conference. Although some quite useful discussion took place between the three Western allies, this was essentially an occasion which would have been much more valuable earlier in the year, but which had had to be postponed because of the stroke that Churchill suffered in April. Dulles accordingly used the Bermuda Conference as another opportunity to come back to the attack over the European Defense Community, which he said constituted the principal aim of America's European policy. He emphasized, for instance, to Eden that:

> the United States Congress was in a mood in which, unless there were some positive action towards European unity in the next two or three months, its foreign aid appropriations would be so rigid and so qualified that there would be very serious repercussions on the NATO program.

It was later in that same month that Dulles made his famous public statement about an "agonizing reappraisal" at a press conference in Paris, while attending the Atlantic Council meeting there shortly before Christmas. What he deliberately did was to put into public form the kind of threat which he had been using for several weeks in private to Eden and to other European statesmen, particularly of course to Bidault and the French. If EDC failed to pass the French Assembly, Dulles said in Paris, the United States would be forced into an agonizing reappraisal of its whole European policy, and of the world strategy which involved the stationing of American troops on the continent of Western Europe. It was a shocking and brutal threat not only to the French but to everyone in Western Europe, and that is what Dulles meant it to be.

The intriguing question, however, was how far he really thought it was valid. In fact, as we now know, the French Assembly did reject EDC six months later in August, 1954, and America did not pull out of Europe. But the fact that Dulles was doing more than merely prodding the French with words is suggested by two other considerations, which were certainly operating in his mind at that time and to which he gave expression both before and after the famous "agonizing reappraisal" in Paris in December. Both concerned the development of nuclear weapons. First of all, 1953 had been the year in which, four years after the original Soviet explosion of an atomic bomb in 1949, the Russians had managed to leap forward to the detonation of their first hydrogen bomb. Atomic strategy was therefore very much in the air, and by the autumn of 1953 Dulles had begun to cause a certain amount of alarm in Europe by suggesting that atomic weapons, including the new atomic cannon recently sent to the American forces in Germany, would probably end by reducing the need to keep American troops overseas. And he was certainly genuine in so expressing his thoughts.

Indeed, assurances had already had to be dragged out of Washington that the Administration was not contemplating the reduction of American forces in Europe, at least until local forces could be built up to take their place. It was in fact in this connection that the United States was insisting that, however much people might boggle at EDC, the equivalent of twelve German divisions must somehow be added to the NATO ground forces in Western Europe. Dulles had already laid it down as a principle that, while over-all deterrence was provided by American nuclear power, the aim must be to equip local forces to provide a shield for their own areas. This was to apply to Western Europe as much as to the Far Eastern theaters of Japan and Indo-China, where Dulles and the State Department were now talking about the need "to equip Asians to fight Asians."

Secondly, of quite equal significance with Dulles's rather confusing threats and warnings to Western Europe was his famous address to the Council on Foreign Relations on January 12, 1954. This was the occasion on which he said that the National Security Council had taken the basic decision "to depend primarily upon a greater capacity to retaliate, instantly, by means and at places of our own choosing." Dulles declared that this enabled more basic security to be achieved at less cost. He coupled his remark with the statement that the traditional policy of meeting aggression by direct and local resistance was too costly to be continued indefinitely without grave economic and social consequences. He then went on from the general to the particular by giving warning that, if aggression were renewed in Korea, the United Nations' response would not necessarily be confined to Korea. Nor, he added, would the position be any different if there were open Chinese aggression in Indo-China.

Within a year of taking office Dulles had thus challenged the world with three of the most remembered policy statements associated with his name—"liberation," "agonizing reappraisal," "massive retaliation." "Liberation" was soon dropped. The "agonizing reappraisal" never came to anything. And "massive retaliation," although he was to refer to it again fortunately never came seriously near to being applied. Massive retaliation, nevertheless, did hold the key to the power situation of the early nineteen-fifties. It was all very well for Dulles's critics to pour scorn on his head, and for later observers to scoff at the bluntness of the truth which he put into words. But at that time, when the United States still possessed great nuclear superiority, the ultimate threat of intervention by America's long-range striking power was indeed an active factor in preventing bigger and more numerous Communist military adventures.

Where Dulles was wrong was in taking the line that massive retaliation could be either as flexible or as possible as he implied. It was essentially a negative weapon. But he showed his own recognition of this fact when he later pointed out that all he had really said to the Council on Foreign Relations was that America possessed a "capacity" to retaliate. He had merely given a fairly loose warning about the possibility of being compelled to use it. Moreover, his words were at least not lost on the Russians, even if they caused dismay among his allies. And it is in this sense that his speech to the Council on Foreign Relations should be judged. What he said on that occasion was in fact the counterweight to what he had said two months earlier about the possibility of offering security guarantees to the Soviet Union. This stick and carrot method of preparing for the Berlin Conference appealed to Dulles, as combining his sense of reality with his strong desire not to let the endless Soviet notes, that were going back and forth in preparation for the foreign ministers' meeting, confuse the issue.

By the time that January, 1954, arrived Dulles felt that the chances of reaching any significant agreement with the Russians, never more than slim, had grown ever slimmer. He was inclined to think that, if a conference had been possible immediately after Stalin's death, or if the famous riots in East Berlin had never taken place, the chances of a breakthrough would have been better. But, with the passage of time, the psychological elements in the situation were hardening as it was inevitable that they would in a period when the realities of nuclear power were so patently shifting. Although the Americans were approaching the end of their nuclear superiority, the United States was still in a much better position than the Soviet Union to contemplate the use of its weapons, because it now had a good many of them. The Soviet Union, nevertheless, by exploding a hydrogen bomb and by beginning to build up a bomber striking force, was sooner or later going to be able to retaliate in kind directly against the United States, and it could expect to be in a far stronger bargaining position once it had achieved this capacity. The one point that emerged most clearly of all was the one that so many people too easily forget. The Americans could never use their superior power to compel the Russians to come to the conference table. American willingness to negotiate, even if it had been less grudging, was in fact bootless without an equivalent willingness on the part of the Russians. But the Russians were unwilling, partly for the very reason that made the Americans willing, namely American superiority of power. It takes two to agree, just as it takes two to disagree.

Meanwhile, many associated arguments went on about the changing character of America's strength. Dulles was right to point out in public that the ability of the United States to use atomic weapons could never be a complete substitute for the maintenance of American, as well as allied, armed forces in or near the potential trouble spots. So far from being a man whose only activity was to rush to the nuclear brink, he fully realized that American troops must not only be present, but must also be seen to be present, if they were to play a proper part in holding America's allies together and supporting American policy. In saying this, he was in some ways doing little more than continuing the former Democrat policy of containment. But it was more difficult to do this now since he had, on the one hand, to warn Americans that they would have to keep at least some troops overseas whatever the nuclear developments, while, on the other, he felt bound do warn the Europeans that, if they could not do more to help themselves, an agonizing reappraisal might involve greater reliance on purely nuclear retaliation. At the same time, Dulles was in no sense wrong to maintain his warning to both Moscow and Peking that the United States could not be expected to have developed its nuclear power, without any will whatever to use it, if pushed too far. Dulles in fact was riding three horses at the same time, and, if he occasionally appeared to find this too much for him, part of the blame at least lay with the horses.

Associated with the development of an American philosophy of the deterrent, there also grew up at this time the thesis that came to be known as a "peripheral" strategy. Later, in effect, given the name of the "Fortress America" concept, the basic idea was that the United States could protect itself by means of its power to deter global war with long-range weapons; and that to a much lesser, though still possibly significant, degree this ultimate strength could also be used to deter war on the periphery, that is to say among its allies. Dulles himself knew too much about the problems of working with allies to allow himself to become publicly committed to the peripheral strategy idea. There was, all the same, some element of it in his own thinking, as was shown by the tone of the further remarks which he made at the Council on Foreign Relations on January 12, 1954. After talking about massive retaliation, he emphasized that it was a permanent potential reinforcement to the first-line defenses sustained by his allies. "Local defense," he insisted, "must be reinforced by the further deterrent of massive retaliatory power." And he went on: "We need allies and collective security. Our purpose is to make these relations more effective and less costly. This can be done by placing more reliance on deterrent power and less dependence on local defensive power."

Inevitably, however, this kind of talk raised the gravest doubts in Britain and elsewhere in the alliance. There were doubts about America's ultimate intentions, as well as about the means by which Washington expected to be able to carry out even existing policies. In the most practical terms, the question was asked what kind of

aggression "massive retaliatory power" would be used to oppose.
Was this, in fact, deterrence or defense? Would this power really
be used, for instance, in Korea, as had been suggested? And, if so,
who would use it? Would it be on the initiative of the American
President alone? Or in combination with the British and French
Prime Ministers? Or in the name of the United Nations?

These, in fact, were the beginnings of the kind of detailed and
increasingly sophisticated debate which has continued ever since
about the characteristics of nuclear strategy and about the deploy-
ment of nuclear power. Since those days a great deal more has come
to be understood, for instance, on the subject of the difference
between deterrence and defense; and, if it was in some ways Dulles
who promoted this kind of thought by the bluntness with which
he spoke, it is to his credit that he did so. Unquestionably, the kind
of language he used could not be used today. But he lived at the
end of an era, in which it was possible for the man in control of
American foreign policy to think in these terms, and the fact that,
in doing so, he shocked and frightened his allies must be considered
as only one aspect of a very complicated situation.

Before considering what actually happened at the Berlin Conference, a word should be said about the standing of the Eisenhower Administration as it reached the end of its first year in office.
There was a good deal of truth in the comment made at the time,
that it had spent the first year in finding out what could not be
done, and entered its second with the growing need to show what
it could do. A remarkable factor was that, in spite of a good deal
of indecision during the first twelve months, together with a rather
higher than average failure to carry out election promises, President
Eisenhower's personal popularity in January, 1954, was virtually
the same as it had been in January, 1953. As for the Secretary of
State, John Foster Dulles had definitely emerged with a good deal
more prestige than he had had when he took office. But for him
too, indeed perhaps for him above all, the second year represented
both a challenge and an opportunity. In spite of the criticism and
sometimes hostility which his more provocative statements had
aroused, he was recognized by his detractors as well as by his friends
as a skilled and experienced figure in his own field. In private, allied
politicians and diplomats had begun to feel that they could get on

terms with him, while he himself seemed to understand that it was no longer possible for his words to be directed only to one type of audience; what he said for the benefit of the more intractable members of the Republican party was also heard by the rest of the world, and vice versa.

Another way of looking at the opportunity that still awaited the Eisenhower-Dulles team as it entered 1954 is to compare it in one important respect with the Truman-Acheson Administration. Although Eisenhower and Dulles had had to eat a good many of their words of criticism about the Truman-Acheson Policy of containment, and had in practice only produced instead a policy which could be termed a kind of "containment plus," President Eisenhower's personal popularity did insure both for him and for his Secretary of State—if he chose, as he did, to give Dulles his full backing—a chance to pursue moderately unpopular policies. By the time that President Truman and Dean Acheson came to the end of their term, their room for maneuver when dealing with the Russians was very small indeed. Although they had proven successes behind them, in standing up to the Russians and in winning the trust of their allies, any concessions to the Communist world would have brought the ceiling down on them within the United States itself. Even the full flowering of Senator McCarthy's vicious campaign against the State Department never put President Eisenhower and John Foster Dulles under quite such a restraint as their predecessors.

At the Berlin Conference of January, 1954, Molotov was in his element. He had spent the previous few months trying to divide the Western allies, by hinting at one thing to one of them and another to another in a seemingly endless flow of diplomatic notes. When it came to meeting them face to face, therefore, the ground was ready for him to pursue the same tactic. Since his demotion and loss of power it has become easy to forget what he was like in his heyday. This Berlin Conference was his heyday, and, in spite of his frigid and expressionless exterior, he could be a formidable figure across the conference table, particularly for Dulles who was clashing with him for the first time as leader of the American team. Thus, it was something of a triumph almost at the start of the conference for the three Western foreign ministers, Dulles, Eden and Bidault, to cause Molotov a moment of surprise and discomfiture by agreeing at once to the virtual acceptance of the agenda as he had proposed it.

Although everyone attending this conference, held in the heart of Germany, had the need to tackle the problem of German reunification uppermost in their minds, Molotov had characteristically led off by proposing an agenda which put Germany only second on the list, and the Austrian peace treaty third. His first item was a vague generalization about methods of reducing international tension and convening a five-power meeting, at which Communist China would be present. Molotov no doubt calculated that this proposal would naturally introduce a whole host of other problems for the United States and could be trusted to confuse a good many issues right at the start. Without batting an eyelid, however, Dulles accepted the agenda on the calculated view, which the three Western foreign ministers had discussed among themselves, that the Communist powers always attempted to weaken the position of Western negotiators by wrangling over the agenda in such a way that public opinion became impatient. This time the Western ministers were determined to avoid the trap. They also felt that, by accepting the agenda and thus showing their determination to get on with the conference, they would demonstrate specifically to the peoples of both Germany and Austria that they were not going to be deflected by irrelevancies. In addition, they considered that, by showing themselves willing to discuss the question of China, they would weaken Soviet efforts to use arguments about the Far East as a means of holding up progress on the problems of Europe. Although implicit Chinese recognition was a question on which Dulles ran into a good deal of trouble at the end of the conference, at the beginning he was able to grasp the nettle without provoking immediate screams from Congress at home in Washington.

In some ways the conference never really captured the momentary sense of agreement which Western acceptance of the Soviet agenda produced. On Molotov's first item, there was a great deal of argument about China, with the Western powers making it quite clear that it was useless to suggest their agreeing to another conference, so long as the Chinese were holding up the political settlement in Korea and doing nothing to reduce the tension in Indo-

China. When the conference did turn to the German problem, there was never any sense of genuine negotiation. On the Soviet side, Molotov made a series of set speeches in the classic Communist tradition, and, although there was a certain amount of clarification of ideas in the private meetings which took place away from the conference table itself, it was obvious that the Russians were using the conference as a platform from which to attack NATO, the EDC project, and the Adenauer government in Bonn.

When challenged by the West, with proposals for holding free all-German elections and for then establishing a government which could sign a peace treaty, Molotov did little more than repeat what he had said in March, 1952. At that time the Soviet Union had demanded a peace treaty under which all occupying troops would be withdrawn from Germany, all foreign bases on German territory closed, and a united Germany would be pledged not to sign any military pact against any of its former enemies. These Soviet proposals were based on the more fundamental attitude which Molotov harped upon again and again, particularly in private, that the Soviet Union could accept no central German government not jointly nominated by the allies before the proposed elections. His aim, as the Soviet aim has remained ever since, was clearly to avoid any genuine freedom of choice for the Germans about the composition of their first all-German government, and, by the nomination of a substantial Communist element in that government, to insure instead the existence of a built-in Soviet veto.

This Berlin conference was historic in that it established the formal pattern inside which the East-West argument about Germany was to be carried on for several years afterwards. There have, of course, been differences of emphasis since, but no fundamental change of stance by either side. Thus, although Berlin proved in some ways the exact opposite of successful negotiation, it did clear the air, and after it was over both sides knew far better where each stood. This was no mean achievement.

The Western case on Germany was put primarily by the British, though Dulles personally accepted and backed the points they made. Indeed, he worked more harmoniously with Eden during this conference than at any time in the entire careers of either of them. The Western view thus came to be known as the Eden Plan

—one of several so-called Eden Plans at various times and on various subjects—and it involved five stages. First, there would be entirely free elections throughout Germany, including that is, the Soviet occupied zone of Eastern Germany. Different ideas have been discussed at different times about the methods of supervising and thus insuring the genuine freedom of any such elections, but the point of principle is that the elections should take place with full safeguards and complete individual secrecy. Secondly, a national assembly would be convoked as a result of those elections, which would, thirdly, draft a constitution and take part in the initial negotiations for a peace treaty with Germany's wartime enemies. Fourthly, the new constitution would be adopted and an all-German central government would be formed, which would, fifthly, sign and carry out the peace treaty.

Molotov's rejection of the Eden Plan was absolute. For many obvious reasons it clashed completely with the Soviet conception of a united Germany, in which the Kremlin would maintain a final voice through the participation of an outright Communist element —which would go even further, if it could, and try to seize complete power. On the Western side, one of the key points was whether this proposed all-German government should have a completely free choice as to its alignment in international affairs, which would mean either for or against the West; or whether it should be obliged to align itself with the West (which was the counterpoint to Molotov's own veto inside it); or whether it should be "neutralized" in the sense that it would be bound under the peace treaty to align itself with neither side. Naturally this was, and has remained, a most important issue. Dulles was out of step with Eden and Bidault on it when he first reached Berlin, insisting privately that the all-German government should be automatically aligned with the West against the Soviet Union. However, he shifted his ground as the conference proceeded, so that the point came when he himself proposed, on February 4, that "the all-German government shall have authority to assume or reject international rights and obligations of the federal government and the Soviet zone of Germany." The gamble was of course a good one from the Western point of view in that a freely elected all-German government would in fact certainly choose an anti-Soviet course. But it was a far

healthier position for the West to take this stand than to stick out
for Dulles's original attitude.

It was, of course, a telling point for Molotov to make, that a new
all-German government could not reasonably be bound by any
treaty previously entered into by a mere portion of itself. This
meant specifically that, even if Adenauer's government signed an
EDC treaty, it would be quite invalid the moment that agreed steps
could be taken to reunite Germany under a central government.
Dulles's instinct was wrong in making him so overzealous in his
opposition to the Soviet Union that he wanted to bind the new
Germany automatically to the West. And he was justifiably criticized throughout the Western alliance for adopting an attitude
which the Russians could obviously not accept. The fact that the
Russians were going too far, in their bid to win Germany to their
own side, did not justify the West in doing the same, if the West
was genuinely anxious to have any negotiations at all. Dulles,
moreover, alienated a good deal of West European and particularly
German opinion in his original stand, by giving the impression
that he was not genuinely in favor of German reunification at all.
Since this Berlin Conference of January, 1954, it has become quite
clear that the Russians are in fact opposed to German reunification
on any terms that look conceivably possible. But this is not really
the Western point of view, and Dulles made a mistake in letting
people think it was.

Apart from the instinctive rigidity of Dulles's original position,
nearly everyone who observed him at this conference agreed that
he handled Molotov extremely well, making jokes with him, being
very friendly in meetings outside the conference, and marshaling
his own arguments with consummate legal skill. His two leading
colleagues have each recorded their own particular impressions of
the conference. Eden, with the later bitter memories of Suez in
mind, wrote cryptically in his memoirs in reference to Dulles: "The
Berlin Conference was the first occasion when I negotiated with
him as a partner. We were able to keep closely in step with each
other and with M. Bidault, with good results, I think, for our
countries. My later experience was not so fortunate." Bidault has
been reported as saying of Dulles at Berlin: "He was considerably
more moderate than was generally understood. It is true that he

was very firm on principle. He was also sometimes very rough and rigid. But the truth is that he carefully avoided being the one to close the door to Molotov."

The one weakness which Dulles could not, unfortunately, do anything about was inherent in the whole public image which he created throughout his career. In spite of his affability and reasonableness in conference, and in spite of his shift of ground over the vital point about German alignment, almost all his speeches were phrased in such a way that when reported outside they irritated many people in the West by their sententious moralizing. Dulles was always a preacher and the Berlin Conference was no exception. Hence his able leading of the Western team on this occasion was to some extent lost on the wider audience, and he did not emerge from the conference with the amount of personal credit that he should have had.

Within the United States, indeed, he came in for a good deal of attack, and he was made to appear to have failed in his first major dealing with the Russians, although in fact he had succeeded brilliantly in holding his ground and had never at any time seriously expected anything but a deadlock. The attack came from both sides, from those who were disappointed that more could not have been done and, what was far more insistent and dangerous, from the right wing of the Republican party where he was blamed for having sold the pass to China. This absurd and unfair accusation arose from the fact that, at the very end of the conference, Bidault succeeded in getting all four powers to agree to discuss in private the desirability of an Asian conference, which would try to bring the war in Indo-China to an end. In agreeing to these soundings, Dulles necessarily committed himself to a line which inevitably implied the participation of Communist China in the proposed Asian conference, and that was diametrically opposed to the highly emotional attitude on the subject adopted by many Republicans. Dulles himself was always uneasy about this aspect of the Berlin meetings, and he did his best to make it clear that the proposed Geneva Conference would confine its agenda to the problems of Korea and Indo-China, thus making it seem that Communist China had not been brought into anything like a general five-power conference. But the fact that he felt impelled to do this was later also reflected in his own extraordinary attitude to the Geneva Conference itself. This was the one great international conference during the whole period of his Secretaryship in which, although he attended it briefly on the opening days, he played no active part and indeed did his best to minimize.

On Berlin itself, the real lesson was that no genuine possibility existed for serious negotiation with the Russians on the vital issues of Germany and Western Europe. In spite of the changes in Moscow since Stalin had died, this was still as true as when he had been alive. But it required the Berlin Conference to prove it, and, in knowing from the start that it would, Dulles was right to attend. To condemn him in these circumstances for not making bricks without straw, however, is both futile and unfair. As regards the West as a whole, the conference did succeed in proving to the majority of people that nothing immediate could be gained by negotiating with the Russians. And for Dulles personally it was the best bit of allied teamwork he ever achieved.

CHAPTER 8

Peace in Indo-China

BETWEEN the end of the Berlin Conference in February, 1954, and the opening of the marathon Geneva Conference about Indo-China in April, Dulles was involved in two significant developments outside the scope of either meeting. One was the sharp renewal of the debate about massive retaliation, following the explosion of America's Bikini hydrogen bomb on March 1. The other was the success which he achieved in rallying Latin American support against Communism, when he flew down to a special conference at Caracas. When the Bikini bomb went off in the Marshall Islands in the Central Pacific, it made the biggest bang in human history. Inevitably this fifteen-megaton H-bomb gave another twist to the wheel of argument about massive retaliation, and those who had already criticized the Dulles philosophy became even louder and more insistent. Adlai Stevenson, for instance, speaking within a week of the explosion, put the doubts in a nutshell when he demanded:

> What if we are confronted with something less than a clear case of overt aggression? What if we had relied exclusively on a policy of "massive retaliation" since the close of World War II? Would we have resorted to global atomic war in order to meet the Communist threat in Greece and Turkey? To counter the Berlin blockade? To resist aggression in Korea? If the answer is "No," then the so-called "New Look" in foreign policy is no "new look" at all, but merely a continuation of the policy of adapting our methods of resistance to the methods of attack.... Instead of greater freedom of choice, does not this decision to rely primarily on atomic weapons really narrow our choice as to the means and places of our retaliation? Are we leaving ourselves the grim choice of in-

action or a thermonuclear holocaust? Are we indeed inviting Moscow and Peking to nibble us to death?

A few days later it was Lester Pearson, the Canadian Secretary of State for External Affairs, who succinctly expressed the point of view of America's allies. Although many Canadians respected Dulles, incidentally, few liked him, since he took Canada's views and position far too much for granted. Lester Pearson declared that, if this new policy was to have any effective meaning and to be operated successfully, it was absolutely essential that the word "our" must mean "those who have agreed together, particularly under the North Atlantic Treaty, to work together." What he deplored, and was of course by no means alone in deploring, was the danger inherent in unilateral American action. The kind of situation, which might conceivably warrant a joint allied Western threat against Russia, was by no means necessarily the same as one in which Dulles and Eisenhower might see fit to issue it alone. With the growing stalemate in the nuclear position, the idea of the West actually threatening Russia has looked increasingly absurd; but the point about whose finger is to be on the button, in the event of having to retaliate against a Soviet move, has, of course, been thrashed out from that day to this without any satisfactory answer being found. And Dulles's provocative language at least served a useful purpose in stimulating the argument.

Dulles himself naturally felt impelled to explain more carefully what he meant. At a press conference on March 16, he remarked: "If you will read my address of January 12, you will see that what I advocated there was a 'capacity' to retaliate. In no place did I say that we would retaliate instantly." This was the disclaimer, which he had already put out privately, and which was in any case inherent in his original remarks, for anyone who cared to examine them carefully. Indeed it was only common sense, however much some people might doubt whether Dulles would really apply his policy in a common-sense way. In order to explain himself even more fully, he put his name to an article for the April issue of *Foreign Affairs,* in the course of which he said:

Initially this reshaping of our military program was misconstrued in various respects. Some suggested that the United

States intended to rely wholly on large-scale strategic bombing as the sole means to deter and counter aggression. What has already been said should dispose of this erroneous idea. A potential of massive attack will always be kept in a state of instant readiness and our program will retain a wide variety and the means and scope for responding to aggression.

The heart of the problem is how to *deter* attack. . . . The essential thing is that a potential aggressor should know in advance that he can and will be made to suffer for his aggression more than he can possibly gain by it. This calls for a system in which local defensive strength is reinforced by more mobile deterrent power. The method of doing so will vary according to the character of the various areas. Some areas are so vital that special guards should and could be put around them—Western Europe in such an area.

Two further comments helped to put the matter more fully in perspective. The day after Dulles had spoken on March 16, the President also held a press conference. At it Eisenhower observed that all the "new look" was meant to do was to attempt to keep abreast of the times. "To call it revolutionary," he said, "or to act like it is something that just suddenly dropped down on us like a cloud from heaven is just not true." In spite of the President's characteristic lack of grammar, his meaning was clear enough. The following day Walter Lippmann also came to Dulles's assistance, writing in the more detached columns of the *New York Herald Tribune:*

> There is no doubt that the words . . . convey the impression that something momentous and novel has been decided. But everything that has been said . . . makes it plain that there has been no radical change in our strategic policy.

With that the dispute appeared to cool off, though it never stopped entirely, and even now Dulles is still regarded by many people as having been crudely unwise, if not downright irresponsible, in the words he chose to use. On the whole, however, his critics were wrong and he was right, since his frank and blunt statements about the deterrent represented no more than the truth at the time at which he spoke.

Where he does bear a very heavy responsibility, nevertheless, is in the political doubts which he sowed among his allies about America's reliability as a life and death partner in the cold war. By talking so much about purely United States action, he made them feel that, if their salvation did not suit him, they might just possibly be thrown to the wolves. Thus, it was Dulles and the revelations which emerged about his own character that tipped the scale in favor of the British continuing to develop their own nuclear deterrent. Without this period of American diplomacy and the implications which appeared to lie behind it, Britain might well have decided to abandon the race. If this had happened, the French would not have felt the same compulsion to go ahead and the problem of the spread of nuclear weapons, the nth power problem, would almost certainly look far less forbidding than it does today.

The Conference of the Organization of American States at Caracas in Venezuela on March 1, 1954, was the tenth in a general series. But it now has even more interest than it did at the time, as a result of the success which the Castro regime has achieved in Cuba since 1959 and the extent to which this success has helped to foment the same kind of upheaval elsewhere in Latin America. Dulles flew to Caracas determined to push through an anti-Communist resolution, giving formal embodiment to the idea of a modern Monroe Doctrine, in return for a more liberal approach by the United States to the problems of aid and trade in Latin America. The Secretary of State's attitude was as warmly supported at home in North America as it caused initial heart-searching among the assembled delegates from the states of South America. In the event, the resolution was passed with only the vote of Guatemala against it, Mexico and Argentina abstaining. At that time Guatemala was regarded as having the only neo-Communist government among the Latin American countries.

The resolution declared that the arrival in power of a Communist regime in any American state would represent a threat to the independence of them all. The fears of the Latin Americans, that this might provoke intervention by the United States in the internal affairs of other countries in the hemisphere, led to the passing of an amendment to the original resolution, which asserted the right of every American state to choose its own form of government. This was not quite what Dulles had wanted. But he saw the dangers and he handled the conference with skill and tact. The net result was a general promise of collective action which, although difficult to define and unlikely in all honesty ever to be directly applied, nevertheless served due warning on the Communist elements of 1954 that their activities in the American hemisphere would not go unchallenged. In terms of domestic policies within the United States, the success of the Caracas Conference was a definite asset to Dulles's public balance sheet at a time when the attacks against him were mounting up on the debit side.

If Berlin saw the peak of allied co-operation in that period, a private duel developed between Dulles and Eden during the months that followed from which neither was ever again to feel fully able to withdraw. It is this tragic duel which provides the main—though not the only—clue to the extraordinary performance Dulles put up over the Geneva Conference, at which a settlement in Indo-China was successfully negotiated. And it was the characteristically different reaction which they each had to the situation after the final defeat of EDC in August, that explained Dulles's curious dash to Adenauer's side while Eden was still touring Europe picking up the bits—a job which in itself Dulles always quite genuinely felt Eden did well. In fact, 1954 was probably Eden's best year.

The story of Geneva began as soon as Berlin was over, though nearly two months elapsed before the conference actually assembled on April 26, 1954, for its marathon sessions which lasted through May and June and most of July. On the spot in Indo-China the French position was already becoming critical and desperate. Although the French Army did not face immediate defeat in the sense that it would be driven from the Red River delta and out of the country, its ability either to maintain its more exposed garrisons or to insure any real political control had already been reduced to a level that was untenable and self-defeating. This was the somber background against which the outlying, fortified French camp at Dienbienphu became invested by a growing avalanche of VietMinh Communist guerrillas. Even by mid-March the view was gaining ground in Washington that this symbolic place would fall, in spite of the gallantry of its defenders under

Colonel (later General) de Castries, a view which the French authorities in Paris still vigorously disputed.

Dulles himself felt that the crucial moment had come, when the whole American policy of containing the Communist thrust southward from China must meet the challenge. And his mood was crystallized by a decisive visit to Washington towards the end of March by the French Chief of Staff, General Paul Ely, on the latter's way back from a tour of inspection in Indo-China. Ely told Dulles that Indo-China was doomed unless the United States came to France's rescue. This was not a formal request for more American intervention; indeed Paris was still whistling in the dark and trying to keep up an optimistic attitude. But to Dulles it had the dramatic quality of truth, and, as the news from Dienbienphu got worse during the next few days, he put the wheels in motion in Washington which led to a full and heart-searching re-examination of policy during the Easter weekend of April 3 and 4. As a result of consultations with leading Congressmen and a fateful session which Eisenhower had afterwards with Dulles and Radford, a decision was taken to commit the United States to all practicable support of the French in Indo-China—on one condition. This was that, irrespective of the method chosen to apply force—and clearly that was a separate headache of its own—America would not go in without some form of effectual collective effort by its allies as well, notably the British.

It was here that the special Eden-Dulles factor began to operate. Dulles flew to London with the new policy in his pocket. After going on to Paris, he returned to Washington cheered by what he felt to be a favorable British and French reaction to ideas which may best be described as similar to those that took shape in a watered-down form a few months later in the Southeast Asia Collective Defense Treaty, commonly known as SEATO. Eden, however, had in reality asked for time before finally making up his mind and had quite understandably not in fact committed himself as far as Dulles thought he had. A few days later, therefore, Eden told Dulles that he could not agree to an immediate course which might be expected to lead rapidly and inexorably to throwing British forces into Indo-China.

Eden gave, in effect, three reasons. One was that it would be folly to widen the war, with the obvious risk of a global showdown, just at the very moment when a vital conference was to take place at Geneva, with at least some genuine chance—as later proved justified—of an acceptable settlement being reached. Secondly, the British considered that, from the point of view of the urgent military situation at Dienbienphu, there was no practical step which the allies could take in time to relieve the beleaguered garrison. Thirdly, Eden made it clear that, if Britain were to find itself involved in a military adventure in Indo-China, this would not have the support of all the members of the Commonwealth, and it would in particular be strongly opposed by the Indian Prime Minister, Nehru; nor did it seem likely in London that, since the struggle against Communism in Indo-China was political as well as military, authentic victory was possible in the teeth of India's categoric opposition.

There was a fourth reason for Eden's rejection of Dulles's proposals as they stood, which he could hardly communicate explicitly to the American Secretary of State, but which was the decisive factor governing his actions. This was that Eden simply did not trust Dulles and the Americans not to leave British forces in the lurch. He felt that, if the Administration found itself committed to a politically awkward campaign, it might well decide to withdraw and leave everybody else to follow suit as best they could. This was a particular danger, as London saw the position, in that another Asian campaign would be desperately unpopular with American public opinion coming so soon after the frustrations of Korea, while at the same time there would be little chance of its succeeding, unless it did receive the fullest and most uninhibited backing that the United States could give it. Obviously, the ostensible reasons which Eden advanced for holding back were also perfectly valid. But it was basically Eden's rooted distrust of Dulles which made him go all the way and thwart the American plan.

The next stage was the unfortunate, but virtually inevitable, corollary of the first. Dulles became bitter and disillusioned, and did not fully trust either Eden or the French again during this crisis. He felt he had made a supreme effort in what he regarded as a vital cause. He had in a sense done what the British had been asking him to do for years—namely to promise active American resistance against Communist pressure on the mainland of Southeast Asia. He knew that he had taken grave risks with American public opinion, in advancing even secretly the full and to him epoch-making proposals which had come out of the critical Easter meetings. He also believed that nothing less than the kind of major allied operation which he proposed would work. It was all or nothing. He had proposed all and been rejected. So it would have to be nothing. Perhaps this is an oversimplification of the thoughts which chased themselves through his mind. But the fact is clear that, from this moment onwards, Dulles hung back rather than pressing forward. And, although he did put as firm a public face on the situation as he felt he could for the benefit of the Communists, it was henceforward a question of the sort of half-measures which at heart he always believed were wrong.

Shortly before the Geneva Conference was due to open Dulles flew to Paris for a meeting of the NATO Council, and it was then that the French Prime Minister, M. Laniel, officially asked for an emergency, unilateral, purely American move to relieve Dienbienphu. Although Bidault knew that Dulles had now rejected any broad American commitment to Indo-China, because of all that had been said in the previous fortnight, he begged the Secretary of State for at least an American air strike, mounted from the carriers of the U.S. Seventh Fleet, in order to save the gallant Frenchmen dying at Dienbienphu. Once again Dulles was wracked with the full range of emotions, which were inevitably roused by the tremendous arguments for and against such action. Looking back now from several years afterwards, even quite well-informed people seem dumbfounded to be told that serious consideration was given to the use of atomic weapons against the besiegers of Dienbienphu. But it was so. And Bidault has since been quoted as saying that Dulles offered him three atomic bombs for use by the French air force, which, however, he declined.

The full truth of what was said at this time may be very slow to come out. But the main outlines are clear. Dulles himself almost certainly did not make the atomic offer as categorically as Bidault is now said to claim, first, because he never had the authority to do so, and, secondly, because those who were close to him during the crisis do not believe that he was ever quite decided that the use of atomic weapons was even feasible; quite apart from the great political imponderables, the military value of an atomic bomb in relieving a besieged fortress is extremely difficult to visualize. What Dulles may well have done was to put the question hypothetically. *If* three atomic bombs *were* to be made available, *would* the French be willing to use them? And it is interesting that this suggests that the Americans would not do so themselves.

There was a school of thought in the American services which did give serious consideration to the possible usefulness of atomic weapons. But whatever some of its advocates may have thought individually, the final decision always in fact rested with the President, and it was Eisenhower who finally vetoed any of the more extreme forms of action favored by Admiral Radford, partly for the widest political considerations and partly because he was persuaded by General Matthew B. Ridgway, the Army Chief of Staff, that the dispatch of supporting forces on the ground was logistically far more difficult than the optimists supposed. In any event, therefore, Washington did not agree to the French government's request, and in the end, in spite of the heroic efforts of its garrison, Dienbienphu fell on May 7.

Behind Dulles's ultimate caution on this dramatic issue lay three further elements. One was that if, as many people say, brinkmanship implies a bluff that can be called, Dulles's essential approach to the Indo-China problem was one which involved this kind of brinkmanship. He deliberately acted in such a way that the Communists had good reason to fear that America would go further than in fact it did. In reality, although Dulles was willing to go a long way, as he had indeed made abundantly clear during this fateful month of April, 1954, he was not willing to go to the end alone. The second element in his thinking was quite simply that he was deeply opposed in principle to any move which would involve the use of American troops overseas so soon after the end of the Korean war; and in this he was quite right, since any such proposal would have been bitterly unpopular with the broad mass of American public opinion. Thirdly, Dulles was, as always, chary of getting committed to anything that might look like the support of colonialism. Although the French had become much more liberal since the early days of the war in Indo-China, opinion in Washington was by no means happy that their declarations about Vietnamese independence meant all that they appeared to mean.

From the Chinese and Russian points of view, events in Indo-China were certainly going well. Ever since the end of the fighting in Korea in mid-1953, Communist military supplies had been pouring into Vietnam at a constantly increasing rate, and already by the end of March, 1954, well over two thousand Communist Chinese were estimated to be supplying military and technical assistance to the forces under the Moscow-trained Vietnamese leader, Ho-Chi-Minh. With Communist China released from its need to supply forces in Korea and also having toned down its immediate threat to Formosa, both Soviet and Chinese propagandists were successfully claiming that Communism was on the march southwards. As Dulles had told the Overseas Press Club of America on March 29, the Communist purpose was "to dominate all Southeast Asia." If they succeeded, he went on, this would mean "a grave threat to the Philippines, Australia and New Zealand, with whom we have treaties of mutual assistance. . . . The entire Western Pacific area, including the so-called offshore islands chain, would be strategically endangered."

Although Dulles had recoiled from military intervention, as a result of the lack of allied support, he was determined that neither this general limitation on American action nor the particular incident of the fall of Dienbienphu should lead the Communists to assume at any time that he had washed his hands of Indo-China. He wanted, that is, to prevent Peking and Moscow remaining in the kind of uncertainty about the American interest in Indo-China which had led to the Soviet miscalculation about the possibility of invading South Korea without provoking retaliation. In this he undoubtedly succeeded, in so far as no major movement of Chinese troops ever took place across the frontier, and, above all, the Chinese did come and negotiate a truce at Geneva.

In this sense it is quite undeniable that Dulles played a vital role in making the Genera Conference possible. Without the American stand the Conference could never have taken place on the basis that it did. And while Dulles rightly felt he had good reason to distrust the attitude of the French when it came to bargaining at the conference table, particularly after M. Mendès-France had become Prime Minister, neither Eden nor Bidault could have kept the conference going without Dulles's shadow in the background. Dulles had in fact warned the Chinese that, however many successes they might achieve in Vietnam itself, the United States could not tolerate a total victory and the fall of Southeast Asia.

Having made the conference possible, Dulles nevertheless virtually refused to take part in it. One general reason was the political difficulty he would have been in at home if he had spent a great deal of time hobnobbing with the Chinese Communist Foreign Minister, Chou En-lai, whom the United States did not officially recognize at all. Admittedly at Berlin he had made it quite clear that, while he could not accept any concept of five-power control in the world, with Peking as a member of that control along with Moscow, Washington, London, and Paris, he was prepared to talk to Chinese representatives about Korea and Indo-China—though about nothing else. But he always had to reckon with the China lobby in Washington and the strongly expressed points of view of people like Senator Knowland. Knowland considered that the war in Indo-China would almost certainly end in an almost complete victory for the Communists, if any negotiation were undertaken with the Chinese. He also regarded any such negotiation as the thin end of a wedge which would force a way into the United Nations for Peking. Nor was Knowland alone in these fears, with the result that Dulles had to give undertakings that, in negotiating with the Chinese Communists on the two particular problems of Korea and Indo-China, he would not in any circumstances allow this to lead to either recognition of China or Peking's entry into the United Nations.

This criticism from the Republican Right was, moreover, not by any means all that Dulles had to contend with. Quite apart from the things that were being said about him in allied capitals, two distinct Democratic criticisms were also leveled at him on the home front in Washington. The first was that Dulles's heavy-footed, blundering diplomacy was leading the United States into an untenable position on the Asian mainland. The second was that, in the search for an agreement with the Chinese Communists and the Russians, the Administration had not only dangerously under-

mined its own original stand, but in doing so had put the Western
alliance under an almost intolerable strain. This second view was
one which, while hardly fair to Dulles, gained some ground as the
events of the early summer of 1954 unfolded.

As regards the unhappy French themselves, Dulles's line was
certainly not one that was likely to endear him to the government
in Paris. Nor did he find it easy himself in the light of his own
Francophile past. M. Laniel, the Prime Minister, and his Foreign
Minister, M. Bidault, were of course in a desperate plight over Indo-
China and could not afford the luxury of breaking with America
at such a time. But they also could not help being aware of Dulles's
cold and cruelly detached calculation, that they must be given
just enough support to prevent them from being overthrown by the
French National Assembly, but little more. They knew he thought
that, if the Laniel government fell, anything which succeeded it
would be bound to offer less resistance to the Communists and
might indeed capitulate entirely; and Dulles's initially severe distrust of Mendès-France, when he first replaced Laniel, was the
direct result of this line of thinking.

French public opinion as a whole also tended inevitably to be
bitter about what was happening on the spot in Indo-China. There,
America's backing had come too late and represented too little to
take the real burden of a terrible war off the shoulders of the
French nation. Thus, the American purpose, which was in fact to
enable and persuade the French to go on fighting long enough to
win the possibility of a favorable truce, could not fail to make
Dulles and France feel they were opponents of one another, rather
than allies. And while the only possible Western objective, with
the Geneva negotiations coming up, was to keep France from
capitulating, for the French themselves the situation was both a
tragedy and the source of immeasurable mortification.

The actual conference at Geneva, which lasted from April 26
to July 21, was one of the strangest episodes in postwar history.
The Western allies got into it at sixes and sevens, in spite of last-
minute efforts of Dulles to rally his colleagues by proposing a kind
of "united declaration" to prevent direct Chinese Communist intervention in Vietnam. The idea was quickly dropped, because it
begged all the questions and was naturally associated in many

minds with the policy of "instant retaliation." Dulles himself spent only a week in Geneva, departing on May 3 never to return, although Eden later begged him to do so. Even in the brief moment that he was there he did all he could to avoid any meeting at all with the Chinese Foreign Minister, Chou En-lai; he was aloof from the British and deeply suspicious of the French.

The precise reasons for his extraordinary behavior are even now not entirely clear, and they undoubtedly lay buried in the complex fastnesses of his own involved nature. Some former members of his staff declare to this day with the most unconvincing disingenuity that, as he always knew it would be a long conference, he calculated at the beginning that it was no use staying there himself, as he had far too much waiting to be done at his desk in Washington. And the conference did indeed adjourn on several occasions, so that the leading members of the Western delegations could return to their capitals. During one such adjournment, on June 24, Eden in fact accompanied Churchill on a visit to Washington. But, while the American Secretary of State obviously could not stay away from the State Department for a solid three months, to believe that this was his overriding motive is to be naive.

In reality Dulles had three general reasons for his bizarre performance and they all interacted. In the main, as regards the French, since he thought they were going to capitulate to the Communists, he was absolutely clear in his own mind that he personally was going to have no part whatever in such a performance. Nor would he in principle be a party to negotiating the formal acknowledgment of the transfer of any territory to Communist control. Secondly, as regards public opinion in America, he had already come under sharp attack from Knowland and a number of other Republicans on the Senate Foreign Relations Committee for attending the conference at all, and, considering his own thoughts about it, he felt it was just too absurdly ironic to fall out with Congress or anyone else over something which he did not believe in anyway. Thirdly, but at times almost more important than any other factor, as regards the British, he blamed Eden for destroying the only plans which he felt could have got the conference off on the right foot, and he was damned if he was going to work with him. He eventually answered Eden's entreaties by sending Bedell Smith to take his place at the conference table, and in the circumstances he felt that this was being pretty handsome about it.

Two-thirds of the way through, the French government fell and Mendès-France came in as Prime Minister, with the arresting promise that he would bring peace to Indo-China within a month or resign. The Chinese, on their side, behaved throughout with the tough inscrutability that one would expect from a combination of that remarkable race and the Communist creed. In the end, the fact that an agreement was reached at all which was not disastrous to the Western cause was one of the greatest triumphs of Anthony Eden's career. As British Foreign Secretary he stepped in, held the negotiations together and gradually achieved a solution. In spite of Dulles's misgivings, Mendès-France turned out to be a determined and clever negotiator. Although he was out for peace, he did not intend to capitulate. Whether more satisfactory terms could have been wrung from the Communists, if Dulles had ever been willing to return to the conference in person, is perhaps an open question. But with Bedell Smith almost as an American observer in the closing stages, the British and French, negotiating virtually alone with the Chinese and Russians, secured an agreement which was to last for many years.

Under the armistice which was reached on the night of July 20, 1954, a dividing line was drawn in Indo-China across Vietnam at approximately the 17th parallel; Mendès-France had argued for the 18th parallel and the Communists at one time had insisted on the 14th. This final line placed about 12,750,000 people under the Communist rule of the VietMinh in the north and about 9,300,000 under the non-Communist Vietnamese Republic in the south. French forces in the Red River delta were to withdraw completely within ten months, and there were certain withdrawals of Viet-Minh Communist troops in the south to be completed within eight months. Elections were to be held throughout Vietnam within two years, that is to say by July 20, 1956, with the opening of negotiations between the Vietnamese and VietMinh representatives about the actual running of the elections by July 20, 1955. India, Poland, and Canada were to provide a neutral international armistice commission to supervise the work of the mixed commissions representing both sides; the international commission was to take most decisions by majority vote, but, if it failed to agree on a matter involving a threat to peace, it was to report back to the nine Geneva Conference powers. In Laos all VietMinh troops were to withdraw and there was to be a regrouping of Laotian dissidents in the two northeastern, or Pathet Lao, provinces. Four separate states were thus established, North Vietnam, South Vietnam, Laos, and Cambodia, and in them no foreign bases were to be established. In spite of the many obvious potential weaknesses of these arrangements, they did in fact endure virtually unchallenged until the reopening of serious Communist pressure on Laos towards the end of 1960, six years later.

Throughout, Dulles had said that he would never put his name to a document condoning any Communist acquisition of territory. And he never did. He gave instructions from afar that the United States should not itself be a signatory to the armistice agreements, using the excuse that America had not been a participant in the fighting. But then neither had Britain. Two declarations were accordingly made at the end of the conference, one by the United States alone and the other by the representatives of the eight other states taking part, namely, Britain, France, Russia, China, Vietnam, Laos, Cambodia, and the VietMinh. The eight governments joined together in declaring that they were convinced that the agreed provisions would permit Cambodia, Laos, and Vietnam "to play their part in full independence and sovereignty in the peaceful community of nations." The United States, on the other hand, took note of this declaration and added that it would view any renewal of aggression in violation of the agreement with grave concern, and as seriously threatening international peace and security. The French, Cambodian, and Laotian delegations made further additional declarations, and everyone expressed the hope that the partition of Vietnam would not be permanent. When it came to the eventual election date two years later, however, no agreement was in fact reached whereby the two sides should reunite, and both Vietnamese states, one Communist and one non-Communist, have continued to exist on the same kind of provisional, but unfortunately enduring, basis as that which has for so long divided Germany.

On July 23 Dulles made a statement to the press, in which he said that two main lessons stood out from the Geneva negotiations. One was that the Western allies must recognize that resistance to Communism requires popular support, and the other that any arrangements for collective defense need to be made well in advance of aggression. Nobody would seriously quarrel with either observation. But they hardly represented more than a passing comment on a highly complex situation and they ran the risk of being merely wise after the event. Dulles had seen to it that the United States should not become too closely involved in the clearing up of an ugly mess, and it was no fault of the other allies that the mess had ever arisen in the first place. The seeds of the Indo-Chinese struggle had been sown in the upheavals of the Second World War and the Japanese occupation. This whole problem was a legacy of events which no one, least of all the French, could control. And in judging Dulles's record in the Indo-Chinese affair one is forced to two conclusions, both of which are extraordinarily characteristic of the rest of his career as Secretary of State. One was that, in spite of all the criticism which was flung at him, he was shrewd and effective in analyzing Communist behavior and devising ways and means of countering it. The other, however, as he himself sometimes recognized, was that for this he needed allies, but that his handling of those allies was all too often a clumsy mixture of ambivalence and an excessive sense of his own authority.

On balance, the Geneva Agreement clearly enabled a new start to be made in Southeast Asia, even if no permanent settlement had been reached. Admittedly the conference had failed to get anywhere on the other almost forgotten item on its agenda, a political settlement in Korea. But no one had seriously expected that it would, and in Indo-China the conference achieved at least as much as the Korean truce, indeed rather more. Peace had been brought to the peoples of Indo-China themselves; their neighbors had been relieved from a nagging fear that the war might spread; and the French had been enabled to put a stop to an impossible drain on their resources. As for the Communists, the VietMinh had gained formal possession of the city of Hanoi, together with the opportunity at last to establish an official Communist government; and Communist China had won a definite puppet state on its borders, together with practical recognition of its own position as a great power in the complex of Southeast Asia. At the same time the Chinese thrust southwards had undoubtedly been checked for the time being, and the whole of Southeast Asia breathed again. The British in particular had won a release from any immediate threat to the territorial integrity of Malaya, and both the Americans and the Russians had achieved a definite slackening of the tension which was still a hangover from the Korean War. This, moreover, had been achieved without either of them losing face.

For the West as a whole, there were three broad lessons to be learned from the Indo-China affair. First, as Dulles himself always pointed out, the success of the Communists in identifying themselves with nationalism proved how important it was that the West should be frank and sincere in its approach to colonial problems. Secondly, neither the French nor the British could any longer expect to act without American support in any context which brought them up against either of the two great Communist powers, a lesson which was finally rubbed home by the Suez crisis two years later. Although Dulles handled the Geneva Conference badly, he did manage to bring to bear the influence of America's strength and determination, and without this none of the skill of either Eden or Mendès-France would have been of any avail. Thirdly, again as Dulles himself was well aware, it was impossible for the West to meet the dynamic and intensely organized drive of the Communists without some form of unity. There was shortly to be a mutual security treaty for Southeast Asia and, although this was to be strongly criticized, its weaknesses reflected more the inadequacies of a military approach than the lack of need for a common political purpose.

All through the Geneva negotiations in the summer of 1954 the project for some kind of mutual security pact in Southeast Asia had in fact lain on the shelf, always slightly threatening Anglo-American relations. Churchill and Eden had visited Eisenhower and Dulles for weekend talks on June 24 partly to clear the air, and, although the problems of Europe probably took up more actual time, it had been the misunderstandings over the Far East which had caused the meeting. In some respects British and American attitudes towards Southeast Asia were never quite as far apart as they sometimes appeared. The difficulties sprang more from differences of national character and personal temperament than from the genuine clash of government policy; if Dulles and Eden had understood each other better, much of the friction over Geneva would never have arisen. Dulles was always unfortunate in getting a bad press in Britain, so that he constantly sounded harsher and less sympathetic than he was. This was sometimes caused by the existence of the common language which the British and Americans use in such different ways. It is, for instance, an American characteristic to overstate a case, a British one to understate it. For individuals of either country who do not fully appreciate this difference of attitude, the result can sometimes cause the most agonizing misunderstandings.

Dulles, moreover, had a strong sense of mission, which drove him forward in the belief that he could cut through the inessentials of a problem and deal with it by discovering what lay at the center; in doing so, he was often apt to regard any check to his progress as something of an affront. Eden's way of looking at things was in many ways the exact opposite. While temperamentally disinclined to yield, he did at heart believe that a complex problem could best be dealt with by patient negotiation between those who really understood it. Thus he normally hoped to see, and was usually prepared to accept, some form of compromise. The differences of approach between Dulles and Eden were also made worse at this particular moment by the fact that they were both to some extent hemmed in by domestic policies. Dulles was always having to address himself in part to a restive, even if not always numerous, body of highly placed critics in Congress, while Eden had to work against the background of a very small Conservative majority in the House of Commons.

This was important in that a growing volume of suspicion attached itself in Britain at that time to the whole principle of mutual security pacts. There was an increasing conviction, certainly in the Labour Party and to some extent among Conservative back-benchers, that the problem of containing Communism was rapidly becoming more political than military. Hence, although the British were willing to consider and eventually sign a mutual defense agreement covering Southeast Asia, they did not particularly relish the idea, and they certainly did not feel that it should be put into writing before the end of the Geneva negotiations. A fair section of American opinion, on the other hand, still felt so keenly about military agreements that it believed a security pact could have nothing but a salutary effect on the Geneva negotiations, and they accordingly branded the British as appeasers, using words like "sabotage," which represented a travesty of the facts, but effectively raised the political temperature on both sides of the Atlantic. In these circumstances Dulles himself ranked as something of a moderate. He could see that the real disagreement between London and Washington had been more on the approach to the problem than on the actual solution to it.

Accordingly, in spite of all the acrimony and misgivings, Dulles worked steadily forward during the summer of 1954 to achieve a Southeast Asian security pact. Eventually, he himself reached Manila in the Philippines on September 6 for the conference which produced the SEATO treaty. With him were representatives from Britain, France, Australia, New Zealand, Pakistan, Thailand, and the Philippines. It was a brief and successful occasion, having been carefully prepared, as a result of the endless discussion of the previous five months. At the opening session Dulles declared that America had no territorial interests in the area, but felt a sense of common destiny with those nations in it which were threatened by the danger of Communist ambition. His use of the word "Communist" raised the only major issue on which there was disagreement.

Dulles was very insistent that the Southeast Asia Collective Defense Treaty should be specific about the Communist threat. But his colleagues opposed him, and the Marquess of Reading, the British spokesman, defeated the American proposal with the argument that a *general* security treaty would make a far better impression on Indian and other opinion in Asia than a pact which could be branded as interference in the developing Asian countries. As events have turned out, SEATO has never ceased to be strongly criticized in Delhi and elsewhere, and it has very largely failed to receive the general support of public opinion in the countries which belong to it, with the possible exception of the United States. If Dulles had had his way, this latent opposition would almost certainly have been even stronger.

The solution reached at Manila was that Dulles signed a special

appendix to the main treaty, stating that the United States's acceptance of its obligations was on the specific understanding that these
were only in respect of armed attack or other aggression by Communist powers. In addition to being primarily concerned with his
own crusade against Communism, Dulles always argued that, unless
his signature to the treaty could be clearly seen in Washington as
an anti-Communist move, the pact would be rejected by Congress;
and in this he was probably right.

Apart from the problem of whether or not to mention Communism, the other major question mark over the negotiations was how
to define the area which the treaty was to cover. It could be argued
that, in view of Asian doubts about being committed to the West,
the precise area should not be defined at all. There were, moreover,
three particularly problematical cases. First, the three little anti-
Communist states which formed the unconquered remainder of
Indo-China, namely Laos, Cambodia, and South Vietnam, held
aloof from the Manila conference, their security being covered in
any case by the Geneva agreements; but they were certainly in the
direct line of Communist ambition. Then, secondly, there was the
political dynamite of the whole Formosa question; although obviously threatened and indeed owing its entire existence to the fact
of its resistance to Communism, for the regime of General Chiang
Kai-shek to have joined SEATO would have wrecked the treaty's
chances of receiving even a minimum of public support among the
bulk of its members. Formosa's adherence would also have practically eliminated any hope of getting other countries to join the
treaty in the future. Thirdly, there was the delicate question of
whether to include Hong Kong.

To be indefinite in matters of this kind, however, ran directly
counter to one of Dulles's main principles. While he believed in
leaving the enemy guessing in what might be termed fringe areas—
such as Quemoy and Matsu—he was adamant that, in territory
which he regarded as important, the value of any deterrent depended more on the certainty of its being applied than on the
nature of the application. And having had to compromise on the
use of the word "Communist" in the treaty, he was in no mood to
accept any vague phraseology about the area to be covered. The
upshot was a clever formula whereby the treaty was defined as

covering the "general area of Southeast Asia, including also the entire territories of the Asian parties and the general area of the Southwest Pacific, not including the Pacific area north of 21 degrees 30 minutes North latitude." In spite of the use of the words "general area," this meant that the treaty was quite specific about the territories of the Asian members, namely Thailand, the Philippines and Pakistan, and also in deliberately leaving out both Hong Kong and Formosa.

There remained something of a question of what to do about Laos, Cambodia and South Vietnam, particularly Laos where the northern provinces were going to continue to be occupied by Communist-supported forces. The dangers in Laos were indeed only too clearly demonstrated six years later by the international crisis of 1960 and 1961, which in a lesser key bore a depressing resemblance to the Indo-China situation of the early nineteen-fifties. Under pressure from Dulles a protocol to the treaty was therefore drawn up, in which the signatories unanimously named Laos, Cambodia, and South Vietnam as being an area in which they would themselves invoke the treaty, if an armed attack were made.

The actual commitment in the event of armed attack, or aggression in that treaty area, against any designated state or territory, was for each signatory to "take action in accordance with its own constitutional processes," and to report any measures taken to the United Nations Security Council immediately. But it was not laid down that the action taken should necessarily be military. In addition, a permanent organization was to be created to help consultation between members and, for the first time in history, to exchange information about internal subversive activities. After some hesitation, this SEATO headquarters organization was eventually set up in Bangkok, where it has functioned with considerable success. Oddly enough, once the SEATO treaty had been signed, it met with relative public indifference and apathy, which compared markedly with the emotional debate beforehand. SEATO has in fact neither failed nor been outstandingly successful. But its existence has meant the continued pledge of American support for those who resist Communist aggression in Southeast Asia, and until 1960 at least no further threats did in fact appear in that area after the treaty was signed.

In the light of all that has happened since 1954, one of the most interesting aspects of SEATO is that in practice it marked the beginning of a new phase in the pattern of behavior of the uncommitted. After that summer the idea of bipolarity began to lose its grip. Instead of the feeling of increasing compulsion to join one side or the other in the cold war, a more flexible international order began to appear. There were two main reasons for this. One was that many of the governments not directly involved in the great power struggle, particularly those of the newly independent nations of Asia and later of Africa, found the perpetual stalemate and their own impotence so intolerable that they started to ignore the great powers whenever they could. The other and more important reason was that, once it had become clear that the Russians and Chinese had won virtually all they could by force of arms, without running too dangerous a risk of global war, the main emphasis of the Communist drive for world domination changed to being more political and economic in character; this was shown up most clearly by China's pacific line at the Bandung Conference in 1955, and by Russia's wooing of India with the Khrushchev-Bulganin visit. Thus, the great powers on both sides were forced to realize the futility of either demanding total loyalty to themselves or seeing total opposition in the other side. With American support the Western alliance had successfully stopped Soviet and Chinese military expansion; but, from this period on, the leaders of the West were increasingly obliged to defend, to counterattack, and to try to stabilize the situation by political rather than military means.

For Dulles this meant a certain amount of mental readjustment. Although he had been the clearest and most consistent of Western statesmen in never forgetting that the aims of Communism were fundamentally political, it was no accident that his whole public posture had become associated in many people's minds primarily with military resistance. His underlying argument had been that, unless the military basis of resistance to Communism could be made secure, the prospects for adopting a successful political stand were poor. But now a new stage had been reached, and Dulles took some time to recognize that the original argument could, and indeed should, be reversed. The chances of offering successful military resistance to a Communist threat, that is to say, really depend more on being able to take a firm and convincing political stand than on lining up allies whose heart may not be in the fight. It is in fact more the military which depends on the political than vice versa.

It is quite untrue that Dulles did not change his views on neutralism and on the best handling of uncommitted countries, though he was slow to do so and his conversion was never exactly like that of Saint Paul on the road to Damascus. As he originally saw the position, if you really kept your eye on what the Russians were up to, as he did, it was impossible not to believe in the need for some form of collective security system. From this the neutrals benefited indirectly without contributing a single penny. Not only that, they went out of their way to be offensive to the West without ever even offering a word of thanks for what was being done. Such an attitude was nothing less than immoral, and Dulles certainly began by feeling very strongly indeed about it. At the same time, he recognized that in certain cases it might be dangerous for a small country to come off the fence, and he would then accept its decision, so long as this did not mean, as it sometimes seemed to do, a kind of neutralism on the Communist side.

What he could not stand was the apparent hypocrisy of some of the things that outstanding men like Nehru sometimes said. Although Dulles never liked Nehru, they did both come to respect each other. And for Nehru to add insult to injury, by actually piling on blame of the Americans from a moral point of view, seemed to Dulles inexplicable, except on the assumption that he was soft on Communism. For Dulles the most vivid reality in the world was the history of the immediate postwar years, with the development of the Soviet danger. Thus, even if he could see the neutrals' point of view, he simply could not at first accept it emotionally. But gradually a change did come. It came because Dulles was too intelligent not to follow what was happening to international relationships; because he did talk at great length with Nehru in particular, but with other neutrals as well, in an effort to understand them; because people under him in his own Department of State worked on him steadily about the sheer importance of the neutral Asian bloc; and finally, because, as he traveled about the globe and saw the problems at first hand, he slowly came to feel a growing sympathy for the peoples of the underdeveloped countries, which he never had when he first came to power. Although the strength of Dulles's views made him slow to learn, in fact, he did learn in the end. And while he can legitimately be criticized for his slowness, it is quite inaccurate to say that he never understood at all. By the end Dulles was a far better Secretary of State than he had been at the beginning.

CHAPTER 9

Western Europe Turns the Corner

THE summer and autumn of 1954 were an extraordinarily active diplomatic period, and one of the most decisive in both Europe and the Far East since the war. Dulles himself spent hour after hour in the air and traveled the equivalent of several times around the globe. He visited Western Europe on an average of more than once a month, in addition to his Far Eastern trip in September. Before considering the drama which played itself out in August and September, however, with the collapse of EDC and the entry of the Federal German Republic into NATO, two other events should be noticed. One was the signature of the Anglo-Egyptian Treaty under which the British withdrew from Egypt, and the other was the introduction of amendments in the United States to the Atomic Energy Bill of 1946.

Eisenhower and Dulles each went out of their way to express satisfaction that the new Anglo-Egyptian Agreement was finally concluded at the end of July. Although Dulles was partly responsible for the Anglo-American misunderstandings in the Middle East, he had played some part in this problem of the Suez Canal Zone by counseling moderation on both sides. On July 27, 1954, after many months of negotiation, Anthony Head, the British Secretary of State of War, and Colonel Nasser, by then Prime Minister of Egypt, initialed an agreement embodying a number of principles to cover the proposed arrangements for the military base in the Suez Canal Zone. Valid for several years, the agreement provided for a complete withdrawal of British forces from the Canal Zone within twenty months from the date of signature, in return for which the Egyptians would keep the existing base in efficient working order, and would afford all the necessary facilities to operate it in the event of war brought about by an armed attack on Egypt, or on any member of the Arab League, or on Turkey. At the time it was hoped that the spirit in which the agreement had been reached would reverse the long-term deterioration in Anglo-Egyptians relations; but two years later it was only a very few weeks after the final withdrawal of the British troops in 1956 that Colonel Nasser exploited the new opportunity open to him to take over the ownership of the Suez Canal, thus setting off the great Suez crisis of that year.

The succession of events, which culminated in President Eisenhower signing a new amendment to the Atomic Energy Bill on August 30, showed Dulles at his best. As Secretary of State, he was called upon to give evidence before a Joint Committee of Congress in support of the proposed amendments, and he unequivocally placed himself on the side of the angels. In 1946, immediately after the war, when the close wartime co-operation with the British on atomic energy had already ceased, and when it was already certain that Soviet spies and sympathizers were getting valuable atomic knowledge from the West, the overwhelming view in Washington was that total secrecy must be preserved, in the interests of humanity as well as of the nation. But eight years later the American monopoly no longer existed, and Dulles was among the most prominent voices to emphasize that three circumstances had arisen which created a definite need to relax at least some of the provisions of the original bill. These were the obvious developments which had already taken place in the Soviet program, the fact that the United States still depended at that time on foreign sources of uranium and, by no means least, the legitimate hopes of America's allies that they would in time be able to develop both military and industrial nuclear power of their own. Dulles also supported a change in the law, which would permit the disclosure of certain military information to help in the defense against atomic weapons.

All these lesser events pale into insignificance, however, in comparison with the crisis which hit Western Europe when France finally rejected EDC in August of 1954. Dulles is reported to have called it, a few weeks later, "a crisis of almost terrifying proportions." Admittedly this was partly in his own mind, because he had previously committed himself and the prestige of the United States to the passage of EDC so deeply. But it is certainly true nevertheless that the two months following the final decisive vote in the French National Assembly on August 30 marked a turning point in Western European affairs, with long-term implications even more important, if that were possible, than the Far Eastern settlement at Geneva earlier in the summer.

In the final vote on the European Army proposal the French National Assembly turned it down by 319 votes to 264, with 43 abstentions, including some members of the Mendès-France government. Every single party in the Chamber was split over the voting, except the Communists, who were of course solidly against. Thus ended well over two years of heartbreaking effort. What had started as a French plan, put forward by M. Pleven, was finally killed by the French themselves, after everyone else concerned had first accepted and then begun to have active doubts about it. For Dulles personally the vote in the French Assembly was a severe defeat, but the events which followed showed that it was by no means the disaster for the Western world that he had so publicly said it would be.

In the United States, nevertheless, the collapse of EDC, following so soon after the formal acceptance at Geneva of considerable Communist gains in Indo-China, was widely taken as evidence that Dulles's policy in Western Europe, as well as in the Far East, had been torn to shreds. Was he right to have thrown so much of his own prestige behind EDC, considering that for months everyone had known that the chances of ratification were dwindling fast? To understand the answer it must be remembered that the starting point lay on that faraway day in September, 1950, all but four years earlier, when in the full flood of the sense of emergency caused by the outbreak of the Korean war, Dean Acheson had startled his British and French colleagues, Ernest Bevin and Robert Schuman, by demanding the rearmament of Germany. Bevin, well aware of the way the wind was blowing, had sided with Acheson, albeit grudgingly and unhappily. Schuman did not. Those were still the days when the French went in distrust and fear of a German military revival, and out of this situation had sprung the rather desperate French proposal that, if arms were to be given to the West Germans, then this must be allowed to happen only if German soldiers formed part of an integrated European force rather than a national army. Received at first with skepticism in Washington and also in London, this awkward hybrid of an idea gradually took root and flourished.

Eventually, somewhere down the long road of discussion and gradual ratification of the provisional treaty by the parliaments of the other five countries which were to form the six-nation European Army with France—namely Germany, Italy, Holland, Belgium, and Luxembourg—it came to be realized that the purpose of EDC had changed. Instead of merely rearming the Germans, momentous though that decision itself undoubtedly was within little more than half a decade from the end of the Second World War, the key purpose of EDC had come to be to tie Germany firmly into the Western community of free nations before it was too late. And it was this aspect of the problem which came to divide Washington and Bonn on the one hand, and London on the other. For Dulles, as for Adenauer, the need to hold Germany for the West was even more important than either a large German military contribution to Western defense or the actual French-German rapprochement required to make this possible. For Eden and the British the proposition never quite took this form. The priorities were different for a mixture of emotional and traditional reasons. Eden and many other people in Britain never quite believed in the danger of Germany slipping away from the West, as Dulles and Adenauer did, and this was the basic cause of a whole host of differences between them. It encouraged the Dulles-Eden duel, it fostered their personal misunderstanding, and it explained Dulles's dash to Adenauer's side in September.

Who was right? Was it really more urgent to tie Germany to the West than either to secure a Germany military contribution or to insure a French-German rapprochement? This is the sixty-four-thousand-dollar question, which the continued life and Chancellorship of Konrad Adenauer have in practice made it much less necessary to answer than it seemed to be in 1954. The fact that Adenauer continued in office right through to the nineteen-sixties has minimized the importance of the dangerous corner which Western Europe had to turn that critical summer. But one of the factors which made it so agonizing at the time was the possibility that the collapse of the EDC policy, to which Adenauer, just as much as Dulles, had pinned his reputation, might bring the Chancellor down with it, if not at once then at the next election. For Adenauer was certainly a lonely and heavily criticized figure in Bonn in the immediate aftermath of the French Assembly's vote. And it was this among other things which Dulles saw so clearly, while Eden either did not or attached too little importance to it. On the plane of personal relations, the friendship between Adenauer and Dulles really dates from the visit which Dulles paid at that moment to the lonely Chancellor.

The truth was that world conditions had changed between the autumn of 1950 and the summer of 1954. By the time that EDC came up for its final decision in the French Assembly, the Korean War had been over for some time, and the apparent urgency of getting the equivalent of twelve West German divisions into the field had slightly receded, though it was still, of course, an important long-term requirement. On the other hand, during these four years the political and economic consolidation of the Federal German Republic had been going steadily forward, and the slate for replanning Germany's role in Western Europe was not as empty as it had been. By now, West Germans were beginning to adopt a more positive attitude to the position of their country in the post-war world; and the question had already begun to arise, by the time the French vote was finally taken, whether the ends of EDC could be fully achieved either with or without the passage of the treaty.

In spite of the overriding importance which Dulles attached to tying Germany in with the West, opinion in Washington had not by any means accepted all the priorities as he saw them. The Pentagon was not at all sorry that this awkward creation, which even the months of argument had failed to elaborate sufficiently to make convincing, would never now come into being. And Dulles himself, in spite of his commitment to EDC, was quite aware that, apart from the specific issue of linking the Federal German Republic to Western Europe while Adenauer was still in control of it, what was needed was some means of creating confidence between France and Germany, as well as adding to the strength of the NATO forces. The beauty of EDC had been that it looked like doing all these things, while also adding to the still shaky, but by now definitely established, superstructure of supranational agencies in Western Europe. This in itself was something to which Dulles, like all Americans, attached great importance, much greater than anyone really did in London. As Dulles commented after EDC broke down, its charm had been that it would at one stroke have made Western Europe "immune from war as between its members and defensible against aggression from without."

Dulles's attitude after the collapse of EDC was different from Eden's, as has already been suggested, by the greater importance he attached to the problem of Germany's position in Europe. But American views on German rearmament certainly also had their effect on Dulles's calculations. In Washington it is quite difficult to make allowance for the legacy of suspicion which two terrible wars have left on Germany's neighbors, and which in 1954 were much stronger than they may be today. The United States itself is not only physically remote from Germany across the other side of the Atlantic, not only a country which has never been occupied by German forces or of course even threatened with such an occupation, but also a great power in quite a different category from any other except the Soviet Union. Americans therefore naturally do not fear the Germans as many Europeans do.

Thus, Dulles was able to make a more detached and analytical estimate of the needs and possibilities of Germany rearmament, for instance, than Eden could. Since then, some American commentators, looking back on this period, have also accused Eden and the British of even going beyond their understandable inhibitions about German rearmament to the point of opposing a full German-French rapprochement, because this would rob the British of their traditional role in the balance of power on the continent, a position which had been given unprecedented strength by the collapse of France as well as of Germany in the war. But, while there was just something in this, to treat it as a dominating motive in the actions of the Churchill-Eden government is to let the tail wag the dog.

Eden disagreed with Dulles's approach, mainly because the British were a good deal more cynical than the Americans about the Germans making a deal with the Communist East. After all, Adenauer was not alone in being bitterly anti-Communist; his views on Communism were shared by almost the whole of the population of Western Germany, many millions of them refugees from the East who had had personal experience of Communist rule. Nor did the British feel that any strong political movement existed in Bonn to take the initiative in negotiating with Moscow. Indeed, when Macmillan later came to claim the part of "honest broker" between East and West, he was as unpopular with many Germans as he was in the United States. Admittedly, the German Social Democrats were far more interested than Adenauer in the possibility of demilitarizing German territory, but this was not the same as wanting to come to terms with the Communists. Eden also had to recognize that there was a coherent internal opposition in Britain, by no means confined to the Labour Party, to the idea of recreating German national forces without taking any steps to control them.

When it came to the EDC method of taking the sting out of potential German nationalism, the British were inevitably less keen than Americans, since it called in question their own possible membership and the partial sinking of their sovereignty in a broad West European organization, which was certainly never proposed for the Americans. Dulles rightly laid part of the blame for the failure of EDC at Britain's door, because the absence of the British tipped the balance in France against the scheme; but he never made this a major issue. Admittedly, the malicious American accusation that the British opposed a French-German integration, through fear of losing their own influence, appeared to be given some substance a year or so later, when they refused to take the negotiations for the Treaty of Rome seriously. But, looking at the position as it actually was in 1954, with Churchill as Prime Minister and Eden as Foreign Secretary, it is simply inaccurate to assert that the British Government was opposed in principle to supranationalism in Western Europe after the collapse of EDC. What they would not do, as Eden said again and again, was to back a horse which they were quite certain was a loser.

There was another factor behind the British attitude, which Dulles consistently played down. Part of the reason why Eden welcomed the eventual NATO solution for Germany, instead of weeping crocodile tears over the temporary eclipse of European supranationalism, was that NATO provided the framework within

which the British felt they could maintain their links with the
United States, while not in any way dissociating themselves from
Europe. Dulles never fully understood British thinking on this
point about Atlantic unity, partly because it did not suit him to do
so. And in so far as he ever carried out his threat to make an
agonizing reappraisal of his own European policy, it has been said
that he chose to support even the tenderest shoots of European
supranationalism which remained after EDC, at the expense of
British wishes. This, however, seems to be stretching the meaning
of words. Dulles did not in the end carry out what everyone understood to be the meaning of his threatened agonizing reappraisal,
namely at least a partial withdrawal from American commitments
to Europe, because the London Conference and the Paris Agreements ultimately brought Germany into NATO, confirmed the
emergence of Western European Union (WEU) with Britain as a
member, and instituted an acceptable measure of control over
German rearmament.

The immediate sequence of events leading up to this moderately
satisfactory conclusion began when Eden left London for his
notable tour of the West European capitals on Saturday, September
11, 1954. He was going to Brussels, Bonn, Rome, and Paris, with
two aims in mind. One was to test the atmosphere after the patient,
EDC, had finally died; and the other was to suggest that some
solution for Europe should be found along the lines of what
eventually emerged as Western European Union, that is to say
drawing Germany and Italy into a new version of the Brussels
Treaty of 1948 which bound Britain, France, and the Benelux
countries to come to the others' aid if they were attacked. This in
fact was to convert a treaty which was originally aimed against
Germany into something more like a regional defensive alliance
against Russia.

The idea of WEU contained two significant elements: it was an
attempt to bring governments together rather than to integrate
states, and at the same time it included Britain among those
governments. As to who really originated this proposal, there is
some dispute. Eden claims that it occurred to him while in his
bath; but Mendès-France has since told the world that the encouraging response which Eden actually got for it on his tour was due

to the French having plowed the ground beforehand. Obviously the idea was one which might occur to anyone, and in various forms it probably did so. But the French claim seems singularly specious considering the state of disarray in Paris at the time, and in any case little would have happened without Eden's energetic diplomacy.

It was in the middle of Eden's tour that Dulles made one of the most extraordinary moves of his career, when he maddened Eden and puzzled nearly everyone else by setting off on a sudden, lightning trip to Bonn on September 16 in order to see Adenauer. From there he returned via London on September 17, where he had an awkward and confusing meeting with Eden, and got back to Washington on September 18. It was Dulles at his worst or best, according to which way one looks at it. To this day Dulles's real motives are a puzzle to Eden. But in Dulles's own mind they were quite clear. He dashed to Bonn because he was deeply concerned at the scale of Adenauer's rage with Mendès-France and the French; because he was aware that it might make Adenauer recoil irretrievably from any solution of the French-German problem; and because he felt that he himself was the only person in the world who could tell the determined, but shaken, old Chancellor not to be so short-sighted.

Although Eden had been in Bonn only a few days before Dulles, the extent of the German government's psychological reaction and the possible dangers inherent in Adenauer's bitterness had escaped him. But this was partly because Adenauer deliberately chose not to confide in him fully, and the fact that his picture differed from Dulles's was not entirely his fault. Thus, although Dulles slightly overdramatized the situation, his idea of what might happen was probably a good deal closer to the truth than Eden's. Adenauer was in fact so angry with the French that he wanted to have nothing more to do with them, nothing at all. He wanted a German-American-British solution to the problem of German rearmament and Germany's ties with the West, in which the French would simply have no part. When this emerged between the lines of an angry communiqué which he issued from his holiday base in the Black Forest, the word "France" was not even mentioned from start to finish.

If Adenauer had seriously stuck to this line of thinking, it would have meant the virtual end of NATO, as well as of the EDC proposals. It would have involved in practice the splitting of the defense of Western Europe between a northern Anglo-German sector and a southern French one. The cohesion of the NATO front has been threatened more than once since the Atlantic Treaty was signed in 1949. But the threat has always so far dissolved under the nightmare of trying to imagine any effective defense system without France. Certainly the consequences of trying to plan American logistical support exclusively through such points of entry as Antwerp and Bremen, without the French Atlantic coast ports, would have the gravest consequences both on the system of defense itself and on American willingness to sustain it.

All this was implicit in Adenauer's attitude, and the results in terms of the cold war might have been appalling. This was why Dulles flew to Bonn. By the time he got there, Adenauer had in fact begun to calm down. But Dulles reassured him about the warmth and reality of American support, and renewed the Chancellor's faith in the policy of linking Germany to the West. Together they discussed in detail the ways and means of achieving the entry of the Federal Republic into NATO. When Dulles got back to Washington, he felt that he had not only conducted a rescue operation but had made a friend for life. In both he was right. The only point where he went wrong was in believing in his rather characteristic way that no one else could be right too. In practice it was to take all the statesmen of the Western alliance to complete the jigsaw.

After the EDC collapsed the central problem was how to give the Federal German Republic some form of parity with the three other major countries in the Western alliance, France, Britain, and the United States. It was generally agreed that the original Bonn conventions, limiting German sovereignty, were no longer quite adequate, and yet at the same time that German rearmament could still not be unconditional. Both these points were recognized in Germany. The question was whether they were equally recognized in France. Whatever solution was adopted, it was desirable to avoid squeezing French neuroses any further. But it was also widely felt that the French could no longer assume the right to impose a further veto on anything that happened.

Although a strong case existed for settling the problem simply by bringing a sovereign Germany into NATO, and then perhaps reorganizing the alliance, the difficulty about any such tightening of the conditions of membership, let alone any discrimination in respect of a particular member, was that it required the revision of the Atlantic Treaty. This would inevitably take time, and the need to take Adenauer's Germany into the Western alliance was extremely urgent. Nor was it at all clear what form revision could take; what undertakings could the members of NATO give to each other in order to curtail the type of membership offered to Germany? Although Dulles was keen on a NATO solution, he fully understood these obvious drawbacks, and it was because he saw the need for something else as well that he genuinely welcomed Eden's efforts to create the Western European Union, deliberately taking an apparent back seat once the WEU negotiations had got properly started. He said afterwards that, while he was always ready to step in if needed, he had not done so because he had thrown his influence in private behind what Eden was doing. It was a slightly double-edged claim, since it also implied that he took what he felt was his proper share of the credit for the satisfactory outcome.

After a month of frantic diplomatic activity, the Nine-Power Conference, consisting of the foreign ministers of Britain, France, Germany, Italy, Belgium, Holland, Luxembourg, the United States, and Canada, opened in London on September 28, 1954. The chief headings on the agenda were, first, arrangements for ending the occupation regime in Germany and restoring full sovereignty; secondly, the project for German and Italian membership of the renovated Brussels Treaty; and, thirdly, the question of German membership of NATO. There were three important moments at this conference, one involving each of the three Western allies in turn, the Americans, the British and the French. Dulles made his most important move in an opening statement, in which he said that he would recommend to President Eisenhower the renewal of the pledge which the President had given on April 16 "in connection with the European Defense Community Treaty," if the London Conference reached a satisfactory agreement about some organization to take the place of EDC. This pledge had stated that upon the entry into force of the EDC treaty, in the President's words,

> the United States would continue to maintain in Europe, including Germany, such units of its armed forces as may be necessary and appropriate, to contribute its fair share of the forces needed for the joint defense of the North Atlantic area while a threat to that area exists, and will continue to deploy such forces in accordance with agreed North Atlantic strategy for the defense of this area.

Given at the time in order to encourage the creation of EDC, the undertaking had been intended to serve that purpose alone and no other. It therefore expired when EDC was defeated, and its renewal by Dulles at the London Conference gave it an entirely fresh significance. In a sense, this was a precise reversal of previous American policy. Instead of threatening to withdraw troops if EDC was not passed, Dulles was now promising exactly the same support as he would have done whether EDC had passed or not. So much for the agonizing reappraisal!

As part of President Eisenhower's statement on April 16, he had made it clear that the duration of the pledge was not limited, and that whatever happened it could be assumed to last until the original twenty years of the North Atlantic Treaty ran out in 1969. "For the United States to cease," the President said, "to be party to the North Atlantic Treaty would appear quite contrary to our security interests when there is established on the continent of Europe a solid core of unity which the European Defense Treaty will provide." For Dulles to renew this pledge now was therefore a new and categoric American commitment of the first importance.

Dulles was also using it, however, for exactly the same purpose as that for which it had been applied to EDC. He carefully pointed out, in fact, that, unless a satisfactory agreement on Western defense did emerge from the London Conference, the American pledge would not hold good. And although one might argue that the United States was still bound by the North Atlantic Treaty itself, on a number of occasions since the degree of positive American support for that treaty has clearly been in doubt, at least in the public mind if not in reality. The effect of Dulles's words on the London Conference was therefore quite striking. Explaining the American point of view, he said that there had indeed been a great wave of disillusionment which had swept over the United States and was particularly manifest in Congress, together with a feeling that the situation in Western Europe was rather hopeless. But he declared that, in view of the efforts which had been made, he most ardently hoped that the conference would succeed in changing the atmosphere; and he added for good measure that, if this could be done by using the Brussels Treaty as a nucleus, he for one would be solidly behind the new project.

Eden, who was chairman of the conference, knew that Dulles was going to make this statement. And the second important development at the conference table was that he himself then got up and gave Britain's equivalent pledge, which in terms of previous British policy was even more epoch-making. Britain, Eden declared, would maintain on the mainland of Europe the effective strength of the United Kingdom forces at that time assigned to the Supreme Allied Commander, Europe, "that is to say, four divisions and the Second Tactical Air Force, or such other forces as the Supreme Allied Commander, Europe, regards as having equivalent fighting capacity." As Eden put it in his memoirs: "The reaction was immediate. All understood the real meaning of what I had said. Britain would hold her military place in Europe, to keep the peace. It was not our numbers that mattered, but our presence." For Britain this was indeed a remarkable step to take. Never before in modern times had specific British forces been committed to service on the Continent, except in wartime. Naturally some people felt that, if Eden had done this a few months earlier, the fate of EDC might have been different. But this seems rather unlikely, since it was not British troops but British membership that was then required. The fact was nevertheless, that at this late hour London had at last begun to see that some British move forward was absolutely essential, and it was to Eden's credit that he made the move when it could still be of genuine value.

The third important moment in the conference was an incident which Eden discreetly leaves out of his memoirs. After giving the new British pledge, "the conference moved rapidly forward," he says. "Only M. Mendès-France, with his sights set on retaining a majority in the French Assembly, was reluctant to match the concessions of the other delegates with some of his own." And Eden adds that: "In addition to the American and British declarations, other countries made contributions of great importance. The Benelux powers renounced the right to manufacture atomic, bacteriological or chemical weapons. The Germans renounced not only this, but also the right to manufacture guided missiles, large naval vessels and bombers. Mendès-France, however, clung tenaciously to his plan for an arms pool to achieve the co-ordinated production and standardization of European armaments, under the aegis of the Brussels Treaty Organization." Then Eden adds: "Under pressure, the French eventually agreed not to make acceptance of their plan a precondition of their agreement to the other proposals before the conference...." What in fact happened was that Eden lost his temper and did so to the best possible effect. "Under pressure" is a splendid euphemism for a violent scene which left Mendès-France shattered. Dulles, for his part, sat tight throughout, knowing full well that for once he and Eden were batting on the same side.

After the London Agreement was signed on October 3, 1954, President Eisenhower described it as "one of the great diplomatic achievements of our time." It covered five main points. First, the three occupying powers in Western Germany announced their intention to end the Occupation regime, to revoke the Occupation Statute, and to abolish the Allied High Commission. This declaration of intent was coupled with a statement that the arrangements would come into effect either before or simultaneously with the German defense contribution. Secondly, Germany and Italy were to become members of the Brussels Treaty, but the original consultative council was to become an organization with powers of decision and authority to supervise the size and character of the German contribution, now formally fixed at twelve divisions and a tactical air force. An agency was also to be set up to control the armaments on the Continent of the Continental members of the Brussels Treaty Organization, a provision which was aimed at the control of German armament and was coupled with a German declaration agreeing not to manufacture atomic, bacteriological, or chemical weapons or to manufacture long-range missiles, strategic bombers or certain types of naval vessels, except with the specific approval of the Supreme Allied Commander, Europe, and of a two-thirds majority of the Brussels Council.

Thirdly, the American and British pledges to maintain their Continental forces were restated. Fourthly, there was an agreement to recommend at the next ministerial meeting of the Atlantic Council that Germany should become a member of NATO and that the machinery of NATO should be reinforced; although Germany did in fact become a member of NATO in May of the following year, 1955, the machinery of NATO was not in practice materially altered. Fifthly, the peaceful and defensive character of the Atlantic and Brussels Treaties was emphasized, the German government undertaking never "to have recourse to force to achieve the reunification of Germany or the modification of the present boundaries"of the Federal German Republic.

There remained only the formal execution of these agreed plans. Dulles flew back to Washington from London, but returned to Paris on October 21. There two days later, in the presence of Adenauer, he signed with Eden and Mendès-France the first of what have become known as the Paris Agreements, which ended the Occupation regime in the Federal Republic of Germany. The rest of the provisions of the London Conference were also signed and out of it all sprang the Western European Union. By October 25 Dulles was once more back in Washington, where he declared that the agreements signed in Paris marked "the beginnings of a new era for Europe."

As events have since proved, he was certainly right. Although Western European Union has not won quite the prestige which at one time seemed marked out for it, since it has throughout been overshadowed by the North Atlantic alliance as a whole, the realities behind WEU have stood the test of time. This was the moment when Western Germany needed to be accepted into the community of Western nations, and it was. And although Dulles had more or less eaten his words about an agonizing reappraisal, he had always in a sense made himself the artificial prisoner of his own stand. As for Europe itself, the fact that the vital issue of Germany's role had been settled satisfactorily led directly on to the reawakening in due course of the urge to see some form of integration in Western Europe. Although Western European Union was only an agreement between governments, its existence and all that went with it made possible the whole later concept of the Little Six. The London Conference of 1954 and the Paris Agreements not only brought Germany into the West, but their method of doing so bought time for the rest of Western Europe to recover its nerve.

CHAPTER 10

The Brink at Quemoy

WHILE Dulles was away in Europe dealing with the paramount problem of Germany's future, a fresh challenge arose in the Far East, as explosive and dangerous as any that he faced in all his time at the Department of State. This was the Chinese Communist shelling of the little Nationalist-held island of Quemoy, just off the Chinese coast opposite the port of Amoy. This shelling had started as soon as SEATO had been signed on September 8, 1954, and the shells were actually falling on both Quemoy and Matsu when Dulles's aircraft put down at Taipei, the capital of Formosa, on his way back to Washington. The period of tension over these offshore islands, at times very acute, was to last for just six months. And during this time Dulles's tough line was to be furiously attacked, both inside the United States itself and by his allies in Western Europe.

When Dulles was in Taipei, Chiang Kai-shek asked him for a definite American security pact. Dulles agreed to take the question up when he got back to Washington. By the time that negotiations were started after his return, the situation on Quemoy itself had become a good deal more serious. In addition, Peking radio had stepped up its abuse of the United States to unprecedented levels. The result was that Dulles felt it necessary to ask for an emergency session of the United States National Security Council, which took place at Denver, Colorado, where President Eisenhower was on holiday. At this session the main lines of America's policy in regard to the offshore islands were laid down, in terms both of the public attitude to be adopted and of the actual military preparations to be made.

The main new development was a request to Congress by the President for what later came to be known as the "Formosa Resolution," authorizing him to "employ the armed forces of the United States as he deems necessary" to defend Formosa. This Resolution was not actually passed by Congress until the next session in January, 1955, when it received overwhelming approval in both the House of Representatives and the Senate. But, in the meantime, the President and Dulles both made a point of threatening China with American intervention, if Quemoy and Matsu were invaded—though mention of the islands had been deliberately avoided in the Resolution, in order not to delay its passage through Congress. At Denver it was also decided to refer the Formosa question to the United Nations; this, however, was little more than a form of words, since Chou En-lai refused to present the Communist case when the dispute eventually came up for consideration in the Security Council.

The Formosa Resolution empowered the President:

> to include the securing and protecting of such related positions and territories of that area now in friendly hands and the taking of such other measures as he judges to be required or appropriate in insuring the defense of Formosa and the Pescadores.

This was the phrase which specifically left unanswered the key question, whether the American guarantee included the defense of Quemoy and Matsu themselves by American forces. Neither during this crisis nor in the later one of 1958 did either Eisenhower or Dulles ever fully commit themselves in public on this question. But they each had fairly definite views about their position, if ultimately faced with a Chinese Communist invasion of the off-shore islands. Eisenhower's instinct was to look at the problem from a strictly military angle; in this sense he kept a fairly open mind, though as a soldier he was clear that the claim, widely heard in the United States, that the offshore islands were essential to the defense of Formosa itself was nonsense. And this indeed it was.

Dulles's own view has not been fully explained, and it may not be finally known until all his papers become available in some years' time. But those who worked closely with him at the time believe that he would not have committed American forces to the defense of the offshore islands. Moreover, the Chinese Nationalist attitude, which became much more definite in the second offshore islands crisis in 1958, was already forming; this was that Chiang Kai-shek would lose face if American troops actually defended Quemoy, and accordingly he never asked that they should do so. At the same time, President Eisenhower is reliably reported to have sent a personal letter at one point to Chiang Kai-shek, assuring him that, if necessary, the United States would help to defend Quemoy and Matsu. But he was not specific about how this would be done, and in the 1958 crisis the U.S. Navy did in fact convoy Nationalist ships supplying the islands.

If both Eisenhower and Dulles would in the last resort not have used American forces on Quemoy and Matsu, in spite of the blank check given to the President by the Formosa Resolution, their attitude was skillfully concealed from the Chinese. In this sense it was one of the outstanding examples of successful Dullesian brinkmanship. It was made more difficult by the fact that the full truth about their attitude also had to be concealed from their allies, and throughout this period, particularly in January, February, and March of 1955, Dulles's apparent intransigence over the offshore islands was being intensely criticized from many different sides. He was in fact in an extremely tight corner, and to the unbiased observer he never showed more diplomatic skill or a finer sense of judgment than in his performance over the offshore islands. What partly enabled him to ride so relatively unscathed through the barrage of criticism from his allies was his knowledge that, if it did come to sending military help to defend Formosa, either including or not including Quemoy and Matsu, the United States would be on its own. The fact that he could expect no help from his allies in Western Europe gave him a feeling of confidence and authority which sprang from his sense of independence in the matter.

At times the tension over the Formosa crisis was as great as during the Korean war and the debacle in Indo-China. This naturally provoked a number of suggestions for dealing with the problem, both from those who thought Dulles was going too far and those who thought he was not going far enough. Among the former a movement developed in Western Europe, and to some extent among the critics in the Democratic party, which held that the only way to secure peace was to let the Chinese Communists have the offshore islands in return for their formal acceptance of the status quo on Formosa itself; unfortunately there was never the faintest possibility that Peking would agree to this. On the opposite side, Dulles was under heavy fire from his longstanding critics in the Republican Party, with the China lobby as ever in the lead, who claimed that the only possible way of preventing war was for the United States to make it categorically clear that it would indeed defend Quemoy and Matsu with its own troops. Dulles had to steer his way between these two sets of critics, as well as handling the realities of the situation in the face of very heavy pressure from Peking. And although a somewhat ineffective attempt was made at one point to land Communist troops on Quemoy, the fact that the crisis eventually blew over was in no small measure due to his courage and ability.

During January, 1955, a special visit to China by Dag Hammarskjold, the United Nations Secretary General, raised American hopes that the several U.S. airmen who had been imprisoned on charges of espionage by the Chinese ever since their plane had been shot down in Northern Chinese territorial waters might after all be released. When it was clear that they were not going to be, Senator Knowland and others declared with renewed vigor that any sort of dealing with the Chinese Communist regime was impossible. Dulles, however, had throughout regarded the incident as a Chinese trick to weaken the American will. He felt confirmed in this view when, shortly afterwards, his own kite-flying about a possible cease-fire between the Nationalists and Communists was answered by the Communist seizure of the small island of Yi Kiangshan, one of the Tachen group some two hundred miles north of Formosa.

Strategically the loss of the island was of no consequence whatever; the Tachen islands do not even lie between Formosa and the critical offshore islands of Quemoy and Matsu. But the attack did show that, even if the apparent determination of the United States to defend the offshore islands was too convincing to risk challenging, such an obviously outlying area as the Tachens was a legitimate place to probe. In terms of American public opinion, however, the loss of Yi Kiang-shan, following quickly on the disappointment about the American airmen, strengthened Dulles's hand. In the middle of the following month, by which time the Chinese Communist bombardment of Quemoy and Matsu had been pushed up to a new peak, Dulles made a foreign policy broadcast which throws light on his own thinking. Speaking on February 16, 1955, he said:

> It has been suggested that Nationalist China should surrender to the Chinese Communists the coastal positions which the Communists need to stage their announced attack on Formosa. It is doubtful whether this would serve either the cause of peace or the cause of freedom.... If the Chinese Nationalists now oblige by making it easier for the Chinese Communists to conquer Formosa, will they be less apt to do so? I doubt it.

He reminded his audience of the specific American commitment to protect Formosa and the Pescadores, but added that there was "no commitment and no purpose to defend the coastal position *as such*." At the same, he said, it should not be assumed that peace and security would be promoted by indefinitely granting one-sided concessions to the Communist nations. "If the non-Communist nations ever come to feel that the Western allies are disposed to retreat whenever Communism threatens the peace, then the entire area could quickly become indefensible."

On February 8, 1955, Malenkov was deposed as Prime Minister of the Soviet Union and replaced by Marshal Bulganin. Khrushchev was already beginning to be the man with the real power, as Secretary of the Soviet Communist Party, but as yet the world was only just entering upon the period in which Bulganin was made the front man. The dismissal of Malenkov was not accompanied by any change at the Foreign Ministry; Molotov still remained. The only immediate result of any consequence was a Moscow radio broadcast on February 12, announcing that the Soviet Union proposed an international conference about Formosa; it would be convened by Russia, Britain, and India, and those invited should include the People's Republic of China, the United States, France, Burma, Indonesia, and Ceylon. Although the proposal never got anywhere, its announcement suggested that, although the Russians were of course backing Peking's claims, Moscow was not inclined to give the Chinese so much active encouragement that the military situation got out of hand and the risk of war with the United States increased.

At the end of the month, on February 27, Dulles flew to Laos, and then from there across to Formosa on March 3, and on down to Bangkok for the first meeting of the SEATO Council on March 6, 1955. The main interest of this visit to Formosa was that he counseled moderation. When taken with the relative caution of the new leadership in Moscow, a common American-Russian interest emerged in restraining both sides in the Chinese conflict from pushing matters too far. Dulles himself had suggested during February that there could be a basis for "practical agreement" with the new Russia, and that instead of attempting to separate China from Russia, the West might look at the problem from the opposite point of view and try to separate Russia from China.

This was a welcome change for the British. It was quite new that anyone in a responsible position in Washington should either hold or put such an idea forward. One of the thoughts behind the original British recognition of Communist China had been that the long-term interests of the West could be served only by trying to separate the Chinese and Russians. By contrast, everything that the Americans had done since the Chinese Communists came to power had tended to drive the two together. On looking back from the nineteen-sixties, Dulles's pronouncement was also interesting in putting forward, for the first time, the now common idea that the divergence of interest between the Russians and Chinese must sooner or later tend to bring the Russians closer to the West.

There were two features of the first meeting of the SEATO Council in Bangkok. One was another head-on disagreement between Dulles and Eden, and the other was Dulles's emphasis on the unity of the Far Eastern problem. The British viewpoint still started from the premise that the first priority in the Formosa Straits must be to get some form of de facto recognition by the Chinese Communists of the Nationalist position. Eden fully realized that this was probably unobtainable, since the Chinese Communists took the view that the whole struggle was a continuation of the Chinese civil war, that it was therefore an internal matter for China alone, and that any interference from outside was intolerable. But since almost any progress in the direction of Communist acceptance of the status quo would be a very distinct success, this only made it a more important objective for the Western powers, not less. Accordingly the British considered that the cession of the embarrassing liability of the offshore islands in exchange for a clear shift in Peking's position on the issue of accepting or recognizing the Formosa regime would be well worth doing. Dulles, however, was adamantly opposed; and, of course, the Republican right-wing leaped in with accusations of British bad faith, hints about Munich, and a general condemnation of Eden. When this happened, Dulles was disinclined to resist it, and so no agreed Anglo-American line could be adopted. He was certainly not going to stand up for Eden on a matter so unpopular and so full of political dynamite.

The other feature of the SEATO Conference was Dulles's estimate that, if the Chinese Communists did embark on open aggression over Formosa, it would probably mean that they had decided on accepting the risk of general war in Asia. The United States, he said, would then have to take into account its treaties with both Korea and with the Chinese Nationalists. "Thus general war would confront the Chinese Communists with tasks at the south, center and north—tasks which would strain their inadequate means of transportation." Dulles carried his thesis further in a broadcast immediately after his return to the United States on March 8, in which he talked about the character of SEATO. He said that he had come back impressed by the spirit both of the governments and of the peoples with whom he had had contact during his Far Eastern tour. And he added: "Almost unlimited Chinese manpower would easily dominate the entire area, were it not for the structure of SEATO, an essential part of which is the deterrent power of the United States and its willingness to use it in reply to a military challenge." He added that the only way to meet this challenge was for American strength and determination to be seen behind each of the separate agreements into which Washington had lately entered. Although his idea of creating organic links between each of these treaty commitments never came to anything, it did help to create a public opinion which looked at the problem of the Far East as a whole.

During this anxious period in the late winter and early spring of 1955, when the Formosa situation reached something of a turning point, British and American official views were by no means as far apart on the day-to-day handling of the problem as public comment in the two countries suggested. The only serious practical point which divided London and Washington was whether American forces should or should not be used to defend the offshore islands. This divergence was fortunately never put to the test, and apart from it the British view on SEATO accorded fairly well with what the Americans wanted.

In general, Eden felt as Dulles did that the ability of SEATO to deter Chinese Communist aggression could not depend on the actual stationing of Western armed forces on the mainland of Asia. Such forces could at best be only very small, and there would be heavy political disadvantages in placing them there at all. It had indeed been part of Dulles's general thesis for several months that, on the ground at least, Asia must be defended by Asians. And Sir Anthony Eden—as he now was—concurred in the sense that he saw that the key to preventing serious military expansion by Peking lay in the long-range deterrent, namely the air and nuclear striking forces available to the SEATO powers from outside the mainland of Southeast Asia. This combined Eden-Dulles attitude cut the ground from under the feet of both the Australian and New Zealand supporters of the idea that Western armed forces should be built up on the mainland.

Eden and Dulles both had serious problems in terms of their domestic public opinions. Dulles was well aware that a good many Americans were far too ready to get into a shooting war in the Far East. Eden understood that the British public was not yet ready to be tough enough in a war of nerves with the Chinese. All through this period there was, of course, the basic difference between the British and American views about the Chinese Nationalist regime. Although Eden felt that there could be no ultimate solution of the Formosa problem without American recognition of the Peking government, he always recognized that this was politically impossible for Dulles to undertake, even if the Secretary of State personally wished to do so—which he did not. It was in these circumstances that there came to be a certain amount of discussion of the idea that Formosa should form a separate state, possibly under United Nations trusteeship. In practice, however, this proposal never got very far, mainly because the physical existence of the Chinese Nationalists depended on American support, and Dulles never let up on his insistence that the Nationalist regime was indeed the rightful government of all China.

The stalemate over Formosa, which had already drifted into a slackening of tension during March, was confirmed by a remarkable, indeed historic, development during April, 1955. In spite of the considerable buildup of Chinese Communist air strength on the mainland opposite Formosa, the attack expected on the off-shore islands in the middle of the month never materialized. And it was either because of this or as a result of it—cause and effect are sometimes difficult to distinguish from one another—that the Afro-Asian Conference at Bandung in Indonesia from April 18 to 24 brought a considerable change to the whole political climate in the Western Pacific. The Chinese Communists went down there, in the person of the quietly forceful personality of Chou En-lai, and suddenly put themselves at the head of the pan-Asian and African yearning for peace. It was a shrewd attempt to leave the Americans high and dry as warmongers. Chou En-lai, while making it quite clear that Peking abandoned nothing of what he called her "sacred right to liberate the territory of Taiwan" (Formosa), declared that China was not going to war to achieve its ends, at least not for the time being. And the way that he said it, together with the whole buildup of the Bandung Conference to which Communist China had committed itself very deeply, confirmed that this was indeed the end of the immediate crisis.

Bandung was a historic event for the ex-colonial powers, and Chou En-lai played his cards there with superb skill. He behaved very humbly and put the six hundred million people of China on exactly the same level, say, as Ceylon or Laos. Although he was disappointed that the conference would not do more to condemn American imperialism, he realized, as the discussions progressed, how immensely strong the forces of neutralism were among the countries which had formed parts of colonial empires, and he played along with them. He saw how easy it would be for the Communists to persuade many of those Asians, who were being urged by the Americans and British to defend themselves under SEATO, that they were merely being turned into cannon-fodder for the West.

Over 60 per cent of the human race was represented at Bandung, and the dominant figures with Chou En-lai were Nehru, Nasser, and Sukarno. It was not a negative anticolonialist meeting; several delegates praised Britain for the help and training they had received in colonial days. But it was a dedicated occasion, sometimes highly charged with emotion, yet with a sense of spiritual unity transcending race or religion. In laying the foundations of Asian and African equality with Europeans there was curiously little bitterness. Bandung has been compared with Magna Carta and the Gettysburg address, and it had the same timeless quality of certainty about it. For the Chinese Communists it was a master stroke to put themselves at the center of such a gathering.

The end of the 1955 Formosa crisis did in fact mark the beginning of a period of three years in which the tension never became as acute again. This development was certainly partly due to Dulles. Although he has been violently assailed from several different sides for his handling of the six months' crisis, events have justified him. Given the political circumstances prevailing not only in Washington but also in London, Moscow, Peking and indeed Taipei, the outcome was as reasonably satisfactory as anyone could have hoped for. Without Dulles's determination and firmness of purpose, however varied the statements by which he chose to express it, Peking would not have accepted a pause. Moreover, Dulles had also succeeded in taming some of the wild men in Chiang Kai-shek's Nationalist regime as well, indeed so much so that, although their position had been saved, many of them became seriously worried and renewed their empty threats about going it alone against the Chinese mainland. At the same time, the toning down of the Communist attitude in Peking was also undoubtedly due in part to the influence of both Moscow and Delhi. Thus, the original forward movement of the Chinese Communist regime, following its advent to power in Peking in 1950, finally ground to a halt in the realistic atmosphere of April, 1955.

CHAPTER 11

The First Summit

WHILE all these great events had been taking place in the context of Asia, the scene had begun to change subtly elsewhere. From April to July of 1955 the approach march to the Summit dominated international politics. The first meeting between the four heads of government, that is of the United States, Britain, France, and the Soviet Union, would almost certainly not have taken place in the circumstances that it did, or at the time that it did, if Sir Anthony Eden had not made himself the driving force behind the idea. To this extent it was Eden's conference, and Dulles has been variously described as going to it grudgingly, or being dragged to it kicking. The one thing that is indisputable is that he was not keen on it.

Dulles and Eden stood in a slightly different relationship to one another after April 6, 1955. On that day Sir Winston Churchill retired for the last time, well over eighty, widely regarded as the greatest Englishman of the century; and Sir Anthony Eden took his place at Number 10 Downing Street as Prime Minister. The new British Foreign Secretary with whom Dulles now had to deal directly was Harold Macmillan, who remained at the Foreign Office for rather under a year, that is until December 22, when he became Chancellor of the Exchequer and was succeeded by Selwyn Lloyd. Until perhaps the last few months of his life, when Dulles began to get on rather well with Selwyn Lloyd, Harold Macmillan was the British Foreign Secretary with whom he felt most readily at home. On the other hand, the tone of the year 1955 was set by the climb up to the Summit and then the climb down again, and during the whole process Dulles could neither rid himself of the feeling that he was engaged in something which he did not basically approve of, nor forget that the main pressure on him came from the Eden government in London.

The British could not, of course, have got everyone to the Summit on their own. In many parts of Western Europe and to some extent in the United States as well, public opinion was genuinely clamoring for a top-level meeting with the Russians in the somewhat naive belief that, if only the people at the top could get together across a table, everything could be straightened out. Dulles at least knew that this was moonshine, and the Western public has indeed become more sophisticated since those days by moving a long way towards his point of view. But he and Eisenhower felt obliged to fall in with the popular clamor, largely because they wanted to help the Conservatives defeat the Socialists at the British general election of May, 1955. It was, in fact, one of President Eisenhower's most indignant complaints the following year over Suez that, whereas he had gone to the Summit for Eden in 1955, in 1956 Eden seemed unwilling to make any allowances for the difficulties of his Administration during the presidential campaign.

Meanwhile, the situation in Russia too was of interest. While Marshal Bulganin was still technically the head of the government, with the Ministry of Defense in the hands of Marshal Zhukov, the role, importance, and characteristics of Nikita Khrushchev were beginning to occupy the attention not only of the world, but also of Russians. He did not yet seem able to act without paying considerable attention to the views of his colleagues, but already he was the obvious power behind the throne. He appeared to be the instigator, for instance, of two unexpected twists that were given to Russian policy that summer. One was the invitation to Adenauer to visit Moscow in the autumn, which was issued in June soon after the formal—and final—admission of the Federal German Republic into NATO in May. So far from turning the heat on Germany, as so much of Soviet propaganda had threatened to do once Bonn had been received into NATO, Khrushchev deftly tried to play the game the other way and to get on terms of his own with the German Chancellor; as things turned out, Adenauer's visit to

Moscow on September 8 did nothing to soften his attitude towards the Soviet Union.

The other twist was the pilgrimage to the little Balkan Canossa of Belgrade, when Bulganin and Khrushchev visited Marshal Tito in Yugoslavia from May 26 to June 3. On this very remarkable occasion Khrushchev metaphorically went down on his knees to Tito and begged him to forget that the break with Stalin in 1948 had ever happened. Dulles, watching these and other Soviet antics from his desk in the State Department, or, perhaps more frequently than ever that year, from the seat of his airplane, found in them confirmation of his view that, once one had really understood the Communist purpose, nothing Moscow ever did was surprising.

In the United States, running parallel with the national debate about the Summit was yet another round in the discussions about the whole philosophy of the nuclear deterrent. Ever since the revision of American defense policy in August of 1953, following the Korean armistice, more and more dependence had been placed on the nuclear deterrent. This, indeed, was the age of those who thought mainly in terms of the deterrent. It was the age in which Dulles was by no means exceptional in his confident references to massive retaliation. It was the age when the expansion of the Strategic Air Command at the expense of America's conventional forces was accepted as an article of faith. Theories were developed about the concept of the "immaculate war," in which, for instance, the otherwise sensible idea of Asians being equipped and trained to fight Asians was sometimes taken far beyond the bounds of common sense. It was even claimed that, if Asians or other allies became involved in war, they could provide virtually all the ground forces, while the United States concentrated on air and naval support.

The chief architects of this dangerous policy were Admiral Radford and the defense chiefs, though many people regarded Dulles himself as coming fairly close to it. In his March broadcast he had said that: "For military defense we shall rely largely on mobile allied power. . . . We shall not need to build up large static forces at all points, and the United States's contribution will be primarily in terms of sea and air power." Politically, however, this was dynamite in Asia, if not also in Western Europe. It spread the impression not only that the Americans would leave others to do the dirty work, but also that Washington was becoming notoriously callous about the destruction which might take place in allied territories, while leaving the home base of the far-flung American air and naval forces unscathed. Increasingly, therefore, this policy also came to be criticized inside the United States too; one incidental factor which helped the process was the publication by the U.S. Atomic Energy Commission of detailed and alarming statistics about radioactive fall-out.

As a result of this nation-wide debate, as well as the gradual easing of tension over Formosa, Dulles himself began for the first time to fine down the roughest edges of his original massive retaliation policy. He was heard to say in public that the punishment would do no more than fit the crime. Naturally this was common sense, and in a way it was what he had always meant. But a long time was to go by before informed public opinion in the United States, quite apart from that in Britain or anywhere else, was to understand how complex is the problem of maintaining a proper balance between nuclear and conventional forces. Only the rise of Soviet nuclear power was to make everyone think the problem through to anything like coherent conclusions. And by the time that happened, Dulles was dead.

A lesser factor, though of some significance, which helped to prepare American public opinion for the Summit Conference of 1955, was the publication in March of the official papers dealing with the Yalta Conference at the end of the war. For years it had been said that at Yalta the leadership of the ailing President Roosevelt had led the Americans into giving away so much that the postwar settlement in Europe had been jeopardized. Dulles did not hold strong views either way about the publication of these documents, nor of course did he particularly want either to clear the name of Roosevelt, or to pave the way to the Summit about which he personally felt only a very tepid enthusiasm. But the basic decision was up to him as Secretary of State, and the manner in which he took it happened to provide a revealing illustration of his own character.

When the question of publication arose, *The New York Times* approached Dulles in a bid to obtain exclusive rights to initial publication in a newspaper, pointing out that it was virtually the only paper which could or would find space for the publication of the Yalta papers in full. After some hesitation, Dulles agreed to let *The New York Times* have the papers first, thus conceding to it a world scoop of a very unusual character. Naturally this caused a storm in journalistic circles, even though the publication rights were freely available to everyone else after *The New York Times* had appeared, and even though *The New York Times* was obliged to publish many columns of not very exciting material as well as the more interesting highlights. When Dulles was tackled vehemently about his action at a press conference, and accused of the kind of favoritism which the press in every country deplores, as statesmen well know, he replied: "I did not give the papers to *The New York Times.*" The innuendo was either that *The New York Times* had obtained the papers without his official sanction or that there had been nothing exclusive about their rights. What was worse was that, in the light of all the apparent facts, the Secretary of State appeared to be telling a deliberate lie. To Dulles himself, however, it was no lie. He salved his conscience with the knowledge that in its most literal sense he had not technically given the papers to *The New York Times.* He had told a member of his staff to hand them over. But it was this kind of legalistic pedantry which struck at the heart of Dulles's moral stature in the world, and in a small way the whole incident reflected an extraordinary narrowmindedness and insensitivity on the part of a man who otherwise possessed qualities which would have been acclaimed everywhere as greatness.

The publication of the Yalta papers actually fell rather flat— although by including a number of historically interesting photographs in their edition of March 17, 1955, *The New York Times* made a much more attractive job of it than the eventual massive tome put out by the State Department. Publication particularly disappointed those who had wanted to use the so-called "shameful secrets" of the period, in order to underline their warnings against any further "settlement" with the Russians; and in the end it was generally conceded that the Eisenhower Administration was by now sufficiently experienced to be trusted to keep its head.

During April and May, therefore, limited sections of the American public gradually came to be mildly favorable towards the idea

of top-level talks with the Soviet leaders. This was in special contrast to the British who have always been the most persistent
sponsors of this kind of contact, the first serious proposal for talks
at the Summit having been made by Sir Winston Churchill during
the British general election of 1950, when Ernest Bevin condemned
his suggestion as a dishonest stunt. Churchill then repeated it as
Prime Minister in his speech of May 11, 1953, and by the spring of
1955 this surge of emotion had gained a great deal of momentum,
both in Britain and all over Western Europe. Dulles himself never
thought that anything much could come of negotiations of this
kind with the Russians, and since the discouraging failure of the
Berlin Foreign Ministers' Conference of January, 1954, had confirmed him in these views, it was only for the sake of his allies that
he went forward at all.

At the Berlin Conference Dulles had always regarded Molotov
as merely an agent at the end of a telephone line and not in any
sense a genuine negotiator. Hence he did regard the Summit as a
somewhat different proposition, since the actual holder of power
in Russia would be facing the West across a conference table. As
he suspected, however, the chances of serious negotiation were even
more limited than they might otherwise have been, in that the
struggle for supremacy inside Russia was not yet over. Throughout
this period Dulles's personal attitude gave rise to a good many
cartoons as well as to some tart comments from columnists. As
events were to prove, he was abundantly right, though his doubts
about the way in which President Eisenhower would himself handle
the negotiations were unjustified—at least they were unjustified in
the sense that, since no real negotiation proved possible, it hardly
mattered so much whether Khrushchev and Bulganin were able
to confute the President or not. The 1955 Summit was merely a
failure. One wonders what Dulles's comments might have been
if he had lived to see the fiasco of the 1960 Summit.

In the Western notes of May 10 the governments of America,
Britain, and France in effect proposed a series of three meetings.
There would first be a meeting of foreign ministers, at which the
issues could be formulated and the methods to be used in exploring
them could be agreed. As a second stage the heads of government
would come together. At a third, the foreign ministers would meet

again to discuss in detail whatever the heads of government might have agreed. In Washington at that time it was generally thought that the heads of government would not meet at the Summit for more than perhaps three days, and that their meetings would be fairly formal. The assumption was that such talks would be no more than the beginning of a series of further meetings, either at the top level or between foreign ministers, which might gradually get to grips with the real problems.

By mid-June, however, American opinion was in general considerably more optimistic than the officials in Washington. And, in the week following June 13, Dulles evoked a good deal of popular support for his exchange of views about the forthcoming Geneva Conference with Macmillan, Pinay, and Adenauer in Washington. When the Western foreign ministers moved across to San Francisco a few days later for a special meeting of the UN General Assembly, in order to celebrate the first ten years of the United Nations, it came as less of a surprise than it might otherwise have done that Molotov should solemnly hand Dulles a note expressing the Soviet Government's regret for the attack on an American naval aircraft on June 22 and offering to pay half the damages. Dulles for his part let it be known that, while he accepted the Soviet regrets with satisfaction, the offer fell short of what he had requested.

Dulles's cautious gloom about the remoteness of any practical guarantees being given by the Soviet leaders that they had abandoned their basic Communist philosophy of world revolution, made him get a little out of step for once with the President. Eisenhower's natural buoyancy and optimism gradually came to epitomize the guarded hopes of the West in a way which Dulles characteristically, and yet wisely too, rejected. In the end both the President and the Secretary of State set off for Geneva with their minds having reached roughly the same point, namely that they would do their best, but would not expect too much. The President, for his part, spoke of his determination to "wage a war for peace," and he left with his reputation just about as high as it had ever stood.

His popularity had been heavily reaffirmed by an event which set the final seal on developments that had been taking place for over a year. This was the ultimate and abject defeat of Senator McCarthy, whose motion at the end of June proposing strict limitations on the President's freedom of action at the Summit talks was utterly defeated by 77 votes to 4. He had argued that Geneva was a trap designed to make the allies lose face, and that the liberation of the satellite countries of Eastern Europe must be placed at the top of the agenda. Neither Congress nor the country, however, were any longer prepared to accept Senator McCarthy rather than the elected Administration as their government, and this marked in effect the end of the McCarthy era. When Eisenhower and Dulles left for Geneva with their hands completely free, they were backed by the trust of the entire nation.

At the end of the previous month, on June 28, Dulles had made it clear that the three foreign ministers of the Western powers and Dr. Adenauer had reached full agreement on the points to be adopted over procedure. He said that specific questions would not be discussed or decisions of substance reached, beyond defining possible areas of agreement. He cast his own particular pebble of doubt into the pool by declaring that he felt the Russians were losing interest in German reunification, now that the Federal German Republic had at last been able to join the Western alliance; and he added that, if the Kremlin was not prepared to discuss reunification in the new circumstances, that fact would in itself throw serious doubt on the genuineness of the Soviet desire to reduce tension. Speaking about the general subject of European security, Dulles claimed that the West had worked out a system of multilateral arms control, which insured that there was enough for defense but not enough for attack. Then, alluding by implication to the ideas of liberation which had played their part in the Republican electoral campaign three years before, he said that it would be a great advance if this system of arms control could be applied to the countries of Eastern Europe.

Challenging Molotov's remarks at a press conference at the end of the San Francisco General Assembly, Dulles pointed out that adoption of the Soviet proposals would mean the liquidation of the North Atlantic Treaty and the substitution for it of a single system for the whole of Europe, a plan which was completely unacceptable to the three Western powers. "You cannot base a security system," Dulles said, "on a joining of forces with those whom you do not trust." On the other hand, he admitted that it might be possible to

work out some balance of forces in Europe, though not at Geneva.
And he rounded off his remarks by repeating that, if the Russians
proposed a five-power conference, that is to say including Communist China, the United States would adhere to its position of
entering no conference dealing with the substantive affairs of China
in the absence of Chinese Nationalist representatives.

Dulles was not in fact prepared to discuss the Far Eastern situation at all at the Summit, if he could possibly avoid doing so. This
was partly because he felt that the de facto cease-fire which had
developed in the Formosa Straits might be disturbed if formal
negotiations were suggested, and partly because of his determination not have any negotiations with the Chinese Communists on
any general topic or great power basis without Chinese Nationalist
representation. At this point there had in fact been consular contact between the Chinese Communists and the Americans for about
a year, and this contact had followed the painfully intimate, though
very strictly limited, negotiations between the American representative at Panmunjom, Arthur Dean—who later headed the
American delegation sent by President Kennedy to the nuclear
test ban negotiations in Geneva—and the Chinese Communists in
order to bring the Korean War to an end. Arthur Dean, incidentally,
was Dulles's successor as senior partner in Sullivan and Cromwell,
and Dulles was partly instrumental in bringing him into public
life. After the Geneva Summit meeting, American and Chinese
Communist representatives met at ambassador level, first in Geneva,
later in Warsaw and elsewhere, and continued their arid talks for
many, many weary months. They met ostensibly to negotiate the
release of the American airmen still held captive in China, but
other subjects were also tentatively mentioned in the course of the
endless and more or less fruitless meetings. Dulles's attitude was
that, while he would not accept recognition of Communist China
as such, he would always sanction hard talk in private with its
intermediaries, or lower-level representatives, if he felt that that
would be to the advantage of the United States.

Dulles, like other Western leaders, felt that of the two main
subjects to be discussed at Geneva, namely disarmament and the
reunion of Germany, disarmament should come first. Already, that
is, the framework for discussion which became familiar at the

second Summit conference in 1960 had begun to appear. The Berlin Conference of 1954 had convinced Dulles that it would be unprofitable to get into the involved question of Germany, without trying to clear the air somewhere else first. Compared with this general view in 1955, the difference between that year and the approach to the Summit of 1960 was that by 1960 it had become quite clear that, while there was still no prospect of getting anywhere on the German problem as such, the chances of making a little progress on disarmament were slightly better than they had been;this was because a more equal nuclear stalemate had developed by then, which gave both sides a direct interest in the subject. In 1955 Dulles was in a minority in being quite certain in his own mind that nothing could be done about Germany, while at the same time the disarmament question was genuinely less pressing for the West, since the United States still retained its nuclear superiority. In this respect, Sir Anthony Eden already held the view in 1955 that the power of the West had probably just about passed its peak, and subsequent events have proved him right.

In Dulles's mind as he arrived at Geneva there were admittedly two mildly encouraging factors about Soviet behavior during the previous few months. The main one was the surprising Soviet *volte-face* in early May which had led to the sudden signing of the long deferred Austrian peace treaty. Dulles himself had publicly embraced Molotov in Vienna on May 15, 1955, when together with Harold Macmillan and Antoine Pinay, they had both just signed the treaty recognizing Austria as a sovereign independent and democratic state. All four foreign ministers appeared outside together on a balcony of the Belvedere Palace amid scenes of moving jubilation. Although the treaty bound Austria to neutrality, it restored the frontiers of January 1, 1938, and promised free navigation of the Danube, the only other important restriction being that the Austrians also accepted a total prohibition of any repetition of the *Anschluss* with Germany.

At the time, many people wondered why the Russians had accepted this treaty after having blocked it for so long. The answer is still not beyond challenge, but they almost certainly argued that, now that Moscow had recognized Western Germany and it had joined NATO successfully, the best chance of breaking its links with the West was to hold out the bait of reunion with an Eastern Germany from which the Red Army had withdrawn. Thus the West Germans might be encouraged to hope for an "Austrian solution" for the whole of Germany. In reality, once Western Germany had been prized out of its alliance with the West, German so-called neutralization would become a virtual alliance with the East, since Germany as a whole is too big, too strategically placed, and too important to Soviet thinking for genuine neutrality to be possible—quite apart from the fact that the Germans themselves are not the stuff of which good neutrals are made.

The other move, which had marked a definite break with the recent past, had been the fresh Soviet approach to Marshal Tito in Yugoslavia. Dulles was somewhat encouraged by this development, since it suggested that the new Soviet leaders might just possibly go a fraction of the way towards honoring some of the pledges given at Yalta and Potsdam, thus allowing the other countries of Eastern Europe a little more political latitude. What neither Dulles nor anyone else could know at the time was that within little more than a year the political détente, both inside Russia itself and throughout the Communist bloc, was to lead the Hungarians to try to take matters into their own hands and to be brutally crushed for their efforts.

Taking Soviet policy as a whole at this period, Dulles was clear that, although fresh forces were undoubtedly at work in the ferment which still obviously existed in the post-Stalin Kremlin, the main Russian objective was to confuse and disrupt Western plans. Dulles did not allow any of his relative satisfaction over the Austrian peace treaty, for instance, nor a conciliatory demarche about disarmament made by Marshal Bulganin at the Communist conference in Warsaw on May 11, to conceal the fact that Soviet tactics were designed in part to cajole the West into making similar so-called concessions. In particular, Dulles was wary about the trap being laid for West German opinion on the subject of reunification as a result of the Austrian treaty. This made him more adamant than ever in rejecting any of the new ideas which the Russians, and indeed certain well-meaning people on the Western side as well were putting about in regard to some kind of a neutral belt in Germany and the possible withdrawal of forces by both sides.

These were the days when the small pilot scheme put forward by Eden at the Geneva Conference, for a neutral belt down the dividing line between the East and West in Germany, was still a fairly new idea. But it was soon to be overtaken by the much wider general debate about so-called "disengagement," and Dulles himself never for one moment accepted any of this thinking. He was always in total disagreement even with Eden's minimum plan, though he thought it best not to make anything of this disagreement in public. Basically, he remained rigid on this question for the same kind of reason that Adenauer did. He believed, first, that it was safer to stand right up to the Russians, so that there could be no uncertainty in their minds about what might happen if they moved forward; and, secondly, that any withdrawal of American forces might end by precipitating a chain reaction in American opinion, so that it ended with a major withdrawal across the Atlantic. Thirdly, perhaps it should be added, Dulles was always intensely aware of the need to sustain morale in Western Germany itself. Unlike many others who understood the Germans less well, he shared precisely the fears and reactions of Adenauer himself, in the sense that a serious reverse to the Bonn government's policy of integration with the West might swing German opinion in favor of those who argued for some kind of accommodation with the East.

The Russians themselves made no bones about their demands, commonly put forward in *Pravda* and elsewhere, that the Americans must return across the Atlantic and evacuate their overseas bases, while the Soviet forces would withdraw no further than East Prussia. The significance of East Prussia was partly that the eastern section of the country had been formally annexed by the Soviet Union, and hence to withdraw there would be to withdraw within the borders of Russia—and no one, after all, could expect more than that. Moscow was indeed demanding, as it constantly has since, the abolition of all military bases on foreign soil as a condition for further progress in the discussions on disarmament.

All through this period the Russians were also piling on demands for a Far Eastern settlement to which Communist China must be a party, thereby implying the abandonment of the American position in Formosa. They were demanding a number of measures in the field of propaganda, such as the ending of all Western broad-

casts to Eastern Europe. They kept up their insistence on the end
of controls on the export of strategic goods to Communist countries.
They repeated again and again the plan which Molotov had put
forward for a security pact to replace NATO in Europe; at the
end of the San Francisco meeting in June, indeed, Molotov had
declared once again that the reunification of Germany depended
on the establishment of the kind of European collective security
system proposed by the Soviet Union. The result of all these hard-
faced and well-worn Soviet themes was to make nonsense in Dulles's
mind of the claim from Moscow that times had really changed,
and that it was now up to the West to make "concessions" before
any further steps towards agreement could be taken. Dulles knew
perfectly well that this verbal barrage meant precisely the opposite.

The Geneva Summit Conference of 1955 took the form of a
struggle over the agenda, as so many conferences with the Russians
do. The agenda, as finally accepted, went in this order: reunification of Germany and European security, linked together; then
disarmament; and, finally, development of contacts between East
and West. The point was that, while both sides knew that Germany
was the central issue, the Russians were determined to make propaganda, if they could, out of their stand on disarmament. At the
same time they worked tenaciously for Western recognition of
Eastern Germany, and to prevent any progress whatever being
made on the Western proposals for German reunification by means
of free elections. The outcome was that no solutions were reached
on either European security or Germany. But the foreign ministers
were instructed to meet again at Geneva during October to go into
the matter further, "taking account of the close link between the
reunification of Germany and the problem of European security."

Dulles fought hard in his effort to thrash out the possibilities
for German reunification, though he was fully aware that it was
hopeless from the start. He was quite willing to take the risk of
appearing to block disarmament, even though public opinion in
Western Europe had fastened on this as one of the great hopes of
the conference, because he reckoned that, unless something could
be done about Germany, disarmament was not to be taken seriously
by either side. At the time this was also Adenauer's adamant view.
Later on, however, both Dulles and Adenauer shifted their ground

in this respect and came to recognize that, since no progress whatever was possible on Germany in the existing atmosphere of tension, it would after all be better to try to reduce that tension first,
by achieving some progress on disarmament, and then return to
the subject of Germany.

Dulles was not particularly keen on the only headline-catching
proposal that came out of the conference, namely the idea of "open
skies" aerial inspection, put forward personally by President Eisenhower. It was an idea which grew on Eisenhower, and he threw it
in partly in earnest and partly to test Russian intentions. Dulles
for his part felt that, while gimmicks of this kind were unlikely to
work, they did no harm so long as they did not raise any exaggerated
hopes. He himself believed that the real impasse lay in Europe
and depended on whether or not the West was prepared to accept
Soviet rule indefinitely over all the satellite territories, including
Eastern Germany. Wherever one started the argument, that is, one
came back to Germany, and since no progress could be made there,
no progress could be made at all. The public image of Dulles
associates him closely with this attitude and some people would
say it was typical of his rigidity. But nothing that happened at the
1955 Summit conference did anything to suggest that he was wrong.

There were five broad results from the talks. The most immediate
was expressed by Dulles himself when he conceded that the conference had, temporarily at least, caused the danger of war to
recede, by eliminating a certain bitterness in the relations between
the Soviet Union and the Western powers. After the conference,
he said, relations with Soviet Russia were now "less brittle." There
was in fact an indefinable something which came to be known as
the "Geneva atmosphere." While Dulles welcomed this if it was
likely to lead to anything else, he also felt it was a danger, in the
sense that Western public opinion might take it as a sign that something of substance had changed. In fact nothing was changed by
Geneva, and the so-called Geneva atmosphere gradually evaporated.

The second point to emerge was that, in spite of Dulles's stand,
the United States did manage to make its peaceful purposes relatively clear. After an era of talk about massive retaliation and
military pacts, Eisenhower personally did manage to put himself
across in his chosen role as the man of peace, and to change the

image of the United States in the eyes of the world. Indeed, he was so successful that the uconscionable Senator McCarthy, down but not out, asked in the Senate whether he did not detect "appeasement in the air."

Thirdly, the Western powers managed to bring it home to their public that the Russians were as rigid as ever. It was they who were made to appear to have no counteroffer to make to President Eisenhower's dramatic aerial inspection proposals, to Sir Anthony Eden's outline of a system of armaments inspection in Central Europe, or to M. Edgar Faure's concept of putting into the under-developed countries the money that might be saved from defense expenditure. The Russians stuck rigidly to their old demands for the withdrawal of American forces from Europe and the end of NATO, making it very plain that the only condition on which they would be willing to agree to German reunion would be the abandonment by the West of its defenses.

One result which Dulles had feared from the failure of the conference did not materialize. This was a reaction in West German public opinion and a swing away from support of Adenauer's whole policy of linking up with the West. This had undoubtedly been one of the gains which the Russians had most hoped to make at Geneva. Having prepared the ground by their swift change on the Austrian peace treaty, they continued to emphasize in their propaganda towards Germany that the best hope for reunification was to unite on the Soviet side. But fortunately the people of Western Germany have understood what this means, and, in spite of the undoubted sense of letdown which followed the Geneva failure of 1955, all shades of opinion, apart from the small Communist party in the Federal Republic, have remained true to the West. In so far as there was any wavering of the kind which Dulles and Adenauer feared, it was entirely removed by the terrible lessons of the Hungarian crisis in the following year, 1956.

Lastly, one of the rather unexpected and indeed unprecedented results of the Summit talks was that Bulganin and Khrushchev provisionally accepted an invitation from Eden to visit London the following spring. This was to be the first of their major sorties into the Western world, and, while Khrushchev's visit to the United States was still four years off, in its own way the projected visit to

London did a good deal to underline the slackening of tension. As President Eisenhower said on a television broadcast, however, the acid test would come in October, when the foreign ministers met to follow up in more detail the discussions which the heads of government had begun.

Between July and the foreign ministers' reunion in Geneva on October 27, one major change took place in Dulles's personal position. It was in September of that year, 1955, that President Eisenhower had his first heart attack. This left Dulles in more or less solitary charge of America's foreign policy, both in theory and in practice. His allegiance to Eisenhower never faltered, but it was one thing to have a President who might be an embarrassment at a Summit conference, because he would say and do things for which Dulles might not have prepared him; it was another to operate in Washington without the one essential source of political power at his elbow, on which Dulles utterly relied.

Moreover, it is also one thing to have to talk the fount of final authority into a particular course, even if you think you can count on doing so; it is quite another to take the decisions visibly alone. Fortunately for Dulles, the first few weeks after the President's heart attack were ones in which he himself was not under particular attack. Later, after the failure of the Geneva foreign ministers' meeting to make any more progress than the heads of government had made in the summer, the Secretary of State came in for one of the waves of criticism which so often broke upon him. But by then the President had recovered sufficiently to be able to reaffirm his faith in Dulles, and to declare that the words and deeds of his Secretary of State had his entire confidence.

The meeting of the foreign ministers in Geneva from October 27 to November 16 took place with far more asperity than the Summit talks in the summer. As Dulles had expected, this meeting finally put an end to any question of a new deal between East and West. Unfortunately, however, there had been a kind of Indian Summer between July and October, in which the more optimistic type of public opinion had hoped that something might after all come out of the so-called "spirit of Geneva." It was therefore natural that the second disappointment was rather worse than the first.

For Dulles personally, the strength of his underlying position had nevertheless improved over the period. Although he had no President to support him, he was backed by a much more bipartisan approach to foreign policy in Washington than had existed for some time. This was partly because in spite of his tough talk, he had shown that he was fully able to sit down and try to hammer out some kind of an agreement with the Russians. Moreover, American public opinion had throughout remained much more skeptical of the so-called Geneva spirit than that in other Western countries. Many Americans, indeed, who had been in Europe during the summer were surprised and worried by the extent of the fears that the United States might come to some arrangement with the Soviet Union over the heads of its Western allies and at their expense. And in so far as Dulles had no intention whatever of letting down the kind of West European spirit of resistance that he recognized so strongly in Adenauer, he gained in stature by refusing either to be carried away by the Geneva spirit or to be bounced into snatching at a bilateral agreement just for the sake of some illusory temporary success.

The clash at the autumn session of the foreign ministers took place on exactly the same lines as the Summit in the summer. The Russians made it even more apparent than before that their aim was to get the Americans out of Europe, to smash the Atlantic alliance, and to make no concessions whatever over Germany, unless they could reshape the entire country in their own pattern. They continued to demand the "liquidation of all foreign bases," by which they transparently meant the withdrawal of both American and British forces from the continent of Europe; the exchange of the North Atlantic Treaty, with its firm guarantees between allies, for a "European security system" which would depend on nothing more than the Communist word; á system of disarmament which could not be checked or controlled; and an inviolable status for the East German regime, whatever might happen immediately or even in the long run over the question of the reunification of Germany. Dulles came in for some of the strongest and most formidable criticism of his career after the breakdown of these final talks with the Russians. But he was never in better form or more confident of his ground, and the passage of time had only

served to show that there was no genuine alternative to the course
of action which he took.

For the West to have accepted the terms offered by the Russians
would have been to destroy every vestige of security which had
been so painfully built up over the previous decade. As Dulles
always insisted, no Western government could possibly treat the
abandonment of the Atlantic alliance as being on a par with the
cancellation of the Warsaw Treaty between Russia and its satellites.
Once NATO had gone, there would be no firm guarantee left
among the former allies, and their weaker brethren would almost
certainly have seen no alternative to seeking terms with the East.
Compared with this, the dismantling of the Warsaw Treaty would
not in reality modify one jot or tittle of the Soviet hold over the
East European satellites.

The West's dilemma was so simple and fundamental, in fact,
that its statesmen had little opportunity to deviate. It was either a
matter of accepting German reunion at the expense of the security
of the whole of Western Europe, or of maintaining that security
at the risk of deferring German unity indefinitely. In trying to
make the Russians understand that they were sincerely willing to
take risks in order to achieve agreement of some sort, Dulles,
Macmillan, and Pinay surprised Molotov by pulling out of their
pockets again the Eden plan for Germany, which had originally
seen the light of day in January, 1954. They now added that, if
Germany were united, it really would have in their eyes a genuine
freedom of choice whether to join NATO or not. Dulles's argument in taking this risk was that, since by definition a freely elected
united German government could not in any case be compelled to
do anything by the West, it was better to insist on the reality of
this fundamental freedom rather than to try to pretend that it did
not exist. For while the freedom of choice would be genuine, no
one seriously doubted that, if it were, in the circumstances of the
time Germany would join the West. Knowing this too, Molotov
of course recognized that it was a risk he could not possibly take.

When all was over and the cold draft of disappointment had
spread across the world, there was naturally an inquest on the
Western side. Dulles himself was accused of many things, including, oddly enough, overoptimism. This was partly due to a pre-

arranged plan whereby his two colleagues, Macmillan and Pinay, did most of the talking in the early stages of the conference, while Dulles, by agreement and contrary to his traditional position, did what he could to lay stress on the possible points of agreement. But, of course, for his time-honored critics like Walter Lippmann and George Kennan, Dulles's known toughness was the outstanding point of attack. He was accused of adopting "rigid sterile positions without alternatives and without latitude for maneuver." Those who spoke in this way, however, have never made it clear just what alternatives they themselves had in mind. Walter Lippmann, to do him justice, had constantly spoken of the neutralization of Germany; on this particular point his theories have nevertheless met with an exceptionally cool response over a long period, and he has never been able to explain satisfactorily how a country as big and dynamic as a reunited Germany could possibly remain neutral for long.

The ultimate result, therefore, of the foreign ministers' meeting was to demonstrate beyond any shadow of doubt that the Russians were in fact totally opposed to German reunification by free elections, and that their only picture of moving forward was to begin by rendering Western Europe defenseless. This turned out to be not only a clarification of the position, but also a help for Western propaganda. All the Western leaders returned home able to convince their publics that the failure at Geneva was due to the harsh realities of the Soviet character and ambitions. In Dulles's own final speech before leaving Geneva, he had reiterated how much he hoped that the Soviet Union would sooner or later come to realize the advantages to be gained by better relations with the West. He said that the Soviet attitude at the conference had already done a good deal to impair the development of confidence, and he castigated Molotov for undoing even the small amount of good which had been achieved by the Summit conference four months earlier.

He then also referred to the position in Eastern Europe, a matter which had loomed so large in his own election speeches three years before. Moscow, he said, had shown that it would not allow the East German regime to be subjected to the test of free elections, and, while this was a refusal which indicated Russia's determination not to allow German self-determination in any form, it also had a significance far beyond the boundaries of Germany. "It highlights, as no words could, the situation throughout Eastern Europe." Dulles said that he realized that conditions in Eastern Europe might be such that the Russians were afraid of the contagious effect of free elections in any part of the Communist world, but it was unfortunate that this had not been foreseen by the Soviet government before Bulganin and Khrushchev had subscribed in principle to the possible idea of German reunification at all.

So ended the aftermath of the first and only Summit which ever took place in the nineteen-fifties. If Dulles can be honestly blamed in any way, it was more for permitting himself to express an optimism which he did not feel than for adopting a perverse posture which events did not justify. With the added experience gained from the fiasco of 1960 many people have now come to see, who did not see before, that Summitry is a very special form of exercise, which holds out only the slenderest possible chances of success, unless all the conditions are right on both sides. At no time since the end of the war have the conditions been anything like right, and Dulles's own view that only small gains can be expected, and then only after arduous and careful preparation, has come to be more and more generally held. It really is no use the wishful thinkers asserting otherwise. The crisis of our age, in which men have literally achieved the power to destroy the human race without first mastering a technique for controlling themselves, is too serious, urgent, and final to be met merely by the symptoms of weakness and fear, by deluded optimism or malevolent appeasement. Anyone who puts his own head in the sand deserves to forfeit not only the respect of others who face the facts, but his right to criticize those who, understanding the truth, attempt to grapple with it.

To the specific charge that Dulles was too rigid in the hour of America's strength, the answer is that, on the one hand, he was a good deal less rigid than the Russians, and, on the other, that it takes two to strike any bargain. The critical meeting of 1955 might admittedly have been handled differently by different people. No two men will necessarily adopt exactly the same tactics in every situation. But that the substance of the Western position should have been anything materially different from what it was has never been proved, and the passage of time seems only to have made this proof harder and harder to find. The strength of Dulles's record is that it shows him to have been more nearly right in his views of Soviet motives and behavior than any of his critics. And the farther we get from the events in which he took part, the more this judgment is likely to be reinforced.

CHAPTER 12

The Road to Suez

DURING their private conversations at Geneva in October, 1955, the foreign ministers of the Big Four spent a surprising proportion of their time discussing the Middle East. They had not expected or meant to. But events there were now moving so fast that a totally new type of crisis seemed to be on the horizon. For the first time since the cold war began Moscow was taking a hand. The result was that the latest round of renewed tension between the Arabs and Israel had started to look more dangerous than anything since the end of the Arab-Israeli war, following the partition of Palestine in 1948.

Soviet lack of interest in the Middle East in previous years had always been puzzling, and there had appeared to be two general reasons for it, neither of them wholly convincing. One was that, since the potentially explosive Middle East situation lay so close to Russia's southern frontiers, Stalin and his immediate successors were always unwilling to stir up trouble there for its own sake, the reverse, that is to say, of their basic policy in virtually every other part of the world. The other reason was a corollary of this, namely that an active Soviet policy in this region, as Stalin once pointed out to Ernest Bevin, would "attract American intervention"; he therefore preferred that the United States should be discouraged from taking an active hand by the absence of apparent Soviet interest. In the critical early debates of the United Nations in 1947 and 1948 before the partitioning of Palestine, the world had therefore witnessed the unusual scene of the Soviet Union and the United States voting consistently on the same side, in favor of the establishment of the new state of Israel. By 1955, however, the memory of Moscow's role in supporting Israel was carefully veiled, and the essence of Soviet intervention, both in 1955 and 1956, was to back the more extreme of the Arab nationalist claims.

It was partly Dulles who had prompted this new Soviet attitude, though from his own point of view he did his best to extricate himself from a tricky situation once he saw where it was leading. Ever since his original trip to Egypt in May, 1953, he had hoped in some way to extend the NATO system of military alliances to the Middle East. Later, after SEATO had eventually been created in 1954, the defense gap in the Arab world looked all the more noticeable. Accordingly, the moment came when Cairo was sounded out from Washington on the possibility of starting a proposed Middle East Defense Organization, allied to the West. On Egypt's blunt refusal, Dulles turned his thoughts to the idea of a defense arrangement limited to the so-called "Northern Tier," and he strongly encouraged the first move in what later become known as the Baghdad Pact; this was a defense treaty between Turkey and Iraq, signed early in 1955. Unfortunately, while he himself had not thought the problem right through, and therefore held back from any formal association of the United States with the new treaty, this striking development provoked concern and anger in Moscow and Cairo respectively—for the Russians because they knew that Dulles had had a hand in it, and for Cairo because this unprecedented alliance of an Arab state, Iraq with the nearest member of NATO, Turkey, looked like being the thin end of a NATO wedge in the tree of Arab unity.

Meanwhile, Dulles encouraged the British to join the new team, which they did with the definite, but as it turned out misplaced, expectation that the United States would shortly join too. By now, however, Dulles had got cold feet and he deliberately backed out, leaving the embryonic defense pact without that degree of American support which it certainly required if it was to have any effective meaning. His line of thinking was that the plan for Persia to join the Baghdad Pact was too dangerous, given the long background of Russian concern about that country, and that the whole of American and British thinking about Middle East problems was becoming too military in any case. It was this second consideration which inclined him to go into reverse and to attempt to play along with Arab nationalism, thus leaving the Baghdad Pact high and dry. Instead of consolidating the West's position in the Middle East, this uncertainty and divided counsel weakened it considerably, particularly after Colonel Nasser in Egypt had reacted with particular suspicion and resentment when he saw that Iraq, not content with undermining Arab unity, of which the Egyptians felt they were the leaders, was specifically trying to take the lead from Cairo.

Nasser resolved to reassert the leadership he claimed by the only means open to him, namely by whipping up a new burst of Arab frenzy against Israel. After stepping up Egyptian raids across the Israeli frontiers, he tried to buy more arms in the summer of 1955, going first to each of the major Western powers, since they were the only suppliers with whom anyone in Egypt had dealt before. The British refused politely but categorically, saying that they could not break their undertaking not to supply extra arms either to the Arabs or to Israel. The French would agree to supply weapons only in return for an acceptable modification of Egyptian policy towards North Africa. And the Americans, under Dulles's guidance, indicated that, if he wanted to buy arms, it would be desirable that he should after all join in some kind of collective security arrangement covering the Middle East as a whole.

Taking all this as a complete rebuff, Nasser inevitably turned to the Communist powers. By September 27, 1955, he announced in Cairo an agreement with Czechoslovakia for the supply of arms in exchange for cotton and rice, calling it a simple trade agreement "just like any other." Such a dramatic move, however, could not possibly have been taken without the Russians being a party to it, and so for the first time the Soviet Union plunged into the muddy waters of Middle East politics, arm in arm with a specific Arab power.

The background of American policy against which Dulles was operating needs a word of explanation. Following the foundation of the state of Israel, in which the American government had been deeply involved, there had been a period of relative detachment. With considerable misgivings and inhibitions about colonialism, the United States had more or less supported the British position in the Middle East, in so far as it did not seem to conflict with

America's own interests or international prestige. Early in the nineteen-fifties, however, two new and important factors had arisen. One was the development of the American oil interests in Saudi Arabia, and the other the establishment of the big American air base at Dharan, also in Saudi Arabia. These two commitments, the one private and the other official, marked a significant change in the situation not only for the United States but also, as events were to prove, for the Soviet Union.

In general these new interests accentuated the rather schizo-phrenic Washington attitude towards Anglo-American relations in the area as a whole. Although a good many Americans admitted that it was against their interests that the stability hitherto fostered by the British presence should be undermined, they never really accepted the logic of the situation, which implied that they should give active support to British policy; to do so seemed to some of them to mean backing what they regarded as a system of imperial-ism, which throughout the history of the United States had been considered abhorrent—even though the crucial years of uninter-rupted American development in the nineteenth century had been made possible partly by the existence of Britain's imperial navy and the *Pax Britannica*. While American emotions were thus con-stantly involved on the side of those elements in the Middle East which were determined to overthrow the British, not for the first time American strategy appeared to dictate the need for the exact opposite.

For Dulles himself, the dilemma was peculiarly insistent, since a fundamental part of his whole philosophical attitude to world affairs, as he once expressed it, was that "to oppose nationalism is counterproductive." Already in the early summer of 1954, during the Anglo-Egyptian negotiations over the evacuation of the Suez Canal Zone, he had felt that the British would be well advised to get out before they were thrown out; and yet at the same time he had undoubtedly disappointed the Egyptians in not twisting the British arm more visibly and publicly. American difficulties were also enhanced by the fact, which has become more obvious since than it was to many people at the time, that by the early nineteen-fifties the British had entirely lost the emotional sympathy of the younger Arab leaders. Fundamentally this went back to the establishment of the State of Israel in 1948, which left the Arabs with a sense of betrayal by the West under British leadership. The result was that from then on the British position in the Middle East began to crumble fast.

At first the trend towards disintegration had nevertheless been held in check by three factors. One was the practical working of the Anglo-French-American Tripartite Declaration of May, 1950, which said, first, that the three Western powers would supply arms to either Israel or the Arabs in the light only of "internal security and legitimate self-defense needs," and, secondly, that "should they find that any of these states (Israel or Arab) was proposing to violate the frontiers or armistice lines . . . (they would) immediately take action, both within and outside the United Nations, to prevent such violation." Next was the fact that, in spite of Arab disgust at the foundation of Israel, the leaders of the Arab states continued to act on the implicit assumption that Arab foreign relations must be founded on their contacts with the West; this was due partly to the absence of any coherent Soviet effort to disprove it, partly to the inherently anti-Communist character of leading Arabs, partly to the traditional belief that the British at least supported the Arab League, and partly to not unjustified hopes of Western economic aid. The third and last factor making for stability had been the physical presence of British troops in the Suez Canal Zone. Unpopular though they might be, they stood solidly across the battle lines between Egypt and Israel; and it was a notable feature of the Suez crisis in 1956 that Nasser made his announcement about nationalizing the Suez Canal within six weeks of the last British troops actually leaving the Canal Zone.

By 1955 all these factors of stability had either diminished or vanished altogether. Although the British had not yet left the Canal Zone, they had already agreed to go. By adhering to the Baghdad Pact, the British were claimed throughout the rest of the Middle East to have taken sides between individual members of the Arab League. And above all, with its new interest in Egypt, Moscow had deliberately and irretrievably intervened.

This was the general position, when Nasser let it be known that he proposed to build a new and much higher dam than the one which already exists at Aswan in Upper Egypt, and put out feelers for Western help. The project was so big that its extra water for irrigation and power promised to enable the leaders of the new Egyptian regime to carry out a substantial proportion of their social promises to the peasantry and workers. Accordingly, when Nasser approached both the British and Americans, Eden and Dulles each saw in the scheme an opportunity for what might prove to be decisive Western intervention. It was Eden who at first made all the running. Unable to promise British aid on anything like the total scale, he managed to persuade Dulles, who was at first a good deal more cautious, to back a joint Western offer with American help. The final details were not fixed, but an announcement was made on December 17, 1955, that the United States and Britain had assured Egypt of support in building the Aswan Dam. Such, then, was the position as the year 1955 came to a close.

In other respects Dulles himself had had an extremely busy autumn and early winter. He used the occasion of the Geneva Foreign Ministers' meeting to throw in additional trips to Spain and to Yugoslavia, while in early December he also visited Portugal. Although these three countries had it in common that they were all dictatorships, Dulles saw them each playing a special role on the political and military checkerboard of the cold war. His conversations with General Franco in Madrid covered the working of the existing U.S.-Spanish agreements on mutual defense assistance, economic aid and defense support, and he declared at the end that "the visit was not only to demonstrate U.S. friendship for Spain but to tend to increase such friendship." He never allowed the considerable criticism from many parts of Western Europe, of America's friendly contact with Spain, to deflect him from something which he regarded as essential to the defense of the United States.

The visit of Marshal Tito in Belgrade was to offset the Soviet visit earlier in the year from Bulganin and Khrushchev, and Dulles had a wide-ranging talk with Marshal Tito, covering the Middle East and the position in Eastern Europe, as well as the Geneva Conference. At that time Dulles was still highly critical of Tito's brand of neutralism, though he later came to have rather more sympathy for it. Perhaps the most interesting product of the visit was Dulles's conclusion that the yeast of freedom was working in Eastern Europe. After leaving Belgrade, he was quoted as saying:

> I don't mean to suggest that there will be an early breakaway of the satellites from Moscow. But I think there will soon be visible signs of an evolution toward governments which command more popular support than those which now exist, and which are markedly less the paid hirelings of Moscow.

It was less than a year to the Hungarian revolt. Portugal, by contrast, Dulles valued because of its role in NATO, and he did not hesitate to make some rather injudicious pro-Portuguese comments in a speech which angered Nehru in neutral Delhi, because of the Indian dispute with Portugal about the status of the Portuguese colony of Goa.

Apart from Dulles's own journeys, which were reckoned in the first three years of office to have covered 226,645 miles and to have taken him to no less than thirty-four countries, one of the fascinating features of the closing weeks of 1955 was the trip made by Bulganin and Khrushchev to India, Burma, Kashmir, and Afghanistan. They arrived in India on November 18, carefully trying to play up Indian irritation with Pakistan, because Pakistan had joined Dulles's SEATO and was no longer strictly a neutral. They combined a campaign to ease Indian neutralism into the Communist camp with careful pressure to insure that Delhi would resist the growing influence of Communist China. Although the trip was in general a valiant and historic effort, it did not succeed in changing India's long-term relations with Russia. And only China's much later attacks on India's Himalayan frontier were to convince Delhi of Peking's aggressiveness.

The year 1956 opened for Dulles with a storm over the notorious article in *Life* magazine on January 16, in which James Shepley, the chief *Time-Life* correspondent in Washington, set out the whole philosophy behind the Secretary of State's policies, apparently as the result of an interview. Dulles later denied that he had seen the article before it was published, and this was no doubt true. But, since it had without question captured the mood and spirit in which he worked, it is worth a certain amount of study. Before analyzing it, however, the domestic political background against which it was written should not be forgotten.

At the turn of the year, the Democrats opened a withering cross-fire against the Republican Administration for lack of leadership and smugness about a deteriorating international situation; they quoted, for instance, the Bulganin-Khrushchev visit to India as evidence of the Soviet Union's growing strength and prestige, and charged that the failure of the Geneva meetings suggested appeasement in Eastern Europe, compared with all the high talk of liberation at the time that the Republicans came to power. Dulles's problem at this, the beginning of a Presidential election year, was consequently to back the Republican Party's claim that the first three years of the Eisenhower Administration had brought America "peace and prosperity," while at the same time trying to keep Americans alert to the ever-changing threats in the cold war.

He also had difficulties within the Republican party. One particular aspect of the problem was the foreign aid program, to which he personally attached the greatest importance. By 1956 the atmosphere of the Korean war years was passing, and aid, having started as fundamentally economic under the Marshall Plan, then swung through a period of military priority and was now going back to the nonmilitary field again, in order to meet the rising Soviet challenge of economic competition under "peaceful coexistence." Dulles's desire for maximum flexibility was, however, vastly complicated by a powerful Republican groundswell in favor of balancing the budget, rather than listening to all his pleas for more over-all foreign aid. For all these reasons, then, his attempt to propound his views through the *Life* article was not surprising. But he was unlucky that it misfired so badly that President Eisenhower felt impelled to use his press conference of January 19, the first since his September heart attack, to issue his second formal endorsement of Dulles's position in as many months, by describing him as "the best Secretary of State I have ever known," and declaring that he was devoted to peace.

The article itself dealt with virtually all the points on which Dulles has been most notably attacked. Its central theme was that the enemy must be left in no doubt about the limit which he can cross only at the risk of global war, even if there is an area near the brink which is open to varying degrees of risk, according to the different interpretation of the situation at different times. Dulles's

THE ROAD TO SUEZ

trouble was that he put it all in such a way that he appeared to be so insensitive as to accept the actual possibility of war, even of nuclear war, with equanimity. He did so because he knew that only by appearing to have nerves as cold as those of the other side could he hope to deter them. What he meant was that there is less risk in standing firm than in running away. He was adamant that the idea of backing down at first, with the mental intention of holding on later if things get worse, is one that Munich proved to be an almost certain road to war, since no aggressor will believe in one's last-minute resolve even if one does so oneself; and that in any case is apt to be doubtful. Unfortunately, this kind of talk is almost always unpopular in a democracy, where people readily lull themselves into a false sense of security, either willfully because it is easier and cosier to live like that, or for reasons of passing political expediency in that any electorate naturally prefers peace to war.

There are three famous examples which Dulles himself claimed as successful brinkmanship. The first was on June 18, 1953, when Syngman Rhee with unexpected malice suddenly released all the North Korean and Chinese Communist prisoners of war on the eve of the truce agreement in the hope that this would restart the war. Dulles let it be known that if full-scale fighting were resumed, American planes would bomb Chinese Communist targets in Manchuria.

The second was in April, 1954, when Dulles sponsored the decision which he, President Eisenhower and Admiral Radford, as Chairman of the Joint Chiefs of Staff, made to ask Eden and the French to form a kind of SEATO before the Geneva Conference, and thus threaten joint intervention on a big scale if Communist China continued to back the VietMinh forces in front of Dienbienphu as it was doing. When Eden refused, and thereby earned Dulles's undying contempt, he nevertheless kept up a sufficient barrage of American threat to make the Geneva Conference possible.

The third piece of brinkmanship was early in 1955 when Dulles used the famous Formosa Resolution as the center piece of the threat, which he never fully defined, to intervene with American forces if the Chinese Communists mounted a full-scale attack against Quemoy and Matsu. "Nobody is able to prove mathematically," he himself once said, "that it was the policy of deterrence which brought the Korean War to an end and which kept the Chinese from sending their Red Armies into Indo-China, or that it has finally stopped them in Formosa. But I think it is a pretty fair inference that it has."

It is arguable that one reason why Dulles was not a great man was that he never made any really major decisions. For one thing, in spite of all that he and others said against the previous Administration, it was President Truman and Dean Acheson who made the basic decisions which established the postwar pattern in the West. For another, as Dulles himself observed on one occasion, "It took a lot more courage for the President than for me. His was the ultimate decision. I did not have to make the decision myself, only to recommend it. The President never flinched for a minute on any of these situations. He came up taut."

On the other hand, American policy unquestionably hung in Dulles's hands all through this period, and, clumsy as he often was with public opinion, it is undeniable that he pushed on in spite of the most bitter attacks from his critics, both in the United States and among his allies; that in spite of all the risks he achieved his purpose, without sending a single American soldier into battle; and that, although the tide was undoubtedly running against the West in those years, not a single fresh country became Communist while he was in power, if one discounts North Vietnam, which was virtually lost already, and Iraq, where the coup by no means put the Communists in power.

Dulles always looked at his leading problems in the light of what history might say about them in twenty-five years' time. By then history may well concede that he was a great man. In any case, it was no bad thing that someone somewhere in the world who had the power should play it rough with the Russians. It was no bad thing for the people in the Kremlin to have that nasty ultimate doubt at the backs of their minds, that some idiot in Washington might not after all loose off an atomic bomb, if Russia went too far. Dulles successfully made his brinkmanship and talk of massive retaliation serve this purpose, and the fact that he probably could not have got away with it, even three or four years later, does not detract from his having done so at the time.

Where he went wrong during this period was in claiming too much. He came in for ridicule and incredulity, for instance, when he testified before the Senate Foreign Relations Committee early in March that the West's position in relation to Russia had improved. While it was true enough, as he said, that "the fact is they have failed and they have got to devise new policies," he neither conceded that Khrushchev was indeed doing so with some success, nor did he propose any convincing means of recapturing the initiative for America. At the epoch-making Twentieth All-Union Congress of the Communist Party of the Soviet Union in the middle of February, 1956, Khrushchev had spelled out the new Soviet foreign policy of "strengthening fraternal relations" with other Communist states, "improving relations" with the Western allies, Japan, Persia and other similar countries, and "strengthening," "reinforcing," and "supporting" countries that refused to be involved in military blocs. A distinct new effort was required by the United States to meet this challenge.

On the face of it, although the situation called for a sharp change of tactics on Dulles's part, the whole cold war contest was in a sense moving into a field in which America should have had a natural advantage over Russia. The United States was far ahead of the Soviet Union in terms of economics, and it should have had a huge potential advantage in the competition which was now arising among the uncommitted countries. Admittedly, the Russians gained by being newcomers, and were therefore able to make promises which no one yet knew whether they would keep. But it was arguable that America would throw away its potential advantage only if it stuck too long to an outworn militaristic creed. Yet this was exactly what many people feared that Dulles would do, and, while in a sense he allowed the impression to get about that he placed the main emphasis on the military aspect, the truth was that he was changing his own mind, and that he felt he could back a substantial foreign aid program only if the military situation was first made secure.

Early in February, 1956, the British Prime Minister and Foreign Secretary, Sir Anthony Eden and Selwyn Lloyd, arrived in Washington for three-day talks with the President and the Secretary of State, being brought down from New York in the President's personal aircraft, the *Columbine,* after crossing the Atlantic by sea. Although it was not one of the more successful Anglo-American occasions, it provided quite a useful opportunity for both sides to review the flexible and self-confident approach, which Khrushchev was adopting towards the so-called "neutral nations"; to discuss the West's proper reaction to the upsurge of anxiety and emotion in Western public opinion, especially inside the United States itself, where the Democrats were talking about the weakness of American leadership; and, above all, to discuss the growing Arab-Israeli tension in the Middle East, together with the mounting success of the Communist propaganda offensive throughout the area.

Although no solution was found to the needs of Western policy in the Middle East, both sides felt that they at least saw the problem in the same terms. In this, however, they undoubtedly deceived themselves to some degree, since to anyone outside the circle of government, discussing the Middle East in both London and Washington during that period, their differences of approach seemed too obviously fundamental to be patched up by a single meeting. It was characteristic of this misunderstanding that during the visit the foundations appear to have been laid for the Anglo-American disharmony which later showed itself over the withdrawal of aid for the Aswan Dam, the incident that triggered off the Suez crisis.

What happened was that Dulles, Eden, and Selwyn Lloyd agreed quite genuinely among themselves that the possibility of Nasser finding adequate finance for his own share of the Aswan Dam project was becoming distinctly remote; in addition, the latest information about the pledging of Egypt's cotton crop to Czechoslovakia against arms, under the agreement of the previous summer, showed that Nasser simply would not be able to keep the Egyptian economy viable while the dam was being built. On both the British and the American side it was, therefore, agreed in principle not to go through with the offer of aid. But the intention was to let the offer "wither," rather than to make any public announcement about the change of plan; and it was this agreement which Dulles broke in July without a single word of warning to his British colleagues. In addition, the British at any rate were

quite clear that the abandonment of the huge Aswan Dam support
did not mean withdrawing lesser aid as well. In Eden's memoirs
he says of his time in Washington: "On personal grounds I had
enjoyed the visit and the opportunity it had given me to meet many
friends again, both in the Administration and outside it. Probably
I overvalued the political results, as one is apt to do at a time of
contact with close allies." On the latter point he was only too
dreadfully right.

Two other journeys that spring are also of interest. Dulles himself set off round the world in March, using the SEATO Council
meeting in Karachi as an excuse. After it he flew on to Delhi,
Colombo, Jakarta, Bangkok, Saigon, Manila, Taipei, Seoul, and
Tokyo. It was after this trip that Dulles was accused, with some
justification, of a particularly characteristic example of his flair for
saying one thing to one group of people and another to another.
While in Karachi he offered increased American economic assistance to Pakistan, Thailand, and the Philippines, implying by his
choice of words that he was doing so because they had taken the
plunge of being America's allies in SEATO. In the case of Pakistan,
Dulles had been particularly keen to show his support, since
Nehru's strong reaction against SEATO had given the Russians an
excuse for lining up themselves behind India. Yet when he reached
Jakarta he made apparently very similar offers to neutralist Indonesia, implying that American aid was generously being given
without strings attached. Obviously he was in the difficulty of
wanting to reward friends and to win over the uncommitted at the
same time; but the moral inconsistencies did not seem to worry
him once they had been buried in legalistic phraseology. Mental
gymnastics of this kind in any case suited his own tendency to
compartmentalize his mind.

The other journey was that of Khrushchev and Bulganin to Britain in April of 1956. Although the somewhat indecisive results of this
visit were later overshadowed by Khrushchev's own phenomenal
tour of the United States in 1959, the occasion did at the time mark
a striking new twist in the cold war. The Soviet visitors were not
in fact treated with the enthusiastic welcome from the British
people that they might have expected, nor did they achieve any
change of direction in British public opinion. Nevertheless, there

were many Americans who doubted the wisdom of the visit, and who were considerably relieved when it passed off without achieving more discernible results. Dulles himself, while admitting in theory that the world was entering a period with greater scope for diplomatic maneuver, never liked this odd and slightly disturbing circus turn in Britain.

All this time the Middle East pot was steadily boiling. On April 9, following a renewal of Egyptian-Israeli clashes in the Gaza area, President Eisenhower issued a statement saying that both he and Dulles regarded the situation there with the utmost seriousness. And the British, still smarting from the humiliation inflicted on them some weeks before by Jordan in December of the previous year, 1955, when riots in Amman during the visit of General Sir Gerald Templer had forced Eden and Selwyn Lloyd to abandon their attempt to get the Jordanians to join the Baghdad Pact, thoroughly agreed. But that was about as far as their agreement went. Egypt held the key to the situation, and I well remember my own sense of shock in Washington that May, only two months before the Suez crisis began, when I realized how very differently the situation was assessed by the State Department compared with the Foreign Office. The essential difference lay in the attitude to Nasser personally. In London, while criticism of the Egyptian regime varied from one political party to another, the government view was that the growth of Nasser's prestige and power was such a danger to the West that it ought to be curbed by any possible means. In Washington, on the other hand, Dulles's own attitude received a good deal of support from his staff, namely that the United States must play along with Colonel Nasser as best it could in order to keep the Russians out. Although Dulles did not like Nasser, he accepted him. The British government did not. And therein lay the fundamental difference, from which sprang the great rift between Washington and London, when the storm finally broke after Nasser had nationalized the Suez Canal.

CHAPTER 13

The Fatal Three Months

WHATEVER view anyone in Britain takes of Suez, neither side in the terrible controversy really has a good word to say for Dulles. He put a vast amount of energy and sheer hard work into what he did, but his intervention ended by doing more harm than good. It was not as if he had failed to grapple with Middle East problems beforehand. Days and days of discussion and drafting by the State Department had been devoted for well over a year to trying to find the right policies and the right formulas for the Middle East. Dulles himself had been in constant touch not only with his ambassadors on the spot, but with the British and French ministers with whom he was so soon to be at complete loggerheads. Inexorably, as the fatal three months from July 26 to October 30 dragged by, his words and actions played their sinister part in accentuating the crisis in spite of his ardent desire to damp it down. Both he and Eden were sick men that summer, though Dulles was unaware of his illness while Eden suffered visibly. But the net result was that in some ways the final peak of tragedy in October was Dulles's doing almost as much as Eden's and Mollet's. And in his record at the State Department it marks by far his most humiliating failure.

In America, however, Dulles had the general support of public opinion throughout, and it was only in the recriminations afterwards that his stock slumped to an all-time low. The support for him is shown by Gallup polls and other less sophisticated tests, though the vast majority of Americans would have found it difficult to say at any given moment precisely what it was they were supporting. Naturally there was also an undercurrent of criticism, and the State Department itself was often divided and sunk in gloom. But considering that the height of the crisis coincided with the culmination of the American Presidential campaign, at the end of which President Eisenhower was elected for his second term, because even with his heart attack his popularity represented the only way the Republican Party could win, it was no mean achievement for Dulles to maintain his position as he did.

It was not that American sympathy for the British and French was lacking, at any rate in the earlier stages of the crisis. The American dilemma was felt to be how to dissuade London and Paris from doing something which would ultimately prove to be to their great disadvantage. Americans felt instinctively that nationalism must be given its head. They were by long tradition against anything which looked like colonialism, in spite of the reputation for a new kind of imperialism for which their own country was already becoming a byword in Asia and Africa. They did not see any clear Communist hand behind Nasser, though some of them were a little shaken by the revelation of so much Soviet equipment after the fighting stopped. They were adamantly opposed to any course which might lead to a wider war—though they would have accepted readily enough the fruits of a local engagement if it had succeeded. Above all, they did not consider that the vital interests of the United States were directly affected by the closure of the Suez Canal, except for the remote contingency that this could prove a precedent for the Panama Canal, and except, of course, for the relatively minor consideration that they might end by bailing out Britain and France with economic help if things went seriously wrong—as in fact the Americans partially did.

Thus, many of the factors which influenced the governments in London and Paris cut almost no ice at all in Washington, or in any other American city. And the only really valid indictment which some Americans felt could be leveled against their country's attitude—and the number was not large—was that the United States had let down its allies; this, indeed, was a point about which sophisticated American opinion, particularly on the Eastern seaboard, felt quite keenly. To sum up, while there was an overcast of genuine sympathy for Britain and France, it mainly took the form of regret that their case was not stronger, and this mood naturally gained encouragement from the violent divisions of opinion within those countries themselves.

Dulles himself was actuated by other motives, in addition to those which affected American opinion as a whole, though each of these naturally had a considerable effect on him. Apart from the week-to-week aspects of the crisis as it developed, three fundamental factors were always at work on him, and, in so far as his attitude and behavior have puzzled as well as incensed many people in Britain and France, these three contain the clues which sometimes seemed to be missing at the time. First and foremost, he was from start to finish determined to prevent the use of force at almost any cost, though he never succeeded in convincing London or Paris that this was his purpose. He saw military action as a dangerous spark which was likely to set off the Third World War, and, in spite of his own constant brinkmanship in the Far East and Southeast Asia, he would have absolutely none of it in the Middle East. He was also far more determined than either Eden or Selwyn Lloyd realized at the time not to let a war break out during President Eisenhower's election campaign. After November 6 his attitude in this particular respect would have been quite different. Thus he was always in a sense simply playing for time.

Secondly, he felt an explosively personal resentment that the initiative in such an important matter was being taken out of American hands. Dulles always reacted violently to being thwarted; one of the main things that he constantly held against the British, particularly in the earlier part of his Secretaryship, was that they were so frequently thwarting him. Over the Suez dispute, he felt that in the last resort the ultimate consequences would depend on what the United States did. America would have to pay the piper; so America must call the tune. And while he was of course technically right, as events eventually proved, the emotion that he allowed to creep into his attitude was a frightening reinforcement of the impression of God-given superiority, which he was normally apt to convey in any case. It simply drove Eden and Mollet on. Eden enormously resented Dulles's assumption of an apparent right to hold the British and French on such obvious leading strings; and, if Dulles had been different from the man he was, he would have been much more subtle in his approach, particularly in view of Eden's shortness of temper, made worse by his poor state of health.

The other factor, often overlooked, was the President. The whole Suez affair was something about which Eisenhower felt very strongly indeed on moral grounds. Dulles felt strongly too, but he was also well accustomed to muffling his conscience if other circumstances demanded it, and his calculation of those circumstances could be cold and very hard indeed. In this case, however, the special Eisenhower-Dulles relationship had a highly significant bearing on the issue, constantly reinforced as it was by the exigencies of the electoral campaign. It must be remembered that Dulles never forgot where his own power came from. Although he always tried to win support in Congress, it was axiomatic in all that he did that he must never fail to carry the President with him. Eisenhower personally was his one supreme client. And now, if that vital person—of whom he was also very fond—felt as deeply as President Eisenhower certainly did on the Suez issue, then that clinched it as far as Dulles was concerned.

Rationally Dulles opposed the use of force over the Suez dispute on several different grounds. In addition to the overriding fear that war might spread, he believed that force would anyway be ineffective since, first, the Canal itself could never be run satisfactorily against Egyptian opposition and, secondly, the cost of overthrowing Nasser would be prohibitive in terms of the rest of the Middle East and of Asia, in that its use would open up these fields to highly effective Soviet propaganda against the West. This was in direct line with his original attitude, two and three years before, that the British must evacuate the Suez Canal Zone. There were also the more positive aspects of the general situation. Dulles did genuinely believe in the UN Charter, and that it must be held up as the one hope for an orderly world system. Thus, he considered it very important to be able to rally support against any Soviet use of force. If the West actually indulged in force—apart from talking about it—there was no moral reason for condemning the Russians when they did the same. Moreover, as he is quoted as telling Pineau towards the end of the year, if he had agreed to use force, it would have made it much more difficult for him to restrain

Chiang Kai-shek, Syngman Rhee, or any extreme German nationalist wanting to do likewise.

Given these thoughts in the mind of the American Secretary of
State, the allocation of blame over Suez is neither one-sided nor
simple. It is shared by the British and French governments, for
going ahead in spite of the opposition from America as well as
from their own countries; by the American government for the way
in which Dulles did in actual fact fail to make his own position
clear, and at each stage undid what he had apparently secured at
the previous one; and by the Labour Opposition in Britain, for
tying the hands of the government when it was already in mid-
stream, swimming under great difficulties. Without any one of
these elements the story might have been different. With all three
it ended in chaos and disaster. And while Dulles was obviously not
to blame for the neuroses of London and Paris, he was responsible
for making them so much worse that the Russians felt they could
step in at the very end and deliver a *coup de grâce,* the very thing
which he had particularly wanted to avoid.

On both sides of the Atlantic Nasser's action in seizing the Canal
was regarded as a violation of legal rights, even though this was
never easy to prove; it was also seen as an unnecessary step, dic-
tated by the urgency of the politics of nationalism, in the sense that
within just over a decade the Canal would have legally reverted
to Egypt anyway. But the question was, of course, what to do about
it. And it is in the difference between their basic objectives that
the key to the clash between the United States, on the one side and
Britain and France, on the other, is to be found. Dulles's purpose
was to try to secure a reasonably free right of passage through the
Canal, in some degree insulated from the Nasser regime and Cairo
politics. He was certain this could not be done by the use of force,
and he was equally certain that, even without force, it could not
be done by humiliating Nasser.

Put in a nutshell, the French and British purpose was to humili-
ate Nasser and thereby obtain rights of passage through the Canal.
This was the precise opposite of what Dulles was trying to do,
and there was never at any time in the Suez crisis agreement
between the two sides as to how they were to compose this fundamental difference. It was a difference which sprang from the logic

of the situation as each country saw it. The French quite simply wanted to get rid of Nasser because of Algeria. The British took their stand on somewhat similar ground, as applied in more general terms to the whole of Africa and the rest of the Middle East; for Eden himself, this was made much stronger by his sense of a personal feud with Nasser. The American Administration, by contrast, looked at the question primarily as a problem of checking Communist infiltration, and, incidentally, with a kind of cold detachment which neither the British nor the French could share, in view of Nasser's stranglehold on their oil windpipe.

Beginning in this way from different starting points, Anglo-French tactics inevitably came down to trying to prove to Dulles that they were right, almost as much as seeking to get Nasser to agree to their plans. If Nasser had agreed, of course, or even shown some sign of agreement, all would have gone relatively well. But the interplay between his own determination and the almost incredible series of encouragements he received from Dulles's public statements could not help but make the British and French more and more desperate with frustration. They were driven almost more to trying to corner Dulles, by proving to him that the only possible answer was to get rid of Nasser, than to concerting plans for negotiating with the Egyptians at all. Dulles, however, had not been a top-flight lawyer for nothing. He decided quite early on that this was not what Eden was trying to do, and he was absolutely determined not to be outmaneuvered. As a result of his agility, skill, and experience, he half succeeded. But, as some American observers see it, this practically drove Eden out of his mind, and the crisis rolled on in an appalling welter of maneuvering as well as misunderstanding. Dulles for his part always believed that he in turn could get the better of the British and French, and, in spite of all the warnings, he was taken by surprise when they did finally reach the point of using force.

In bargaining with Nasser, Dulles's general idea was to go as far as possible in threatening the Egyptians with an untenable situation, if they did not come to terms with the maritime powers. At the same time, he never meant it to be clear what he would do if his bluff was called, and indeed he was never really clear himself. In carrying out this tactic, he was undoubtedly hampered by a kind of legalistic respect for the carefully agreed written document, and he also paid far too little attention to the consequences of his own words and insinuations on the realities of the situation. Given the choice in a calm situation, he would not have repudiated the use of force too publicly. But the situation was nearly always far too pressing to permit him to do what he wanted. The one thing which the activities of the British and French kept on pushing him into was being asked publicly by the press whether he would use force or not. However much he hoped to avoid this oversimplification—and much that he said during the crisis shows how hard he tried to play it down without success—he could not help saying more than he wanted to. And to this extent the British and French did in a sense corner him—to their own disadvantage.

Dulles's idea was to use the same tactics over Suez as he had set out to use over Indo-China in 1954. This was to wave a big stick even if he did not mean to use it. The comparison between these two episodes has, however, a special additional significance in the history of the relations between Dulles and Eden. Dulles's line of thought over Indo-China was that the French would throw in the sponge, and that this would make the Communists put forward unlimited demands. For this reason he felt that it was vital to formulate the SEATO idea *before* the Geneva Conference, implying, as it did, determined collective action if the Communists went too far. When Eden undermined this strategy by refusing to give countenance to the SEATO concept at that point (because he already distrusted Dulles), Dulles never forgave him. Now, when Dulles was once again trying to influence a nasty situation, by appearing to threaten something which in the last resort he did not mean, the shoe was on the other foot. It was Dulles who in fact rejected the logic of his own procedure and sold the pass to Nasser by his behavior. Eden never forgave him. Dulles's bitterness with Eden over Indo-China ran a tragically close parallel to Eden's bitterness with Dulles over Suez.

Dulles may be blamed for his share in the Suez fiasco in three respects, though they are not by any means all of the same importance; nor is it so easy to establish his precise position in each case. These three are that he provoked Nasser in the first instance by the gratuitously insulting way in which he suddenly withdrew

American money for the Aswan Dam; that he never made absolutely clear to the British and French that in no circumstances
whatever could they count on American support if they used force;
and that at successive stages of the crisis he undermined the negotiations with Nasser, either deliberately and maliciously or through
an incapacity to grasp the essentials of the struggle, by saying things
which made it clear to Nasser that he was not really on the same
side as Eden and Mollet. Of these three, it is the last two which
are the most insidiously damaging to his reputation.

The first, the matter of the Aswan Dam, has already been partly
put in its right context. In addition to the general argument that
Egypt was already prejudicing its economic viability, which Dulles
and Eden had both agreed on in Washington in February, Dulles
had also decided in principle that American aid ought not to be
tied up in one huge long-term project, since this would leave the
field free for the Russians to come in over the next three or four
years with a whole series of far more showy short-term ideas. But,
as to what should be said in public, nothing was agreed—except to
say nothing. And Dulles had no business whatever to make an
announcement without consulting Selwyn Lloyd.

He did so primarily because, in spite of conscious efforts in the
State Department to prepare a moderate communique which would
give the least offense when it was eventually announced, Dulles
believed that he had been put on the spot by a sudden move
made by Nasser. Nasser had never formally accepted the Anglo-
American offer of aid at the time that the offer genuinely stood.
Now, by the summer of 1956, when the decision had already been
made in principle not to proceed with the offer, he suddenly determined to grab at it. He told the State Department publicly that he
had put his ambassador on the plane to go to Washington to accept
the proposed aid. Dulles decided that he must have a clear refusal
ready for the ambassador when he arrived. This was accordingly
prepared, the excuse being used that certain difficulties with
Congress—which did in fact partly exist—made it impossible to go
ahead with the offer. Dulles was also not sorry to take a calculated
risk in being blunt with Nasser's envoy, since he hoped it would
teach Nasser not to think that he could play Russia off against the
West indefinitely and get away with it. The fact that he did not

give the British adequate warning of what he was about to do pales into insignificance beside the dramatic sequence of events which his action provoked in Cairo.

On the question of whether Dulles made his irrevocable objection to the use of force clear enough to the British and French, the evidence is still inconclusive; indeed it is probably one of the aspects of the Suez crisis that may yet take many years to unravel and will be clarified only by the publication of documents which still are, and will remain for some time, confidential. All that can be said incontrovertibly is that on the American side, first, Dulles was expressing the clear view of most of the politicians and civil servants in Washington, when he indicated that the United States would not be a party to the use of force; and, secondly, in spite of this attitude towards the Suez dispute itself, in the last resort the Administration would nevertheless not have stood by and watched France or, more particularly, Britain be destroyed by, for instance, Soviet air or rocket attacks just because they had transgressed the American will in the Middle East.

On the British side, uncertainty about where the country stood between these two extremes of the American point of view unquestionably existed. Robert Murphy, Dulles's Deputy Under Secretary of State, was told in London within two days of Nasser's nationalization of the Canal of a British Cabinet decision in principle to use force if necessary. This information was the cause of Dulles coming straight over to London. It seems hardly conceivable, therefore, that he could not have made his own position plain either then or later. Yet the fact remains that either he did so and the British did not believe him, or he failed to do so. And here the evidence available in London must be taken into account. This is that Dulles personally was saying in private that "it might in the end come to the use of force"; and his first question, when Selwyn Lloyd went to see him in the hospital after it was all over, is very reliably reported to have been: "Why did you stop?" In any case, Eden and Selwyn Lloyd were not alone in thinking, certainly at first, that if and when it came to the point, the Americans would not obstruct British and French action even if they did not actively lend their support. Later, during the final three weeks before the landings at Port Said, when the British and French did not tell the Americans what they were doing, the American position was undoubtedly better understood. But by then the frustration of Dulles's whole apparently schizophrenic behavior throughout the crisis had irretrievably aggravated the whole situation.

The main blame to be laid at Dulles's door arises out of his behavior during the actual negotiations of August and September. It was not that he held aloof this time, as he had at Geneva in 1954. Throughout he played a leading part in the proceedings, frequently taking the apparent initiative, only to intensify the crisis a few days later by backing out of the implications of what he had done. The first instance of this occurred almost at the beginning over the First London Conference on August 16. When Nasser had nationalized the Suez Canal on July 26, Dulles happened—somewhat typically— to be not at his desk in the State Department, but at a conference in Peru. He flew straight back to Washington and then, because his own withdrawal of the Aswan Dam money had implicated the United States, because the Eisenhower Administration needed to make good its current electoral claims to "peace, prosperity and progress," and because Murphy had told him that the British Cabinet had already decided in principle to use force to secure passage through the Canal if there were no other way, he went on to London, arriving there on August 1. After thirty-six hours of close contact between Dulles, Eden, Selwyn Lloyd, and Pineau, the French Foreign Minister, the three Western powers issued an invitation, based on Dulles's proposals, to all the maritime users of the Suez Canal to attend a conference in London on August 16, in order to establish an international company or agency, which might exercise a supervisory control and see that the Canal dues, pledged by Nasser to the building of the Aswan High Dam, were properly applied to the maintenance and expansion of the Canal.

Back in Washington by August 3, Dulles made a broadcast that night which expressed his initial reactions with the same kind of revealing clarity as that shown by Hugh Gaitskell, the British Labour leader, when he made his first Suez speech in the House of Commons. In the course of his broadcast Dulles said:

> If President Nasser's decision to exploit the Suez Canal were permitted to go unchallenged, it would encourage a breakdown of the international fabric upon which the security and

well-being of all peoples depends. The question is not whether
something should be done about it. I believe that a plan for
international operation of the Canal will emerge from the
twenty-four-nation conference. . . .

It is inadmissible that a waterway, internationalized by
treaty, which is required for the livelihood of a score of nations,
should be exploited by one country for highly selfish purposes;
and that the operating agency required to give effect to the
1888 Treaty should be struck down as a national act of venge-
fulness.

The government of the United States has given no commitments of any kind as to what it will do in the unhappy contingency of the failure of the London Conference. We assume
that the conference will not fail, but will succeed. . . .

After President Nasser's action there were some people who
counseled immediate forcible action by the governments most
directly affected. This, however, would have been contrary to
the principles of the United Nations Charter, and would undoubtedly have led to widespread violence, endangering the
peace of the world. By deciding to call together in conference
in London the nations most directly involved to see whether
agreement can be reached on an adequate and dependable
international administration of the Canal on terms which
would generously respect all the legitimate rights of Egypt,
a different approach has been adopted.

I believe that out of the conference which has been called
will come a judgment of such moral force that we can be confident that the Suez Canal will continue to serve in peace the
interests of all mankind.

Three points stand out from Dulles's words. He was entirely
opposed to accepting what Nasser had done. But he pinned his
whole faith on the force of moral law. And he expressed an optimism about the outcome of the crisis which neither events nor
indeed his own inmost thoughts warranted.

It was in this early period that Dulles also made his first comments about bringing the United Nations into the dispute. The
news from Egypt was clear enough. Nasser had not only acted
with great swiftness and skill on that night that he delivered his
nationalization speech in Alexandria, but he had also made sure of
consolidating his hold by moving the Egyptian army into positions
of strength along the Canal during the following fortnight. Dulles's
main reaction was not so much to condemn these further moves

as to fear that they might be regarded as provocation in London and Paris. To counter this he put out the idea of appealing to the United Nations. But, even so, he said he still placed his main faith in the "hope that the Suez Conference will be successful." Thus he committed himself once again to the London meeting of August 16, which had been virtually his own brainchild.

When Dulles returned to London just in time for that London Conference, he was accompanied by a considerable team of officials and a good deal of publicity, instead of the haste and relative secrecy with which he had traveled a fortnight earlier. By now considerable efforts had indeed been made in Washington to prepare to help Britain and France and the other maritime nations, so long as they pursued policies which were in line with those of the United States. Dulles and the President had naturally discussed the danger of hostilities being opened, partly because, if they did, a special session of Congress would almost certainly have to be called, should there be any possibility of American troops having to intervene; and the very idea of doing this in the middle of the election campaign was appalling. What the Administration did do, however, was to initiate discussions between the Department of the Interior, the Office of Defense Mobilization, and thirteen leading American oil companies to work out plans for making extra supplies available to Western Europe, if the Suez Canal should in fact be closed.

Dulles and his officials in London went out of their way to show their understanding of some of the views being expressed by the British and French, adding that the United States was going into the London Conference with a clear determination that it should succeed, and that above all some form of international control should be exercised. Only one little flicker of doubt could be deduced about America's apparent determination; but it was one which, as events were to prove, was extremely important. Although Israeli ships had for years been prevented by Egypt from using the Suez Canal, Israel was not even invited to the London Conference. Admittedly, as was advanced at the time, it could be argued that, since Nasser had already condemned the London Conference as having no standing, it was only adding fuel to the flames to bring the factor of the Arab-Israeli quarrel directly into the dispute.

Nevertheless, that this longstanding and flagrant abuse of the freedom of the Canal should be glossed over at this point was a fact
of evil omen.

The London Conference got down to business very quickly and
finished within a week. Of the twenty-four nations invited to
attend, twenty-two came, those refusing being Greece and Egypt
itself; but the Egyptians kept themselves informed of what was
happening through the presence of Wing Commander Ali Sabri
as an observer. The conference decided by an eventual majority of
eighteen to four to adopt the plan for an international management body capable of exercising some measure of control over the
Canal. This was the plan which Dulles himself drafted, argued for,
and finally pushed through, largely by his own leadership. In effect,
he acted as spokesman for Britain and France at this conference,
and he was primarily opposed by Krishna Menon, who spoke pas-
sionately against him on behalf of the minority of four: Russia,
India, Indonesia, and Ceylon.

The alternative to Dulles's plan had been the purely consultative organization, through which Egypt and the users of the Canal
would do little more than be kept in contact with one another.
It was a question of management or advice. And, although there
was at no time any guarantee that Nasser would accept either, by
urging the stronger course, Dulles created an even more false impression of his real position than he might have done. He did so,
moreover, in spite of Western hopes before the conference that
a situation would not develop in which the Russians could pose
as the spokesmen for Egypt. Yet this is precisely what the Soviet
delegate and Krishna Menon were able to do.

Two days after the conference was over Nasser agreed to receive
Robert Menzies, the Prime Minister of Australia, in Cairo as
leader of a five-power delegation from the eighteen countries which
had supported the Dulles plan. And Menzies duly set off for a
rendezvous in Egypt with the foreign ministers of Sweden, Iran,
and Ethiopia, together with Loy Henderson, representing the
United States. It was at this precise point, however, that Dulles's
own extraordinarily complex personality took over. Instead of
simply remaining quiet after he returned to Washington, he gave
a long press conference on August 28 in which he pulled the rug

from under Menzies' feet. He told the press that he did not really see eye to eye with the British and French. He declared that "the Suez Canal is not a primary concern to the United States." And, in an apparent attempt to play the issues down, he asserted that he saw "no necessity to think in terms of great issues, like nationalism versus internationalism or Asia versus Europe. These and similar attitudes make the dispute almost insoluble." Three days later President Eisenhower joined in by holding a press conference, unusual on a Friday morning, in which he declared: "We are committed to a peaceful settlement of this dispute—nothing else." And he repeated his statement on September 5.

Menzies took as tough a view of the nationalization of the Canal as anyone, and, if the Canal users were at sixes and sevens in their resolution, he was hardly the man to handle the negotiations with Nasser. He did not in fact prove an able spokesman and his mission duly failed. But Nasser's unconcealed relish at the American statements, both on television and during the talks themselves, showed how far Dulles had succeeded in sabotaging the mission—a mission, moreover, which had gone to argue for the very things that Dulles himself had proposed in London. Observers in Cairo were clear that Nasser was convinced of Washington's retreat from the Dulles plan, that he was thereby encouraged to drive a wedge between America and the British-French partnership, and that what little doubt he may have had was banished by the attitude on the spot of Loy Henderson and of the American ambassador, Hector Byroade. As for Dulles himself, having delivered his bombshells, he packed his bags and went off for one of his periods of secluded contemplation on Duck Island.

Not content with his folly in making the statements which he did, on the eve of negotiations that at best could only be extremely difficult, Dulles also began to back-pedal at this stage on the idea of taking the dispute to the United Nations. With the Menzies failure, Eden and Mollet were known to be considering an appeal to the UN, as Nasser was also doing. Dulles, however, had the State Department deny at once the rumors to this effect which began circulating in Washington. And both Eden and Selwyn Lloyd gained the impression that he was opposed to it because he feared the consequences. If Britain and France came off badly, he was afraid that this would push them nearer to the use of force. If, on the other hand, Nasser had to accept a possible UN investigation, Dulles felt it might be highly critical of him—as indeed it probably would have been at that time. Either result would therefore be embarrassing, particularly taking place on America's own doorstep in New York at the height of the Presidential election campaign. But all this meant that any semblance of genuine Western unity on the problem had gone. Nothing was therefore done about the UN at this point, since the British and French felt it would be unwise to go to the Security Council without at least American co-operation—a fear that proved fully justified in harsher circumstances later on.

In the light of Dulles's observations that the Suez Canal was not of primary importance to the United States, with the implication that Washington would not therefore go to the limit in defending any American interests there, it is worth noting what the United States' position is in relation to the Panama Canal, and indeed what was going on in Panama at this eventful time. In the middle of September, 1956, the Americans felt obliged to make two concessions to Panamanian opinion, under the threat of further violent clashes between Nationalist demonstrators and the United States authorities in the Canal Zone, like those which had taken place on November 3, 1955. One concession was to display the Panamanian flag alongside the Stars and Stripes in the Canal Zone, and the other was to abolish segregation between American and Panamanian employees there in respect of such things as sports grounds, swimming pools, movie theaters, and the use of separate shops. Washington might well have been expected to have made these concessions long before; but the fact that they came only in 1956 was an interesting reflection on the sensitivity which the United States felt about its own affairs as a result of the tension in Egypt.

While it was easy enough for many Americans, as Dulles well knew, to regard the Suez Canal as a faraway waterway of which they knew nothing, the Panama Canal is a familiar trigger spot in the American political anatomy. Fortunately for Dulles, his series of sharp exchanges with the Foreign Minister of Panama, Señor Alberto Boyd, took place against a background of more strongly entrenched American control over the Panama Canal than that which America's allies had over Suez. Until 1903 the territory through which the Panama Canal runs had formed part of the Republic of Colombia. When Panama became independent in that year, with American support, and signed a treaty with the United States, it leased in perpetuity a strip of land ten miles wide across the isthmus. In this zone, which was specifically designed for the construction of the Canal, it granted authority to the American government, "as if it were sovereign," over the operation, maintenance, and defense of the Canal. In return, the United States agreed to pay to Panama a lump sum of ten million dollars and an annual fee of $250,000. This annual payment has since been raised twice to very much higher levels. The actual tolls on commercial vessels using the Canal now amount to about thirty-three million dollars a year, and about half is absorbed by operating expenses.

Dulles claimed that, as a result of the original agreement, the United States "holds the sole right to exercise sovereignty in the Canal Zone to the exclusion of every other government." But Panama itself retorted with some justification that all Washington had originally been granted were "certain powers expressly for the purpose of the Canal and nothing else." This difference of view has never been entirely resolved; but, in comparison with the position whereby the old Suez Canal Company operated the waterway through Egypt, the Panama Canal always has been run as a government organization by the United States. Moreover, no international convention, such as that of 1888, exists to guarantee freedom of transit through the Panama Canal, and there is indeed no time limit to the duration of the American position, as there was with the Suez Canal in the sense that by 1968, even if Nasser had taken no action whatsoever, the Suez Canal would have reverted to Egyptian ownership. Dulles, it should not be forgotten, had always been very much aware of America's interests in Panama and the possible threats to them, ever since his visits to Central America on behalf of Sullivan and Cromwell in his early twenties.

With the failure of the Menzies mission to Cairo, the first stage of the Suez crisis ended. In the second, which opened on September 12, Dulles was again to be not only the prime mover but also the chief cause of the failure to make any progress. On Wednesday, September 12, the British House of Commons assembled for an

THE FATAL THREE MONTHS
THE FATAL THREE MONTHS 221
a proposal to set up a provisional emergency organization to be
by its initials, SCUA. But the real originator of the proposal was
Dulles. In Eden's speech he said that "We have decided in agree-
should be set up without delay to enable the users of the canal to
exercise their rights." Neither then or later, however, was it ever
made clear how they were to exercise those rights in the face of
Egyptian opposition. Once again it could only be a matter of
In order to work out the details of SCUA, Dulles first of all flew
Out of his visit there emerged the Second London Conference,
which opened on September 19 and lasted for just over two days.
The eighteen countries (including Spain) which had supported the
more to discuss this second stage. And once again, as a month
ence, taking the initiative in outlining the six main proposals for
Dulles proposed that SCUA should exist because it was useful.
Secondly, it should be based on the ideas which were put forward
at the First London Conference. Thirdly, it should consist of a
small operating staff to work on a practical basis with the Egyptians,
goings of the Canal as such. Fourthly, SCUA should be run by
a small government board, which would keep an eye on future
projects. Fifthly, a small working fund should be set up, with which
to begin operations. And, lastly, it was to be hoped that members
"would voluntarily take such action with respect to their ships and
the payment of Canal dues as would facilitate the work of the
Association and build up its prestige and authority...."
Although this was a milder proposal than the one suggested by
the words Eden had used when he made his first public introduction of the scheme in the House of Commons, it still went far

beyond anything that Nasser had so far shown any sign of accepting. The adoption of these proposals therefore implied further intense negotiation with Nasser and the planting in Nasser's mind of the thought that, if he did not accept the proposals, he would lose by doing so. This after all is only basic to any negotiations between any two parties. And while there was nothing explicit in the SCUA proposals, designed to make it clear what would happen if they were entirely rejected, it would have been childish to put them forward from such a totally weak position that Nasser was under no pressure whatever to consider them. This did not imply being precise about the use either of economic sanctions or of more forceful means, but it did at least suggest that the West should give some impression of having a card or two up its sleeve.

Dulles was therefore crippling SCUA quite gratuitously when he suddenly came out with his famous press statement shortly before the Second London Conference, that, whatever else happened, "We do not intend to shoot our way through; we might have the right to do it, but the United States does not intend to do it. If we are met by force, we do not intend to get into a shooting war. . . ." This was the second specific occasion on which Dulles went out of his way to undermine not only the bargaining position of the Western allies, but also the implications of the whole stand which he himself had just taken, by assuring Nasser that, whatever happened, his opponents would not get tough with him. Some people feel that the only coherent explanation of Dulles's extraordinary behavior is that he was indeed mainly playing for time, either deliberately or in part subconsciously, with the idea of spinning out the period of indecision until after the American Presidential election on November 6. But, if so, considering what was at stake in the rest of the world, it was a cruel and cynical performance.

Dulles had, among other plans, given a good deal of thought to the proposal for an economic boycott of Egypt. This was to take the form of rerouting ships round South Africa, and it inevitably involved at least temporary American help for Britain and France. American oil was required from the Western Hemisphere to replace some of the Middle East oil which could not physically reach European markets, and American tankers were needed to help transport such Middle East oil as could be carried on the much longer haul around the Cape. In pursuit of this plan Dulles made a public statement, saying that American tankers which had been laid up were being taken "out of mothballs" and prepared for sea. In this respect the actions of the United States were both generous and sensible. But it was a great pity that Dulles's public pronouncements did not leave matters on this economic level, without saying anything about other steps that might or might not be taken. Whatever he said to the British and French in private, he had no need to make any public reference at all to the use or nonuse of force. In fact, if he had been as explicit in private as he went out of his way to be in public, he would have served the cause of peace and reason a great deal better.

At other times and at other places of his own choosing, Dulles had no hesitation in either speaking only part of the truth or rattling his sword. One of his own axioms as a lawyer was that he was under no obligation to point out the weaknesses of his own case to the other side. In spite of his iron streak of conscience, he usually had no moral scruples in taking a legalistic and narrow view of the meaning of words, if it suited him to do so. It was a key to his whole approach to foreign affairs that a bit of brinkmanship was both legitimate and useful. And on top of all this it is a known fact, reported by people in Washington who were in close contact with Dulles during the Suez crisis, that from the start he believed the maritime powers needed to employ the same kind of tactics as those which he himself had used over Indo-China two years before —talk tough, that is, even if you do not mean to go to the limit in the last resort. In 1954 he went on talking tough, even after he felt that Eden had let him down. In 1956, when Eden needed encouragement and a steadying sense of support quite as badly as he needed restraining, Dulles failed him completely.

If Dulles really had been a great man, this would never have happened. Those who share what we now know to have been Dulles's basic view, that force should not have been used in any circumstances, may well argue that he was morally right to proceed as he did. But there are two answers which they should at least consider. First, in that case it was dishonorable to have taken the leading part he did in drawing up the SCUA proposals at the

Second London Conference, since he never had any intention of following them through. Secondly, since at this date, the middle of September, the information in Washington was that the British and French had postponed, if not abandoned, the measures started early in August to use force, Dulles had a certain duty to treat his allies as allies, by giving them the benefit of the doubt instead of positively provoking them to act independently. The truth was, of course, that Dulles did not regard the British and French case as his own, and, in so far as he led them to suppose that he did, he behaved with a chilling dishonesty which has done permanent damage to his own reputation.

The next stage in the Suez tragedy was the discussion of the dispute at last by the United Nations Security Council. On September 23, two days after the end of the Second London Conference and before any further steps could have been taken to implement its decisions about SCUA, the British and French governments asked the Security Council to consider the "situation created by the unilateral action to the Egyptian government in bringing to an end the system of international operation of the Suez Canal ... (under) the Suez Canal Convention of 1888." In going to the United Nations, they beat the Egyptians to it by one day. As ever, Dulles was against their move—which the Labour Opposition in Britain had demanded for a long time—and when it finally came he did not even associate himself with it. He merely noted that they had made it and "accepted" what they had done.

Meanwhile, during the last few days of September and the beginning of October, tension on the Suez Canal itself was rising and the preparations being made by the Suez Canal Users' Association were going badly. It was not until October 1 that a definite meeting was called in London to draw up the details of the SCUA plan. By then, however, Dulles had virtually withdrawn from sponsorship of the scheme, and in his own mind he had now come around to the conviction that the British and French were making specific preparations for the ultimate use of force—as indeed they were. In the uncomfortable act of backing away from even his own conception of SCUA, Dulles managed once again to anger even quite moderate opinion in Britain, as well as the two governments in London and Paris. For by now he appeared to be whittling down even what he himself had previously said, so that his own plans for an economic boycott looked weaker and weaker. Admittedly, it would have been difficult for the United States to impose the kind of Treasury control over shipowners which would have been necessary, for instance, to prevent them paying canal dues to Nasser; but no serious attempt was even made to devise, let alone to put into operation, any such control. Dulles, while pretending that SCUA had not changed in character, was already talking as if only time and luck could bring Nasser to any agreement.

It was at this point that, on October 2, Dulles chose to use yet another of his unfortunate press conferences to add the third in the series of striking phrases with which he had managed to undercut any semblance of serious American pressure on Egypt throughout the crisis. "There is talk," he said, "about teeth being pulled out of the plan. But I know of no teeth. There were no teeth in it so far as I am aware." This seemed to be going beyond even the point of denial which he had reached previously. Many people to this day have regarded this statement as showing a curious political naïveté, since to deal in this way with any kind of authoritarian regime, whether Communist, nationalist, or anything else, showed either ignorance or an unwillingness to learn from the lessons of the past. But Dulles was far from being either ignorant or naive, and by this stage the only adequate explanation of his attitude would seem to be that it was governed by his personal anger with Eden—which was equaled only by Eden's anger with Dulles.

When the UN Security Council met on October 2, Dulles stood apart from the British and French and urged strongly on Dag Hammarskjold, the Secretary General, that the meetings of the Council should take place in private. Ostensibly this was because it would offer more chance of reaching agreement, but in reality because he wanted to minimize the occasion, to reduce the publicity given to the British and French case, and to avoid the embarrassment of holding a public United Nations discussion on this highly contentious subject in New York itself in the middle of the Presidential campaign. The debate therefore opened in private, although both the British and French positively wanted the kind of world platform which the Security Council provided, in order to express their point of view. It was well over a week before the sessions became public. By that time six principles had been more or less agreed for the operation of the Canal. These were that:

1. There should be free and open transit through the Canal without discrimination, overt or covert.
2. Egypt's sovereignty should be respected.
3. The operation of the Canal should be insulated from the politics of any one country.
4. The manner of fixing tolls and charges should be signed by agreement between Egypt and the users.
5. A fair proportion of the dues should be allotted to development.
6. In case of dispute, the matter should be settled by arbitration.

The public session of the Security Council opened with the discussion of a resolution put forward by Britain and France, designed to carry out these principles. This was virtually in two parts. The first named the six principles, while the second made two specific recommendations. One ran that the Security Council *"invites* the Egyptian government to make known promptly its proposals for a system meeting the requirements set out above and providing guarantees to users not less effective than those sought by the proposals of the eighteen powers." The other said that the Security Council *"considers* that ... the Canals Users' Association ... and the competent Egyptian authorities should co-operate to insure the satisfactory operation of the Canal and free and open transit through the Canal in accordance with the 1888 convention."

Not surprisingly this was too much for Russia, and Mr. Shepilov, the Soviet Foreign Minister, fiercely attacked the resolution on the grounds that its second part amounted to "coercion of Egypt." Dulles, swinging back in a sense to his moods of the two London Conferences, went along with the resolution. After a brief discussion, however, it became clear that the whole exercise had become academic, since the Russians were going to use their veto. In the event, all the members passed the preamble with its six principles; but the effective part of the resolution was vetoed by the Soviet Union, the seventy-eighth such veto that Russia had imposed.

This, in effect, was the end, so far as the efforts to deal with the Suez crisis by diplomacy were concerned. Following the Security Council debate, there was a period of a fortnight when a great deal of useless coming and going took place between the capitals, and during which a flurry of activity in the Middle East itself did nothing to soften the news that now the Egyptians were once again stepping up their *fedayeen* raids against Israel.

The only outstanding event was the famous visit to Paris on October 16 by Sir Anthony Eden and Selwyn Lloyd to see Mollet and Pineau, in the immediate aftermath of their common dismay at the collapse of the Security Council's activities. Although the full truth about this meeting will probably not be known for many years, its significance is that the fateful decision was undoubtedly made there to go ahead with the Suez military operation, whether or not the French told the British the full details of Israel's intentions. It was also decided that, in view of Dulles's attitude over the last few weeks, Washington should not be kept informed of all the Anglo-French plans. Extraordinarily enough, Dulles appears to have been genuinely puzzled by the lack of information that came to him from London and Paris as a result. Events had reached a decisive turning point which, quite apart from any question of sense of morality, he found it difficult to understand.

At the end of the month the explosion took place. On October 29 the Israeli forces crossed the frontier into Egypt and began their swift and brilliant attack across the Sinai Peninsula. David Ben-Gurion, the Israeli Prime Minister, had told the French what he was going to do, because he needed and obtained from them a guarantee of French air cover for the civil population, if that should be required during the operation. On October 30 the British and French issued their ultimatum to both Israel and Egypt, its terms being that both sides should stop forthwith all warlike action by land, sea, and air, and should withdraw their military forces for a distance of ten miles from the Suez Canal; that, in order to guarantee freedom of transit through the Canal by ships of all nations, Egypt should agree that Anglo-French forces would temporarily move into key positions at Port Said, Ismailia, and Suez; that both Egypt and Israel must reply to this communication within twelve hours; and that, if they did not or if they rejected these undertakings, British and French forces would intervene in such strength as to secure compliance.

Israel accepted on condition that Egypt did so too. But Egypt rejected the ultimatum and the die was cast. Then began the harrowing week in which British and French military action was started by means of air raids against Egyptian airfields and other military targets on the evening of October 30. By the evening of November 2 the Israeli attack over the Sinai Peninsula had been completely successful. Everywhere Egyptian forces were in full retreat, and the Israeli Army was very nearly on the banks of the Suez Canal. For the Anglo-French forces, however, it was not to be until November 5 that the first paratroops landed at Port Said. Commandos were then put ashore from the sea on November 6, and that evening, when their leading units were just short of Ismailia, a cease-fire was accepted.

This cease-fire was the outcome of a week of frenzied activity at the United Nations in which Dulles, together with Cabot Lodge, the American delegate to the UN, led the attack against Britain and France in both the Security Council and the General Assembly. When the British and French had issued their ultimatum, both President Eisenhower and John Foster Dulles had been seized with a personal fury. For Eisenhower there was both the moral indignation that force should have been used at all, and, although American intelligence reports had naturally suggested what was brewing, a shock of surprise that the worst had actually happened. In addition, what particularly angered the President was the point about his having gone to the abortive Summit the year before to help Eden's election, while Eden would not apparently make any concession to help his.

Dulles, for his part, felt a righteously outraged venom at the way the West's use of force had undermined its moral position in relation to Russia. He also bitterly resented being thwarted in the one aim which he personally had really had in mind for the whole of the fatal three months, avoidance of the use of force. At this point, therefore, the President and his Secretary of State reacted violently. Far now from even trying to keep in touch with London and Paris, they deliberately let the bridges go. For Dulles it was the fourth and final decision to put Eden and himself on opposite sides. Now he was no longer just going to withdraw his support from what Eden was doing. He resolved to place himself at the head of the opposition and rub the British noses in the dirt.

Dulles was never someone who readily stood apart if there was a chance of plunging in. Once he felt that he must reject the course the British and French were following, the uncompromising side of his own character took over. Once he had decided to oppose, he had to oppose remorselessly and ruthlessly. In analyzing his motives for taking the lead against the British and French in the United Nations, therefore, many different elements must be taken into account. There was his own Puritanism, stirred by a sense of moral outrage. There was his impulse not only to defeat an opponent but to crush him. There was an irresistible temptation to use his priceless opportunity to prove to the British that they were no longer a great power which could act without America. There was his contempt for Eden and a desire to teach Eden a lesson. In addition, Dulles had his own views on actual policy to support. He had been against the use of force from the beginning and he must now justify his attitude. He had throughout taken the view that, since Nasser could not be destroyed, he must be won over. Lastly, on the one hand, he believed that the British were simply mistaken in their reading of the Middle East situation and they must be shown how wrong they were, while, on the other, he felt as so many people did, that, even in the detailed operational handling of the Suez invasion, Eden and Mollet had behaved with a sickening disregard for morality and truth.

For all these reasons, at the meeting of the Security Council on October 30, the day that the Anglo-French ultimatum was issued, Dulles instructed the American representative, Cabot Lodge, to call for positive action against the British and French. Lodge responded with vigor, declaring:

> Failure of the Council to react at this time would be an avoidance of the responsibilities that maintain peace and security. The government of the United States feels it imperative that the Council act in the promptest manner to determine whether a breach of the peace has occurred, to have a cease-fire ordered immediately, and to obtain the withdrawal of Israeli forces behind the frontier lines. Nothing else will suffice.

It was at this stage that the British and French vetoed the resolution which the United States had put forward, and the breakdown across the Atlantic became absolute and complete.

The following day, October 31, when the Security Council met again, Yugoslavia thereupon moved a resolution calling for an emergency session of the General Assembly by invoking for the very first time the famous resolution of 1950, which had become known as the "Uniting for Peace" resolution. This laid it down that "If the Security Council, because of lack of unanimity of the permanent members, fails to exercise its primary responsibility for the maintenance of international peace and security in any case where there appears to be a threat to peace ... the General Assembly shall consider the matter immediately with a view to making recommendations to members for collective measures." This Yugoslav resolution was supported by the necessary seven votes in the Security Council, with only Britain and France opposing. America, like Russia, voted for it.

When the General Assembly of the United Nations met in emergency session next day, November 1, Dulles made one of the best known of his many speeches in that unique body—and also the last for quite some time. It was his "heavy heart" speech. In spite of all that had happened, in the sense that he had condemned the actions of the British and French in his own mind more and more as the weeks went by, he showed a good deal of emotion as he said:

> I doubt whether any delegate ever spoke from this platform with as heavy a heart as I have brought here tonight. We speak of a matter of vital importance, where the United States finds itself unable to agree with three nations with whom it has ties, deep friendship, admiration and respect, and two of whom constitute our oldest, our most trusted and reliable allies. . . . Because it seems to us that disagreement involves principles which far transcend the immediate issue, we feel impelled to make our point of view known to the world. . . . The resort to force, the violent armed attack by three of our members upon a fourth, cannot but be treated as a grave error inconsistent with the principles and purposes of the Charter, and one which, if persisted in, will gravely undermine our Charter and this Organization.

Sad as Dulles was, he made no reference to any of the steps by which he himself had played such a very prominent part in each stage of the crisis. Instead he went on:

If we do not act and act promptly, if we do not act with sufficient unanimity of opinion so that our recommendations carry a real influence, there is great danger that what has started, and what has been called a police action, may develop into something far more grave. Even if that does not happen, the apparent impotence of this Organization to deal with this situation may set a precedent which will lead other nations to attempt to take in their hands the remedying of what they believe to be their own injustices. If that happens, the future is dark indeed.

After a highly emotional debate, in which the ear of the Afro-Asian countries was sought by both the Russians and the Americans, an American resolution was carried by sixty-four votes to five, with six abstentions. This resolution condemned the British, French, and Israeli governments and called for a cease-fire, irrespective of the issues which had caused the hostilities. The three countries which voted against the resolution besides Britain and France were Israel itself, Australia and New Zealand. Those which abstained were Canada, South Africa, Belgium, Holland, Portugal, and Laos. Neither Britain nor France complied with the resolution, and the delicate yet hamfisted bombing of Egyptian airfields continued, in preparation for the landings at Port Said which were still four days away. The Israelis, however, having completed their task of destroying the Egyptian Army, which had menaced them with its aggressive *fedayeen* raids, complied with the cease-fire twenty-four hours later. The Egyptians for their part saw fit to take this as the opportunity to start the vast and maliciously destructive operation of blocking the Suez Canal with sunken ships, thus insuring that this great international waterway would be out of commission for many months to come.

The next day the General Assembly met again. A number of resolutions were adopted on November 3 and 4, among the most notable of which was one sponsored by nineteen Asian and African countries, demanding a time limit for compliance with the original American resolution; this was carried by a majority of fifty-seven to five with twelve abstentions. Another was a Canadian resolution, adopted this time by fifty-seven to nil with nineteen abstentions, setting up a United Nations Command to take over in the Canal Zone with General Burns at its head. Meanwhile, within a few hours of this happening, Khrushchev threatened the British and French with direct attack by Soviet rockets, and at the same time the French franc and the pound sterling came under very heavy pressure on the international exchanges. As a result of all these factors all fighting stopped on the Canal the following day—to the astonishment of many of the authorities in Washington.

Dulles by now was not in Washington. He was recovering in a New York hospital from his first operation for cancer. His "heavy heart" speech had been late on the Thursday night. The following night at about two o'clock in the morning he suddenly felt severe pains in his side. They got so bad so quickly that his doctor was called, and he was in an ambulance on his way to hospital before dawn broke. Apparently his cancer was such that, if it had not come on so suddenly, he would probably have been dead within six months. As it was, the operation was entirely successful and by the Monday Dulles was dictating notes from his bed, with instructions to the Acting Secretary of State, Herbert Hoover, and to Cabot Lodge.

In spite of his extraordinary resilience and a swift recovery during the next four weeks, however, Dulles was in fact out of active politics for the time being. If he had not been, a good many people believe, events might not have continued to take such a drastically harsh course against London and Paris. Dulles with all his faults was still capable of taking a wide and long-term view. Both Herbert Hoover and Cabot Lodge were narrower in outlook, less experienced and much less able. Dulles, for instance, is reported by those close to him to have reacted quite strongly when he heard about the Soviet rocket threats to Britain and France. The one and only thing which Eden had asked of the United States, in the last period before the Suez attack, had been that, if the Soviet Union came up with any new and aggressive line, the United States should not remain aloof. "We don't want your assistance," Eden had said in effect, "except to take care of the Bear." And this in the last resort Dulles would have done. But in the event it was not required. As Washington saw the situation, Eden lost his nerve at the last moment. If he had not done so, there was nothing irrevocable to stop him going on, and, if he had succeeded, there is evidence for thinking that Dulles would probably have been among those Americans who would have accepted the result.

Some doctors deny that there could have been any connection between the strain of the last few weeks and the onset of Dulles's cancer. But the more experience one has of the effects of the mind on the body, the less one feels inclined to believe them. In any case the removal of Dulles from the scene marked the end of the main part of the Suez crisis. From now on it was a question of picking up the bits, and in terms of Anglo-American relations these were not destined to be put together again for many long months. With the cease-fire, the establishment of the United Nations force, and the gradual clearing up of the situation in the Canal itself, a new phase had begun. In this, after an interval, Dulles was to play once again a major role. But, while for the present even he was out of it, never again were relations between himself and Sir Anthony Eden, the two chief protagonists in the long decline of Anglo-American understanding, to play the part that they had in the past. Whether or not Suez brought on Dulles's illness, which in the end was to prove fatal to him, it was almost immediately decisive in the case of Eden's. Within a few weeks he came near to having yet another, a third, very serious operation, and he was forced to retire from being Prime Minister, his life crippled and his career ruined.

CHAPTER 14

The Year of the Critics

ALTHOUGH Dulles had had the general backing of American public opinion during the Suez affair, a reaction came after the crisis had burst. When he returned to his desk at the beginning of December, he entered upon one of the bleakest periods of his whole career. Everything seemed to have combined against him at the same time, including his own health. Suez was only one element in the problem, though on that alone he was being blamed for having miscalculated in the Middle East, broken up the Western alliance in Europe, and given the Russians a clear road to gain influence and prestige at America's expense. The Soviet standing in the world had, admittedly, received a heavy blow from Moscow's cruel and cynical repression of the Hungarian revolution. But in terms of Dulles's own aims, policies and recorded word, he was in no position whatever to score. All that he had ever said about liberation and the rolling back of Soviet rule in Eastern Europe was thrown in his face by the agonizing, yet inevitable, decision that the United States could not and would not interfere to help the Hungarians. Everywhere, it seemed, American policy was failing, the prestige of the United States was at a new low, and the ebullient, cock-a-hoop Soviet leadership of Khrushchev was on the offensive, based on growing Russian nuclear and missile power, on Moscow's world-wide drive to rival American economic and technical aid, and above all on a sense that the Soviet Union was gaining the initiative.

It may never be clear quite how far American propaganda was responsible for misleading the Hungarians into believing that they would receive positive Western military aid if they revolted against their Russian masters. By 1956 Dulles himself had already begun to realize that it was foolish to encourage hopes which could not be fulfilled; besides being heartless and inhuman, such a policy would lead to disillusionment and the actual weakening rather than strengthening of opposition to Communism. But some of the American sponsors of Radio Free Europe undoubtedly showed less sense of responsibility and rather fewer scruples, with the result that, while the revolt would have taken place in any case, there were longing hopes not only in Hungary, but elsewhere in Eastern Europe, which were bound to be cruelly and bitterly dashed. For one brief moment people held their breath as they waited to see if America would act after all, this America which, to many of those in the bottomless despair of Europe's political jails and refugee camps, has for years stood in the sunshine of limitless hope, a quite unreal kind of symbol for all that mankind has dreamed about and striven for through its ages of mortal suffering. But, when it came to the point, the United States recognized that no action could be taken without the gravest risk of widespread war.

The big question mark is whether the West could have deterred Russia from crushing the Hungarian rebellion if it had not been wracked by its own torture of Suez. If the West had been united and resolute at that moment, would the Russians in fact have acted as they did in Hungary? Although no one was put more on the spot by the combination of Suez and Hungary at the same time than Eisenhower and his advisers, Dulles himself never tried to defend America's inability to rescue the Hungarians by claiming that the Western rift over Suez prevented it. The Suez crisis almost certainly played a part in helping Khrushchev to make up his mind to act as he did in Hungary. At the same time the logic of the local situation there was so strong that, in the light of present knowledge, there seem to be no grounds for believing that he would in fact have ended by acting differently. No Communist-held territory has ever yet been formally abandoned (except a few square miles in Korea); no Western interference in a Communist East European state has ever so far looked remotely possible without going to war with the Soviet Union. And, in spite of the moral odium into which Britain and France fell over Suez, for Khrushchev the issue in Hungary was quite distinct and separate, representing a relatively temporary risk that he felt he could afford to run with world opinion, at a time when Soviet prestige was rising on almost all other fronts. Eastern Europe has indeed become the Achilles heel of the Communist empire, a source of potential weakness, instead of a source of reliable strength. But it is idle to pretend that the Suez crisis was the cause.

The Hungarian crisis, which Dulles was compelled to observe mainly from his hospital bed and during his period of convalescence, did have the effect on him, however, of making him want to start rebuilding Western unity. The very week of his return to active duty, therefore, he flew across the Atlantic once again on December 10 to attend the ministerial session of the Atlantic Council in Paris. Contrary to previous practice, he refused to meet Selwyn Lloyd and Pineau together, but, for the first time since Suez, he came face to face with them individually and discussed with each the problems of restoring confidence and consultations within NATO and of reopening the Suez Canal. Dulles was henceforward going to work for both vital objectives in a serious and chastened mood.

At the same time it was more than his own involved nature could accept to wipe the slate clean and forgive. Accordingly, when the Atlantic Council formally opened on December 11, he showed that, although practical efforts were now necessary to repair the damage that had been done, as a moralist at any rate he had much to say. He made in fact the kind of speech which no American spokesman had ever previously made about his two biggest allies in the Western alliance. He criticized the Anglo-French intervention in Egypt and gave a fresh outline of American policy at the United Nations, declaring that he was totally opposed to the use of force as an instrument of national policy. He went on to say that the Western world now had its greatest opportunity since the war for seizing the moral leadership of humanity and for helping to liberate the suffering peoples of Eastern Europe. Recapturing to some extent the attitude he had adopted in the American electoral campaign of 1952, he used the tragic events of Hungary to drive home the lesson that every moral support should be given to the forces in Eastern Europe which were attempting to undermine the Soviet system.

Unfortunately, Dulles allowed another side both of his own

nature and indeed of the realities of the situation to appear when he went on to speak about the role of the United States. He reminded his listeners that America had treaty responsibilities with thirty other nations besides those in NATO, that it therefore had the right to act in urgent cases without consulting NATO first, and that consequently its special position gave it special rights. This glimpse of power politics brought wry smiles to the faces of some of the British and French. Dulles was virtually saying that, although everyone else must toe the line, the United States was under no such obligation. Again, what he said was, of course, true in the sense that the United States is the essential pillar of the whole Western position. But, after all that had happened over Suez, it hardly seemed the moment for Dulles to mark his return to the scene in quite such a sanctimonious way.

Although Dulles said that Western unity should be repaired, in the Middle East the Americans continued to stand apart from the British and French. But there are grounds for believing that, if Dulles himself had remained in charge throughout, the American position might not have been so unswervingly hostile. The basic dilemma was whether the British and French either should or could lay down any conditions for the withdrawal of their forces; and whether in turn the United Nations either should or would accept the conditions demanded by Egypt, before any practical work could be begun to remove the block ships and to clear the Suez Canal for international traffic.

At first the British and French tried to insist that their forces would be withdrawn, only when the United Nations force could "assume effectively the tasks assigned to it under the Assembly resolution," these including steps to reopen the Canal and to secure free navigation through it. But the Egyptian attitude was to refuse to allow salvage even to begin until all foreign troops had been withdrawn; and since this was in effect endorsed by the United Nations, the only way out of the stalemate was for London and Paris to give way. Thus, under American sponsorship the whole atmosphere at the United Nations, in the weeks after Suez, was to condemn the British and French to such a degree that they were prevented from having any hand in the re-establishment of the Suez Canal as an international waterway. For many weeks the only salvage vessels actually available were those which had been brought to the canal by the British and French, but all through this period they had to lie at anchor without taking any hand in the raising of sunken ships.

With the opening of 1957 the second four years of the Eisenhower Administration began. After his re-election with overwhelming support, President Eisenhower had no hesitation whatever in reappointing John Foster Dulles as his Secretary of State. For Anglo-American relations the new start was marked with almost equal sharpness by the fact that only a few days before, on January 9, Sir Anthony Eden finally had to resign as Britain's Prime Minister on genuine grounds of health, being succeeded by Harold Macmillan. Dulles himself was not to survive to the end of the second Eisenhower Administration, but there could be no question that his relationship with Harold Macmillan gradually reforged at least a working link between London and Washington.

Selwyn Lloyd, who continued as British Foreign Secretary because Macmillan neither wished nor could afford to defy those elements in the Conservative Party which had stood by Eden over Suez, always had a rather uncertain position in Dulles's mind. Towards the close of his life Dulles got on well with Selwyn Lloyd and a real affection sprang up between them, in spite of the bitterness with which each had regarded the other at the time of Suez. But Dulles always tended to feel that Selwyn Lloyd never had any clear policy, was not serious, and jumped around "like a man on a trapeze." Dulles was also uncomfortable with him, in never quite knowing where he stood or what responsibilities he really had.

Dulles respected strong downright men, and it was extremely unfortunate for Anglo-American relations that, during virtually the whole of his time as Secretary of State, the only person who came into that category was Sir Winston Churchill; and then, although Dulles had quite a good relationship with Churchill— apart from some plain speaking in which each of them once or twice indulged—Churchill's operative relationship was direct with Eisenhower rather than through Dulles.

Four days before Eden resigned he had some satisfaction in hearing, while he was still at Number 10 Downing Street, the news of President Eisenhower's special message to Congress of January 5,

1957. This message contained the announcement of what became known as the Eisenhower Doctrine, in which the United States promised American economic and possibly military aid to any nation in the Middle East that asked for it, undertaking in particular to employ American armed force "to secure and protect the territorial integrity and political independence of nations requesting such aid against overt armed aggression from any nation controlled by international Communism." The Eisenhower Doctrine never really stayed the course, but at the time it looked and was a revolutionary change in American foreign policy. Dulles and Eisenhower were proposing direct intervention in the Middle East, to a degree which appeared to deny much that Dulles had said in public during the previous few months. In reality this was not quite the case, since the essence of the Eisenhower Doctrine was that intervention should take place only at the invitation of a government on the spot.

The fact was that Dulles had begun to realize that his policy of dissociating himself from Britain and France had helped to forge a chain of unfortunate circumstances, in which the Russians were gaining a position of quite unprecedented prestige in the Middle East. As a result of the Soviet intervention against Britain and France at the time of Suez, and of their attitude since, the cry in the Arab countries was "the Russians have saved us." Dulles concocted the Eisenhower Doctrine, therefore, for the single purpose of fighting Communism. But in that it involved America directly in the cold war in the Middle East, it was the precise opposite of his original thesis, that, by the United States remaining out of the area, the cold war itself could be kept from affecting events there—as had been the case in Stalin's time.

The Eisenhower Doctrine had a mixed reception abroad, being welcomed in London and Paris, as well as in Australia, Iran, Turkey, Iraq, and Lebanon. Turkish spokesmen went so far as to say that it "vindicated Sir Anthony Eden's policy and the Anglo-French Suez action." In contrast, the announcement of the Doctrine met with a guarded lack of enthusiasm in Cairo and was sharply attacked in Moscow, which in many ways thereby justified Dulles's change of front. Inside the United States, however, the reaction was none too good. President Eisenhower was not very warmly received by Congress when he came in person to present his special message, an act which, occurring only a few days before the customary Presidential State of the Union Message, did in fact steal the thunder of the traditional procedure.

It fell to Dulles therefore to argue the case in detail for the new Doctrine against a somewhat critical reaction. On January 7 he made a statement to the Foreign Affairs Committee of the House of Representatives, in which he said that it was his definite belief that the Middle East would be lost to the Communists, if this American economic and military aid were not forthcoming. He added:

> And if it is lost, it will be the greatest victory that the Soviet Communists could ever have gained, because if they could get into this area they have in effect gotten Western Europe without war.

It was, however, a few days later, on January 14, that Dulles ran head-on into the main storm, when he gave testimony before a joint session of the Senate Foreign Relations Committee and the Senate Armed Services Committee. On being closely questioned by Senators Humphrey, Fulbright, and Russell, he declared that there was no present plan to station American troops in the Middle East, but that there was a very great likelihood of American troops fighting in the Middle East, if Congress rejected the resolution embodying the Eisenhower Doctrine. There was, however, very little likelihood of such an eventuality if the resolution were adopted.

Senator Fulbright demanded that Dulles should justify the whole course of his recent Middle East Policy, and he declared in the name of the Democratic Party that "a disastrous and remarkable collapse of our relations with our closest allies has taken place under the direction of the present Secretary of State. . . ." Although Dulles successfully resisted Fulbright's demand for a White Paper on American Middle East policy, he did accept the preparation of a chronological statement outlining the sequence of events from 1946 to the outbreak of the Suez crisis. Other Democrats joined in the hunt. Dulles's good faith was called in question, as well as his competence. Former President Truman called the Eisenhower

Doctrine "too little and too late," and Adlai Stevenson remarked with his customary wit that "the first vacuum that should be filled is in the State Department and not in the Middle East."

After nine weeks of acrimonious wrangling the Eisenhower Doctrine was passed into law. But this required the President once again to throw into the scales his own full backing of Dulles, with the statement that the Secretary of State was "an outstanding, dedicated man, doing a terrific job under difficulties"—which was, of course, entirely true. Eisenhower let it be known that there was no question whatever of Dulles being sacked, nor would he let him resign. So Dulles survived. This was certainly a period, however, in which he was not far from falling out with Congress in just the way that Dean Acheson had done, and which he had made it one of his prime aims to avoid.

It was during an argument with Senator Morse, in the course of the hearings on the Eisenhower Doctrine, that Dulles came out with one of those classic observations which showed him at his worst. Morse had said that Americans would surely not be required to "go it alone," in fighting on behalf of any Middle East state, while their allies stood by and did nothing. Having already been pressed in cross-examination on his Middle East policy by a number of other Senators, Dulles produced the remark that American soldiers, if involved in fighting under the Eisenhower Doctrine, would naturally feel happier if they did not stand shoulder to shoulder with British and French troops. After all that had so recently happened, it was understandable that, in trying to design a policy to influence Arab opinion, Dulles should wish to follow a tactic of nonalignment with Britain and France. But the remark was a gratuitous insult, which was widely quoted in London and Paris; and it was regarded as typical of a man who, even as late as this, in January, 1957, could still not bring himself to try to repair the Western alliance with any degree of sincerity.

A simpler impulse to punish and condemn also dominated Dulles's attitude, and hence his policy, towards Israel. He had come to power considerably more free from any political obligations towards the Jewish community in the United States than had some of his predecessors, and he had long felt that America's traditional association with the Israeli point of view was a danger-

ous handicap, in trying to compete with the Russians for the hand
of Arab friendship. And whereas his personal bitterness had been
mainly reserved for the British and French at the actual peak of
the Suez crisis, his own basic urge to moralize and preach against
the wrongdoer now found as righteous a target in Israel as it did
in Britain and France. Accordingly, Dulles felt that the United
States must lean over backwards to dissociate itself from any support of Israel; and, at the expense of any proper recognition of
some of the realities in the Middle East, he was absolutely adamant
that Israel should withdraw from every vantage point that it had
gained during the fighting in November. Considered on its merits,
this was unfair as well as unwise. Eden and Mollet may be ar-
raigned for imperialism and dishonesty, but Ben-Gurion's position
was quite different. He was Prime Minister of a little country
whose very existence was gravely threatened, and against whom the
real aggression had begun long before, in the form of the deliberate
Egyptian *fedayeen* raids across the Israeli frontier. In 1956 Israel
fought for nothing less than its life, and Dulles's deliberate victim-
ization of the Israelis after their successful battle showed a hard
and mean streak in his character, which it is difficult to condone.

There were three points at issue in the struggle to get Israel to
withdraw. The first was whether Israel should give up possession
of the commanding position it had captured at the entrance to the
Gulf of Akaba called Sharm el-Sheikh. From this position the
Egyptians had been able to dominate the entrance to the Gulf, and
hence to render the little new Israeli port of Eilat useless. The
second question was that of getting Israeli ships once more through
the Suez Canal. And the third was whether Israeli troops should
evacuate the Gaza strip, without the condition being imposed that
Egypt should not reoccupy it. It had been from here that many of
the *fedayeen* raids had been launched against Israeli territory in
the month preceding Suez. The importance of the first two points
was that, if neither aim could be secured, Israel's whole commercial
drive to build up desperately needed trade with Asia would be
blocked. At no stage, however, was Dulles willing to give Israel
any proper guarantee that any of its three aims would be met. As
events have turned out, Israeli shipping is still even today unable
to pass through the Suez Canal; but the freedom of the interna-

tional waterway of the Gulf of Akaba has in practice been secured, though it has rested on a somewhat tenuous basis. What Israel gained from the Suez affair was nevertheless of inestimable military and political importance. The Arab states realized that they could not attack Israel with impunity, and that, if the great powers did not intervene from outside, Israel was militarily strong enough to defeat them decisively in the field.

February and March of 1957 were at long last the months of reconciliation. First came the French. On February 26 the French Prime Minister, M. Mollet, and his Foreign Minister, M. Pineau, visited Washington for discussions with the President and the Secretary of State. They discussed the European Common Market and Euratom, NATO problems, the question of Algeria and other African territories, and the Middle East. The atmosphere was subdued, but friendly, and at the end of the meetings the sharpest of the hatchets had been buried. Dulles himself was now beginning to be back in form again, and on March 11 he flew to Australia to attend a SEATO meeting in Canberra, at which the British representative was Lord Home, at that time Secretary of State for Commonwealth Relations. Then, not quite a month after the French ministers had visited Washington, Eisenhower and Dulles left for Bermuda on March 21 to meet the new British Prime Minister, Harold Macmillan, and his Foreign Secretary, still Selwyn Lloyd.

Considering all that had happened, President Eisenhower was making a generous gesture in agreeing to go himself to a meeting on non-American soil, and it was in this spirit that the talks were held. For Macmillan, this was the first step on the road back, the road he had set out to tread with determination from the moment that he became Prime Minister. Like Churchill, his mother had been American, and he realized in any case that the breakdown in Anglo-American relations had removed the linchpin from Britain's traditional foreign policy. These Bermuda talks did begin to repair the damage that had been done and even Dulles, who was not exactly the life and the soul of the party, came away feeling that a corner had been turned.

It would have been quite wrong, however, to expect this one meeting to make up for all the spasms of nearly a year of crisis; and it was not until after the royal visit in the autumn that Anglo-American relations really got back on the track again. Little of significance arose out of the actual discussions, the only two points of note being an American undertaking to supply the British with a number of medium-range missiles, and Dulles's promise that the United States would not "participate actively in the military committee of the Baghdad Pact." With the coming of the Eisenhower Doctrine, he no longer took quite the same jaundiced view of this alliance that he had done previously. Perhaps it was a happy and symbolic augury that, only a few days after this Bermuda Conference, the Suez Canal was finally reopened on April 10 for ships of maximum draft after six months of closure.

After Bermuda Mr. and Mrs. Dulles managed to get away for one of their longer visits to Duck Island. They flew out across Lake Ontario in the amphibian, as they always did, and had ten days alone on the island, with Dulles sharing in the domestic work between spells of relaxed contemplation and note-making on his famous yellow pad.

Dulles returned from Duck Island much refreshed, to find yet another Middle East crisis breaking over his head. Early in April, fighting broke out in Jordan between left-wing elements and the supporters of King Hussein. This time, however, the United States was fully prepared. Rightly regarding this as the first major challenge to the Eisenhower Doctrine, Dulles and the President issued a statement, after a telephone conversation between them, declaring that they regarded "the independence and integrity of Jordan as vital." They also ordered units of the American Sixth Fleet to sail at once from the French Riviera for the Eastern Mediterranean; a later announcement was made from Washington that American troops were ready to be parachuted into Jordan "in a matter of days." The effect was immediate. In spite of continued instability in Jordan, nothing further came of the crisis. America's realization that the spread of violently left-wing nationalism was playing into Russian hands had brought a new factor into Middle East politics. For the time being the Eisenhower Doctrine worked.

Compared with 1956, 1957 was a year without any central theme. Dulles, however, was kept extremely busy. He was also constantly under attack from his critics in the American press and in the Democratic party. This was now Eisenhower's second term, and in spite of the President's own popularity the Republicans had lost their former hold on Congress and were much more on the defensive. After the wave of criticism which Dulles had encountered during the winter his position eased somewhat during the spring and summer, only to reach another peak of hostility in the autumn. Indeed, it was in the latter part of 1957 that Dulles probably came under the most persistent and penetrating attack of his career. This was a period of declining American prestige and humiliating frustration for the Administration's foreign policies. It only needed the launching of Russia's first sputnik in October, 1957, to cast Americans into their worst state of gloom and self-doubt for several years. Fortunately for Dulles, his own reputation began to rise again at this point, since he was personally attacked by Khrushchev. From then on, until his death in the first half of 1959, his star slowly rose to a new zenith.

As if to symbolize Dulles's difficulties with his friends as well as with his critics, the month of May, 1957, even saw one of the very few occasions in the long association between Dulles and Adenauer when the Chancellor's chronic suspicion of Washington suddenly leaped into flame. Adenauer had had very little sympathy for the disarmament talks, which had been going on in London since March 18 under the auspices of the United Nations. The flare-up accordingly started on May 8, when President Eisenhower answered a question from journalists about apparent recent Soviet efforts to revive the Eden Plan for a demilitarized zone in West and East Germany, saying that the United States would be very sympathetic in studying any proposals for test areas of disarmament. Although Adenauer had been meeting Macmillan in Bonn only a few days before, the old man's suspicions were instantly aroused both of the British, whom he distrusted anyway, and, what was worse, of the Americans, on whom his whole policy rested.

When the German government asked officially for an explanation, Dulles attempted to settle the matter on May 14 by saying: "We do not accept any arrangement which is based on the present partition of Germany ... (and) ... in anything which touched directly or indirectly upon Germany and its prospects for reunification, we would act only in the closest concert with Chancellor

Adenauer." It took some time for German suspicions to die down. Bulganin must have been very happy at the amount of quite unnecessary friction that had been produced within the Western alliance simply through his mentioning again the proposals which Eden had originally put to the Summit conference of 1955.

German sensitivities had been affected by another development, over which Dulles had no control, as well as by the disarmament talks. This had been the announcement in a British Defence White Paper at the beginning of April, 1957, of the new policy of Duncan Sandys, the British Defence Minister, under which greater reliance would be placed on nuclear weapons, and certain financial and manpower cuts would be made in British conventional forces. Dulles and others in Washington had deplored the effect that this might have on other members of NATO, but they had accepted the policy in the sense that, while there was nothing much they could do about it in any case, this was the period in which the claims of America's own conventional forces were at their lowest priority.

Thus, the first half of 1957 marked a kind of final flowering of the special nuclear emphasis in which Dulles himself had so often indulged. It was, incidentally, also the time when the first tests of the British H-bomb were being carried out at Christmas Island in the Pacific. Although the peak of American nuclear superiority over Russia had in fact passed, there was still a feeling that more could be done with nuclear weapons than was justified. Since then, as thought has matured both on the balance of terror between East and West, and on the best balance between nuclear and conventional forces, the tide of opinion has gradually flowed back again towards more and more emphasis on conventional weapons.

Adenauer was in fact somewhat out of step with the Americans, the British, and the French, in continuing to resist any disarmament proposals which did not at the same time move directly towards a solution of the German question. This issue of priorities had worried him ever since the summit conference, and he was to take some time yet before he really swung round to accepting the view that only through a relaxation of tension by some measure of disarmament could progress be made on German unity. Dulles was himself always skeptical of the prospects for disarmament, but he had been quite sincere in favoring the negotiations, which had begun at Lancaster House in London between members of the Sub-Committee of the United Nations Disarmament Commission on March 18. What had angered him, however, so much that by July 29 he arrived in London to take part himself, had been the behavior of the leader of the American delegation, Harold Stassen. Although Stassen had handled the early part of the negotiations with considerable skill, he had run into trouble in trying to hustle them along by holding separate one-to-one private talks with Zorin, the Soviet delegate, thus bypassing other members of the Sub-Committee. This had naturally aroused the distrust of the other members, and there had also been some danger of Stassen revealing too much of the American plans. Yet in spite of his anger, Dulles only really condemned Stassen for being a "too-eager beaver."

As Dulles found when he got to London, these Lancaster House talks were destined to be peculiarly sterile. As the weeks had progressed, confusion had increased. Even the search for some limited proposition which might start the ball rolling had been extraordinarily difficult. The two simplest ideas were each open to equally simple objections. To stop nuclear tests, it was felt on the American side, risked helping the Soviet stockpile to catch up with the American. Yet to halt bomb production without any form of inspection seemed equally to play into Soviet hands. Dulles at one point reintroduced the American "open skies" proposal, but it was later abandoned, in recognition of the fact that the United States did not really have anything suitable to offer in return for a sacrifice by the Russians of their biggest secret weapon—secrecy.

The major issue was the suspension of nuclear tests. Already at this stage American fears took the form they have done ever since, namely that a long test ban, without any inspection, would enable the Soviet Union to steal a march on the United States by carrying out tests in secret, possibly underground. At the outset of the talks, therefore, Stassen had had instructions to begin with a proposal for a ban on all further production of nuclear weapons, recognizing that existing stockpiles could not be reliably inspected. Zorin retaliated with the stock Soviet demand for total abolition of all nuclear arms. Then, with the Russians having just completed an important series of nuclear tests themselves, he proposed an immediate suspension of all further tests. The Western reply was that any such ban should be linked to the stopping of the further production of nuclear weapons, and to other so-called "first-stage" measures. It was after the Russians had refused to accept this link, but were insisting once more that a ban on production should be tied to a total ban on the possession of nuclear weapons, that Dulles flew to London at the end of July. He and Selwyn Lloyd worked closely together on the whole test problem during this period. But neither of them managed to shake the Soviet position. And the talks petered out when the Russians resorted to their usual tactics in such cases, of taking up a procedural point which had the effect of throwing the problem back to the General Assembly at its autumn session.

In July, 1957, Dulles raised the first of two questions, which were to cause a great deal of heart-searching from then onwards among the various members of the North Atlantic alliance. Later was to come the American request for overseas missile bases, stimulated in part by the shock of the Soviet sputnik in October. But what Dulles put forward in July was the idea that a special stockpile of American nuclear weapons should be allocated for the use of NATO. He argued that, in the event of war, the allies of the United States would not then be "in the position of suppliants." He asked that these weapons should be reserved for the alliance as a group, rather than for particular countries—which would have raised some delicate political problems—and that the stockpile should continue to be owned technically by the United States, with control vested, however, in the Supreme Allied Commander in his capacity as an American general. This marked in fact the birth of the scheme which has since been adopted in NATO. At that time it was a considerable step forward, in that it meant, as Dulles had intended, that nuclear weapons should be held ready more or less at the places where they might be used.

Since then, however, the idea has been somewhat overtaken by events. It never fully achieved one of its main purposes, which was to avoid individual countries feeling that they needed to produce their own atomic weapons if they were to retain their independent status in the alliance. The French have not been restrained in the least from pushing on with the development of their own atomic bomb. Nor have the Western European countries remained satisfied with American control of the stockpiles, since this has failed to meet their growing fears that, with the increasing vulnerability of the United States itself, as the missile race has developed, the Americans might be increasingly chary of embarking on the use of atomic weapons to repel an attack in Europe. At the time, nevertheless, Dulles's proposal was bold, new and useful.

It was in August, 1957, incidentally, that the Chairman of the Military Applications Branch of the Atomic Energy Committee, Senator Jackson, first spoke in public about what has since become known as the Polaris submarine. This followed two years of experience with the first American nuclear submarine, the *Nautilus*, and the launching of the third nuclear submarine that month, the *Skate*, which was regarded as the "first of the assembly-line models." Senator Jackson spoke of mounting on a nuclear submarine a number of intermediate range ballistic missiles with nuclear warheads, capable of being fired for a distance of up to fifteen hundred miles from the submarines when submerged. It was still to be three years before the Polaris weapon as such achieved reasonable reliability, and before there were to be two Polaris-equipped nuclear submarines in actual service. But this period of 1957 marked the beginning of the development of America's crucial second-strike capacity, that is to say the ability to retaliate against the Soviet Union even after a surprise nuclear attack.

Throughout all these major questions of high strategy, disarmament, relations with his allies, and Soviet pressure in the Middle East, Dulles always found himself keeping an active eye on that other permanent source of diplomatic trouble, the Far East. In fact, his upbringing, experience and inclination all constantly combined to make him give its problems a certain instinctive priority. This is a tendency of which many Europeans, physically so much farther away from the Far East, often take too little account. In May and June of 1957, Dulles was involved with Communist China, Formosa, and Japan in turn.

In regard to Communist China, after the State Department had announced early in May that it was considering certain relaxations of the ban on trade, Dulles came under renewed pressure from the

American press to permit at least a few American journalists to visit China. Nothing much came of either issue at that time. But the first, the trade ban, was a symptom of the extent to which America had lagged behind opinion in the rest of the world; and the second, the question of the press, was a follow-up to Dulles's own complete refusal nine months earlier to allow a group of American newspapermen to accept a Communist Chinese invitation. This time he retreated half a step, by admitting that one or two reporters might visit China on a pooled basis, so long as this did not mean a mass of other people, including other journalists, wanting to get there too. But his concession was in practice so hedged around with conditions that it failed to arouse any enthusiasm.

In June, Dulles had two anti-American riots on his hands. The one in Formosa was set off by the acquittal at an American court-martial of a United States serviceman who had killed a Chinese, allegedly in self-defense. The case drew the attention of Chiang Kai-shek's followers to the extraterritorial privileges enjoyed in their country by American servicemen, and it was a searing reminder of the long humiliations which China had suffered over this type of question in the past. Dulles handled the incident well and, as a result of it, set in train a review of the conditions governing the relations between some 250 overseas American military establishments and their host countries. Under the defense treaty between the United States and Formosa, incidentally, the provision that Washington can at any time ask for a base there has never been implemented. The Chinese Nationalist ministers have always urged the Americans not to request such a base, since to grant it would make them lose face; and there is in fact no United States base there to this day. All the Americans on Formosa are there "to teach the use of weapons."

The other incident which occurred at almost the same time, oddly enough, was rather similar in Japan. Known as the Girard case, an American GI was accused this time of killing a Japanese woman on a shooting range. The issue was whether he was on duty or not. If he was, the existing agreement with Japan entitled him to be tried by a United States court-martial; if he was not it was becoming political dynamite in Asia that he should not be tried by a Japanese court. It so happened that, when the case arose, the

Japanese Prime Minister, Kishi, was in Washington and this added to the prominence given to the incident. Moreover, the flurry of anti-American feeling which it provoked in Japan was a sign that events were already moving towards the situation in which, three years later, anti-American riots in Tokyo prevented the visit of President Eisenhower and were the signal for the removal of Kishi from office.

Dulles decided to let the Japanese courts try the case, in spite of a wave of public sympathy for Girard inside the United States. This was strongly fanned by petitions from his home town in Illinois, and by the publicity which his family and their legal advisers were understandably trying to exploit on his behalf. Dulles had undoubtedly made the right decision in view of the pressure that was mounting against American interests in Japan. But the Girard family fought the ruling so successfully that they got the case taken to the American Supreme Court. There, fortunately for Dulles, the ruling was that no constitutional or statutory barriers prevented the United States waiving its own right to try Girard. This Supreme Court ruling had a lasting effect wherever American servicemen were serving, in making it more difficult for GI's to be excluded from the jurisdiction of local courts.

During the late summer and autumn of 1957 Dulles found plenty more to worry about in the Middle East. Although the Eisenhower Doctrine has come to be dismissed as a rather temporary phenomenon, and not a very successful one at that, throughout its first year, 1957, Dulles devoted considerable time and thought to it. He was now finding the United States confronted with many of the old problems which had for so long plagued the British, and for which they had so frequently been criticized in Washington. The main development was Communist progress in Syria, and the specific news of a so-called commercial treaty between Syria and the Soviet Union caught Dulles on a late August holiday on Duck Island. The treaty was accompanied by the promotion of an extreme left-winger, Colonel Afif Bizri, to be Commander-in-Chief of the Syrian army. As a result, the American Embassy in Damascus found itself in a state of semi-siege, and on Wall Street shares with Middle East connections, particularly those of the big oil companies, plummeted downwards. Dulles accordingly hurried back to Washington.

Up till now the record of the Eisenhower Doctrine had been quite good. It had succeeded in calming the situation in Jordan in May and influencing a general election in Lebanon in June. It had also been applied with some vigor on the economic side. When Congress had approved the Doctrine in March 1, it provided that, during the four months ending in June, 1957, the President could dispose of up to 200 million dollars for military and economic assistance in the Middle East. This really represented a more flexible allocation of existing aid rather than any fresh commitment; by waiving some of the restrictions contained in the Mutual Security Act, it gave the President greater freedom in the disposal of the aid. By the end of June, 174 million dollars had in fact been earmarked, of which 123 million dollars were for economic development and 51 million for military purposes. The whole of the military aid and 68 million dollars of the economic had been agreed to by James Richards, the President's Special Envoy during a long tour of the Middle East in March and April, in which he had visited every country from Morocco to Afghanistan, except Egypt, Syria and Jordan. The first two did not want him, and he had avoided Jordan for fear of embarrassing King Hussein. Jordan nevertheless received 30 million dollars in a combined military and economic allocation, even though its government had publicly dissociated itself from the Eisenhower Doctrine for reasons of Arab politics.

Faced with the Syrian drift to the left, however, Dulles could not apply the Eisenhower Doctrine as such, since it did not and could not provide for the arming of Arab states against Soviet penetration, when the West itself was the primary target of their own left-wing nationalists. Dulles, who had spent much of his life thinking about nationalism and emphasizing that to oppose it was useless, was now ironically considered by many Arabs as the arch-imperialist, a point of view assiduously cultivated both by Communist propaganda and by Cairo radio. His concern at this trend played a not insignificant part in changing his views about neutralism in general.

It was only little over a year since he had said, in June, 1956, that neutrality had "increasingly become an obsolete conception and, except under very exceptional circumstances, it is an immoral and shortsighted conception." His use of the word "immoral" had made world headlines and had brought down on his head a whole cascade of abuse. By now, however, he had begun to see that neutrality had its uses. It depended in part on whom one was neutral against. Moreover, Dulles had by now talked to Nehru on a number of occasions, and with the passage of time he had honestly come to see Nehru's point of view, in a way that would have been inconceivable originally. Confronted now with the Syrian position, he therefore decided to shift his ground. When the Syrian Foreign Minister, Salah el-Bitar, came to the autumn session of the UN General Assembly in New York, Dulles sought him out and applied himself with a new understanding to the Arab attitude.

In spite of the beginning of this new trend in his own thoughts, Dulles came off second best when the Syrian affair blew up into an essentially phony crisis in the middle of October, 1957. Just before the Turkish general election, a crescendo of Syrian and Soviet propaganda was directed against the Turks' attachment to NATO, with the strong hint that Dulles was going to use the Turks to interfere in Syria. This hint was finally put in the form of a blunt accusation by Khrushchev in an interview with James Reston in *The New York Times*. Khrushchev, with his happy knack of always giving peace a helping hand, added that in the event of war Turkey would "not last one day." Dulles replied that he felt the situation in the Middle East was not unlike just before the Korean War, with the main difference that an actual outbreak of war was less likely, because the eyes of the world were already focussed on the area.

A few days later the atmosphere of crisis evaporated almost as rapidly as it had arisen. Unfortunately, the net result was that the Russians had managed to perform a trick repeat of their Suez maneuver, whereby they ended up as the apparent saviors of an Arab state against wicked Western imperialism. It was ironic that Dulles, at the very moment of his new thinking about neutralism, should find himself so readily branded as an imperialist along with the British and French. Naturally his enemies in Washington made the most of the failure of the Eisenhower Doctrine to meet the situation, and this added fuel to the flames of criticism with which he was now surrounded.

In the autumn of 1957 Americans were indeed in a confused and chastened mood. Many were baffled and worried at the way in which their scientists had been beaten into space by the Soviet sputnik. Those in Washington who kept their eyes on the world outside were disturbed by the accusations of imperialism leveled against American policy in Asia, and by the unpopularity of the Administration among its allies in Western Europe. Dulles himself was under constant personal attack both in Congress and in the press. Once again the more outspoken of his critics, like Joseph Alsop, the newspaper columnist, and some of the leading Democrats, like Senator Humphrey, were calling for his resignation. They declared that Dulles must go, because the distrust of him among America's allies was so great that it prevented even preliminary direct negotiations with the Soviet Union. The magazine *Look* had just written: "Not since Hitler has any foreigner been so scorned and disliked in Britain as Secretary of State John Foster Dulles."

Everywhere his policies were being reviled and condemned as failures. He had talked about "Liberation," but his régime had seen the Communists move forward. He had talked about massive retaliation, but the Russians were catching up with American nuclear power so fast that their missiles were beginning to constitute a threat to the United States itself. He had talked about the immorality of neutralism, but, if the United States could detach itself from the opprobrium into which it had sunk, the view was gaining ground that neutralism was precisely what Washington ought to cultivate most. He had emphasized that America needed friends and allies; and yet he had made himself hated and distrusted by them.

Although this was the worst revolt against Dulles of the several that took place while he was Secretary of State, it never really came even near to easing him out of office. The main reason was that throughout he had the confidence of President Eisenhower. Dulles as always was shrewd enough to make quite sure that he carried the President with him in every major move. The President was willing to be carried, but Dulles was wise enough never to take this for granted. Secondly, in spite of all the criticisms, Dulles continued to provoke respect for his dogged sense of dedication and his own sheer knowledge of foreign affairs. No one doubted the inflexible quality of his anti-Communism, and most people continued to be impressed by the value of long experience of Communist tactics. Thirdly, what clinched the matter on this occasion, as it had done on others, was the fact that, the more obviously Dulles was attacked in public, the more difficult it became for the President to abandon him. Moreover, in October, 1957, when Khrushchev publicly demanded that the U.S. Senate should investigate the activities and policy of the U.S. Secretary of State, any practical steps against Dulles were rendered virtually out of the question. This unsolicited tribute from Moscow marked in fact the turn of the tide.

On October 20, 1957, Her Majesty the Queen and the Duke of Edinburgh visited Washington, followed a few days later by the British Prime Minister and Foreign Secretary, Harold Macmillan and Selwyn Lloyd. From the point of view of the two governments, the ice had been broken at the Bermuda meeting in March. But, as far as public opinion was concerned, there were still a good many people in the United States who, when they thought at all about Britain, felt that the Suez crisis of the previous year only confirmed their view that the wicked ways of British imperialism were by no means over, even if the British themselves were decadent. There were admittedly quite a number of other Americans who sympathized with the British and French in the dilemma in which nationalization of the Suez Canal had placed them, even if only a very small section agreed with Eden and Mollet in the action which they took. What latent sympathy there was or might have been on quite a large scale, if the Suez operation had succeeded, was largely dissipated by the astonishing abandonment of the landings at Port Said before they had reached their objectives. It was against this background, therefore, that the Queen's visit took place.

From the moment that she and the Duke of Edinburgh landed, they were received with growing enthusiasm. The visit was the most tremendous success. The Queen carried off her fantastic welcome to perfection. Characteristic of the warmth and cordiality brought even to the most formal occasions was the story repeated afterwards about the last moments of the visit at the airport. When

President Eisenhower conducted the Queen to her aircraft, he made the usual polite observation of a host to his guest, but with more than usual sincerity, "I wish you could stay a little longer." The Queen's reply was treasured for just that touch of half-seriousness and half-humor which Americans love. "I wish I could," she is reputed to have said, "but, you see, the Prime Minister needs the airplane." And in the same aircraft, after a quick turn around in London, Macmillan and Selwyn Lloyd did in fact duly arrive twenty-four hours after the Queen had left.

The success of the Queen's visit took the passion out of the breakdown of the previous understanding between Britain and the United States. But this could never quite repair what had once been broken. Just as many people in Britain have long rejected anything that looks like tying Britain to the chariot wheels of the United States, so many Americans have always repudiated even the kind of Anglo-American partnership which existed during the war. But it is undeniable that a special partnership of some kind existed during the war. It did reflect a common sympathy and understanding which grew stronger in the heat of battle; it was something which had, or should have had, a definite part to play in the postwar world. And it was this which the Suez crisis destroyed forever. It is for this that Dulles is widely regarded, in Britain at least, as being to blame on the American side. Whatever happens now, there can only be the building of something different. The old sense of being together has gone. But, in this rebuilding, the Queen's visit in the autumn of 1957 played a genuinely important role, without which the task of the politicians and statesmen would have been a good deal harder even than it was.

Macmillan's visit, following that of the Queen, was also something of a personal triumph in a different way. At Bermuda in March, while neither side had said it was sorry, both had realized that a new relationship must somehow be created. Now, in October, after several months of steady work clearing the ground and replanting, a new confidence was growing up, and on this visit the first fruits were beginning to ripen. Macmillan and Selwyn Lloyd found that there was a much greater identity of interest than there had seemed to be before—over the Middle East, over Quemoy, over nuclear tests—and this almost automatically brought a fresh cordiality to the whole Anglo-American relationship. The word which Macmillan later employed in a number of his speeches to underline the new mood was "interdependence."

After the talks, arrangements were announced to share the results of military research and development between the United States and "other friendly countries," notably Britain. It was stated that the deterrent power of the allies, that is to say basically American power, "would in fact be available in case of need for their common security," and that "it will not be used by any nation for purposes other than individual and collective self-defense." From this it emerged that Dulles and the President were determined to uphold the Western alliance by doing what they could to reduce the fear that America might go it alone and by minimizing the impact of the strict American security regulations against the sharing of defense secrets with allies. Britain and America, in fact, were friends again.

In the same month as the British visits, an article appeared over Dulles's name in the October, 1957, issue of *Foreign Affairs,* in which he sought to defend the Administration's record under the title "Challenge and Response in United States Policy." He began by quoting from the first of the Federalist papers, a source with which he was as familiar as with the Bible, that Americans "have believed that their 'conduct and example' would influence events throughout the world." After referring to the moral stand which he had taken, he went on to talk about the power of the United States in the context of fresh Communist demands to ban the nuclear bomb, and of an increasing public desire in Western countries to halt nuclear tests. Dulles came out somewhat surprisingly with the view that the time was coming when it would be possible to move away from the theory of massive retaliation, because of the technical progress which had been made in the development of tactical atomic weapons. He wrote:

> The resourcefulness of those who serve our nation now shows that it is possible to alter the character of nuclear weapons. It seems now that their use need not involve vast destruction and widespread harm to humanity. . . . In the future it may thus be feasible to place less reliance upon the deterrence of vast retaliatory power.

He went on to deduce that, "in contrast to the 1950 decade," in the nineteen-sixties it might be possible to meet a full-scale conventional attack with small tactical atomic weapons, and thus confront an aggressor rather than his victim with the choice between "failing or himself initiating nuclear war." This interest in graduated deterrence represented a considerable shift in the Dullesian thesis, prompted in part by the pressure of criticism against the theory of massive retaliation. Since then, the wheel has come much further around in favor of conventional forces, but the idea of "forcing a pause" on an aggressor, which Dulles was supporting, has been the official doctrine in NATO from that time to this. His article showed both his interest and his flexibility of mind when dealing with strategy and nuclear weapons.

It was at the beginning of the month, at about midnight on October 4, 1957, that the Russians announced the successful launching of their first sputnik. Khrushchev soon followed this up with the suggestion that the Soviet Union and the United States should make a bilateral deal on the control of high-flying missiles. At first rejected by Washington, this proposal later led to a meeting between Dulles and Gromyko in which the Secretary of State asked for more information. Dulles was in fact in a dilemma, of a kind which occurred with increasing frequency as the initiative was seized by the Russians. On the one hand, he did not want to let Moscow claim that its approaches, even over specific items of arms control, were meeting with no response from the West; on the other, he did not want to be pushed into acting without the rest of his allies. On this occasion, immediate suspicion was in fact aroused in other Western countries by his talks with Gromyko, just as they had been by Stassen's talks with Zorin at the London disarmament negotiations earlier in the year. Dulles, incidentally, sometimes used to have Gromyko to his private house in Washington, a thing which he had never managed to do with Molotov. Naturally, this Khrushchev propaganda approach came to nothing, except that it added, if that were possible, to the urgency of America's re-examination of the whole missile situation. Dulles himself embarked on a fresh round of consultation, including even talks with a number of experts from the previous Truman Administration, and he came out in support of the idea that the United States should push ahead with its plans for missile bases in Western Europe.

On December 16, 1957, these major problems of strategy were discussed by one of the most important meetings of the NATO Council which has ever taken place. For the first time since the signature of the North Atlantic Treaty, the heads of government of all the member states, except Portugal, assembled in Paris, together with their foreign ministers and defense ministers. In order to be present, President Eisenhower, who had only recently recovered from his second heart attack, flew across the Atlantic at a specially low altitude, so as to avoid any undue strain on his heart. At the meeting it was clear that Dulles's stock was by now beginning to rise again. The kind of line which he had followed in his *Foreign Affairs* article had also been the theme of many of his statements and speeches, and he was listened to with respect.

During these last few months of 1957, it dawned for the first time on a wide range of people, who had not otherwise thought in any detailed fashion, that true superiority of power was slipping from American hands. Originally the United States had possessed a monopoly in the atomic bomb. Then it had possessed an undoubted superiority, both in quantities of nuclear weapons and in the means of delivering them. Now this was no longer true. Peace had come to depend on a balance of nuclear deterrence, instead of on American superiority.

The United States still retained, it was true, a much larger manned bomber force than the Russians, and the days of the bomber were a very long way from being over, in spite of much loose talk to the contrary. But in essence the sputnik had proved that the territory of the United States was now vulnerable, and it followed that American efforts must be redoubled, if retaliation against attack was to be quick or effective. Thus, as Dulles argued at the Paris meeting of the Atlantic Council, although the United States might be temporarily lagging behind in the development of long-range intercontinental ballistic missiles, it was already well advanced in the manufacture of both tactical and strategic missiles with a shorter range. But, for these IRBMs to be effective, it was now absolutely vital that they should be provided with launching bases in at least some parts of Western Europe.

This was not well received by the Europeans, though the reasons for the American request were well understood. Coming after the change of policy which Dulles had announced earlier in the year, whereby nuclear weapons were now to be stockpiled under American control in varous allied countries, it was felt that events were tending to make these smaller nations higher priority targets for Soviet nuclear attack. Thus, while the European members felt their own increased vulnerability, so indeed did the United States, but for rather different reasons. At Paris the outcome was that Britain, Turkey, and Italy did agree at once to embark upon detailed negotiations for the establishment of American missile bases within their territory; but the European powers as a whole were determined to extract some concession from the Americans, in return for their acceptance in principle of any missile bases in Western Europe.

This concession was that Dulles and President Eisenhower undertook to renew negotiations with the Russians for some kind of settlement at the highest level. Dulles had good reason to be doubtful about the prospects of "negotiating from strength" at such a moment, since he, like many others, was well aware that the position of strength was moving from Washington to Moscow. He felt bound to agree to pay the price for the missile bases, however, and thus began the long chain of proposals and counterproposals which eventually led up to the abortive summit conference of May, 1960. The way had been opened by the Russians who, immediately before the December session of the Atlantic Council, had written a series of letters to Western governments holding out some prospect of negotiating a settlement, but only, of course, if all American and British forces were totally withdrawn from Germany and the rest of the European mainland. The Western allies had, in fact, all received a very nasty jolt from the proof which the sputnik had afforded of the progress made by Russian missile technology.

When Dulles returned to Washington, after paying a flying visit to General Franco in Madrid on the way, he found that American political reactions to the Paris meeting were split almost precisely along party lines. The Republicans strongly supported the official view that Dulles and the President had achieved a success in securing recognition of the principle that missile bases should be established in Europe; and that they had proved their desire for peace in the eyes of their allies by agreeing to try to reopen talks with the Russians at the foreign ministers' level. Among the Democrats and Dulles's critics generally, two reactions were evident. First, so far from approving any desire for peace shown by the leaders of the Administration, the critics held that Dulles and Eisenhower had lost an opportunity to seize the diplomatic initiative by urging talks between East and West much more strongly themselves. Secondly, they argued that an unnecessary strain had been put on the Western alliance by the way in which the United States had had to force its allies to accept missile bases. Dulles, however, felt convinced that no other course had been open to him than the one that he had followed, and he knew that, in spite of the natural fears of the Europeans, many responsible people on the other side of the Atlantic agreed with him.

Dulles was in fact deeply concerned about the question of American overseas bases, and it had been for this reason that he had gone to see General Franco. He was very conscious that the strategic picture had been fundamentally altered by Russia's development of long-range rockets. He saw that the Russians would redouble their efforts to cripple America's overseas bases, at the same time pushing on with their own development of missiles which could reach United States territory from the soil of the Soviet Union itself, a process that has in fact continued rapidly from that day to this. Bulganin—who was still the Prime Minister of Russia, though Khrushchev was increasingly in obvious command—sent a note to Franco declaring that Spain was running grave risks in having American bases on its soil. While the Spaniards saw this as an opportunity to extract from America more than the total of seven hundred million dollars which they had already received, Dulles realized that the Spanish bases of the U.S. Strategic Air Command had indeed become more important than ever; these four airfields had just been completed at enormous expense and were now available for operational use. He accordingly hastened to Madrid. There, both sides renewed their terms of reference on the existing agreement, Dulles promising more aid and Franco confirming that the bases would continue to be available in a world in which their importance was rising.

The year nineteen fifty-seven had been a cruel one for John Foster Dulles. But he entered 1958 knowing that, without abandoning his principles under pressure, the stimulus of criticism had started his mind moving along new channels. Simultaneously, the fresh burst of Soviet aggressiveness had once more helped the West to sink its own internal differences, in spite of the increasingly complex and difficult nature of the problems it was facing in nuclear strategy. The result was that Dulles's own long experience, and the intense thought which he had lately given to nuclear problems, was beginning to count for more perhaps than at any time in the past. Even if he was never to succeed in rallying the West by any personal magnetism, his intellect, his lucidity, and his resolution were at last commanding the less grudging respect among his allies that had evaded him for so long. Incredible as it might have seemed halfway through 1957, by the end of his last year, 1958, Dulles's presence was to be a reassurance and a comfort to many of his colleagues in the Atlantic alliance. And after he was gone, they missed him badly.

CHAPTER 15

The Last Year

DURING Dulles's last year he was much more effective as Secretary of State than he was in his first. Naturally anyone should learn from experience, but many do not. For a man with views as determined as his the changes were inevitably slow in coming, even though he always tried to see each side of a problem and his immense capacity for work considerably enlarged his normal range of experience. By now, however, he had been through so much that almost nothing was totally new. Virtually all three of the chief crises which he had to deal with in 1958, for instance, were old and familiar ones in a different form. In July the landing of American troops in Lebanon only gave a dramatic new twist to a situation with which Suez and the Eisenhower Doctrine had long made Washington familiar. In August the renewed shelling of Quemoy and Matsu merely reopened a situation which had been dormant for three years. And Khrushchev's challenge in November over Berlin was a very old problem indeed, dressed up in a new coat. And this rapid moving of the area of crisis successively from the Middle East to the Far East and back to Europe found Dulles ready with the arguments and sometimes the answers at his finger tips.

As the year 1958 opened, the main foreign topic of interest in Washington was the continuing question of negotiation with the Soviet Union. Dulles's own star rose and fell with even more bewildering rapidity than usual, according to whose views were in the ascendant at any given time. His general approach was not to deal with the Russians until the United States had regained something of a "position of strength," following the setback over the sputnik, and until the Russians had in some way proved their good faith "by deeds not words." While this line was relatively pleasing to the Republican Party, it provoked a good deal of criticism among the more internationally minded Democrats. They were not particularly effective in pursuing their campaign against him, however, and, when testifying before the Senate Foreign Relations Committee, Dulles was applauded for his renewed emphasis on the importance of meeting the growing Soviet offensive in the underdeveloped countries.

As regards actual tactics, although in February Dulles dropped his insistence on the need for a foreign ministers' meeting before there could be any Summit between heads of government, he stuck to his view that adequate preparation was necessary; but he took the line that at a pinch this could be done through normal diplomatic channels. In some ways this represented a concession to Bulganin's suggestion, in a letter to President Eisenhower, that the presence of Dulles himself at a preparatory meeting would impede the negotiations. But Dulles had already gained considerably from these personal attacks by Soviet leaders, and he certainly did not relish the idea of spending even more time arguing fruitlessly himself with the Russians; at that date it was estimated that, during the previous twelve years, he had already spent the equivalent of a year and a half at the conference table with Soviet leaders. Moreover, by the end of February there was a widespread feeling that the endless flow of letters backwards and forwards between Eisenhower and Bulganin was not an ideal way of conducting affairs. All that Eisenhower personally insisted on was that, in any preparatory discussions, Dulles must himself take a leading part, a view which was naturally also Dulles's.

As February drew on into March, the practical question became whether a Summit meeting should again consist of the Big Four, or should simply devolve into direct contact between President Eisenhower and the head of the Soviet government. This latter point became more significant early in April, when Marshal Bulganin was finally dismissed by Nikita Khrushchev. Khrushchev, however, demonstrated the frivolity of his immediate approach by suggesting that no less than eleven foreign ministers should prepare for a so-called Summit between up to thirty heads of government. Dulles's reply was that he would not take part if the conference was to be merely a "hoax" or a "spectacle."

In the first five months of 1958 Dulles made three overseas journeys, which demonstrated the importance that he still attached to his military alliances. The first, to Ankara on January 27, was notable for being the first occasion on which he himself had attended any meeting of the Baghdad Pact, though even now he was still technically only an observer. Although he denied somewhat disingenuously that there was any special significance in his presence, nearly everyone else took it as showing that, after some disappointment at his inability to make friends with President Nasser, he was willing to let the United States stand more openly for the kind of anti-Communist policy in the Middle East implied by the Baghdad Pact. If so, it was a pity that he should still have given such a dismal impression of hesitancy and indecision by coming merely as an observer. Of the other two journeys, one was to Manila for a session of the SEATO Council, and the other for a ministerial meeting of the Atlantic Council at Copenhagen in May. Thus Dulles did what he felt he could to show his own support for the policy of military alliances, even though the maximum usefulness of such pacts—except perhaps for NATO—was no longer generally recognized by considerable sections of Western public opinion.

The first thing that Khrushchev did on assuming sole power in the Soviet Union in April, 1958, was to announce the suspension of Soviet nuclear tests. It so happened, as Khrushchev well knew, that whereas Russia had just completed a major series of tests in March the United States was about to begin one in April. Hence, he was inevitably able to score a propaganda lead, since neither the Americans nor the British were willing to be hustled into a similar ban. Dulles saw that America was being out-maneuvered, and he therefore hinted at the possible early suspension of nuclear tests. This implied taking a stand against the dogmatically militaristic view of the Secretary of Defense and also the attitude of the Atomic Energy Commission, who naturally thought in terms of the United States's need to develop suitable nuclear warheads for the long-range missiles just coming into service. The position of the Administration as a whole had in fact been equivocal for at least two years. On one side, the experts were pressing for more tests in order to develop smaller and cleaner weapons—clean in the sense that for a given atomic explosion there should be less radioactive fall-out. On the other side were those who felt that America was losing the battle for world opinion, particularly among its allies, where estimates of the dangers from radio-activity had been receiving growing publicity.

Once again the Administration was indeed being widely criticized for having lost the diplomatic and propaganda initiative to the Russians on two important issues—nuclear tests and a Summit conference. On the Summit, however, Dulles felt more sure of his ground. Throughout these months of maneuver he stuck doggedly to his main view, that it was no use attempting to reach the Summit without sending scouts ahead to survey the conditions of the climb. In April Dulles proposed special talks between the Western ambassadors in Moscow and the Kremlin, as the first stage of a three-stage operation, in which the ambassadors would talk first, to be followed by the foreign ministers, and only then by direct personal contact between the heads of government, Khrushchev, however, resisted any idea of dealing with the ambassadors, except individually, and proposed instead a meeting of the foreign ministers for May. But Dulles made much of Gromyko's refusal to meet the three Western ambassadors together, as a reflection of Soviet insincerity about negotiations as a whole; and the result was that by June the prospects for progress were virtually nil. At the end of the month, when Khrushchev again made personal attacks on Dulles at a party at the British Embassy in Moscow, the idea of an early summit meeting more or less went into cold storage. He was to drag it out again as a kind of gimmick to meet the Middle East crisis in July and the Berlin emergency in November, but without success.

On June 7, 1958, Harold Macmillan again visited Washington with a number of his advisers. By now this kind of contact was going very smoothly, and the British Prime Minister scored a particular success when he spoke at the National Press Club. He managed to appear at once urbane and friendly, confident yet casual, solid yet witty and alive. This in fact was a forerunner of the excellent impression he made with American public opinion when he was heckled by Khrushchev at the stormy session of the UN General Assembly in October, 1960. At the end of the three-day visit Dulles said that the talks had dealt with "every subject under the sun"; they in fact covered mainly the fading Summit prospects, the deadlock over the suspension of nuclear tests and over the proposed inspection system, and above all the advances being made by the Soviet economy itself, as well as by Soviet propaganda to the underdeveloped countries. Although the smallness of the sterling area reserves also figured prominently in the talks, Macmillan made it very plain that he was not asking for special aid. He particularly did not want to have his visits to Washington constantly associated with begging missions.

Dulles himself had begun showing more appreciation of America's need for allies than at any previous time. In particular, he was keen to help in any reasonable way that he could the two men in Western Europe with whom he was now in closest contact, Macmillan and Adenauer. Macmillan's visit had in fact induced in Dulles a certain flexibility about the Summit, and he had become less worried about committing President Eisenhower to the uncertainties of another direct confrontation with Khrushchev, since Khrushchev had now emerged as the single key to power in Moscow and no serious business could be done with anyone else. With regard to Germany, Dulles told the Senate Foreign Relations Committee on June 6 that the genius and value of Konrad Adenauer lay in the German Chancellor's own recognition that, if Germany were united without being harnessed to the West, it could again become a menace to everyone.

In this period Dulles also spoke up in favor of a freer exchange of nuclear information with America's allies. Appearing before the Joint Congressional Committee on Atomic Energy in April, he specifically rebutted Democratic criticism that a relaxation of the American law would help to spread the ownership of nuclear weapons, with all the inherent dangers that that would imply. He argued that information would be given only to countries which already manufactured nuclear weapons, knowing full well that at this point the British alone would so benefit, though other allies would also receive information about the effects of atomic explosions in order to help their defense organizations.

Dulles went further and showed marked foresight in his view of the interplay between the distribution of nuclear weapons and allied morale. Under the decisions made at the Atlantic Council the previous December, all members of NATO had become eligible to receive the basic weapons in the nuclear armory, without either owning or controlling the actual nuclear warheads, and Dulles argued that, unless this decision were implemented satisfactorily, the will to resist of his allies would be weakened. He also asserted that only by having nuclear weapons readily available, even though under American control, would they be dissuaded from trying to develop nuclear weapons of their own; apart from thus widening the dangers, their resources would be deflected from far more urgent needs. Since 1958 there has indeed been a considerable growth of the fear in Western Europe that, if the price for using nuclear weapons is now to be a nuclear attack on the United States itself, then American willingness to employ them in the defense of Europe has alarmingly diminished. This is the argument which has been the basis of the case for a so-called NATO deterrent, and its ramifications have certainly weakened the solidarity of the Western alliance. As far back as 1958, Dulles saw this coming.

Another problem which again received a good deal of attention in Washington during the early summer was Latin America. The tour by Richard Nixon, the Vice-President, had been warmly welcomed in some parts of Latin America, but in others had provoked actual violence from gangs of students and unruly crowds. Dulles had always taken Latin America seriously. When he had first assumed office in 1953, he had declared that the Truman Administration had become "so preoccupied with ... Europe and Asia" that it had taken South America too much for granted. Since then, however, he had laid himself open to criticism on the score that, although he had now been in power for over five years, the policy had not really changed. Yet this was not quite fair. Dulles's own passionate concern about the dangers of Communism had led him to recognize for some time that Latin American poverty, when combined with the mood of deep irritation with the United States which is endemic among many Latin Americans, represented a potential breeding ground for Communism. The question was not only how much attention to pay to friends rather than foes, but how to avoid propping up reactionary governments, and how to meet the people rather than dealing with only a small elite. Since then, events in Cuba have certainly more than justified Dulles's doubts.

On May 13, 1958, the revolution which started in Algiers brought General de Gaulle back to power in Paris. It was some weeks before his new government of the French Fifth Republic was ready to receive visitors, but by the end of June the first to come were Macmillan and Selwyn Lloyd, followed a week later on July 5 by Dulles. Four particular problems were on the Secretary of State's mind—the future of French atomic weapon development, France's conditions for allowing American missile bases on its soil, the prospects for a change of policy towards Algeria, and, not least, General de Gaulle's ideas about a Summit conference.

Almost immediately after his accession to power, de Gaulle had approached Washington with the request that the Administration should intervene with Congress, in order to have the amendments to the 1954 Atomic Energy Act altered in France's favor. The French ambassador, Hervé Alphand, had reported that the Senate and the House of Representatives had each already passed the amendments, so framed that they deliberately admitted Britain alone to full association. It was too late for anyone to alter the situation, and, when President Eisenhower had signed the new law, Dulles had to explain to General de Gaulle exactly how matters stood. His visit to Paris was not therefore an easy one, nor indeed would anyone who knew either de Gaulle or Dulles have expected it to be. Nevertheless it passed off in an atmosphere of calm and mutual respect. And to Dulles personally it was not unwelcome that this country, of which he had been so fond when he was young, should have a firm, bold hand at the helm again.

Only a few days after Dulles's return from Paris the Middle East once more blew up. On July 14, 1958, King Faisal of Iraq and his pro-Western Prime Minister, Nuri es-Said, were assassinated in Baghdad, to the accompaniment of exhibitions of barbaric brutality unusual even in the twentieth century. General Kassim was swept to power on a wave of mixed nationalism and Communism. This dramatic event changed the whole balance of politics in the Middle East. Ever since May the situation in Lebanon had been deteriorating under the pressure of a peculiarly tortuous rebellion against the pro-Western government of President Chamoun. While the rebels drew courage partly from Egyptian and Syrian inspiration, the Lebanese themselves were deeply divided. A small corps of United Nations observers had been in Lebanon for several weeks, and Hammarskjold, the Secretary-General, had visited Beirut during June. Now, the crisis in Iraq brought matters to a head.

President Chamoun appealed to the United States for help, and on July 15 President Eisenhower announced that American marines would be landing immediately in Lebanon. The following day Dulles dispatched Robert Murphy as the President's special representative to investigate the situation on the spot, and Selwyn Lloyd flew to Washington at Dulles's urgent invitation for consultations on the Middle East situation as a whole. The next day, July 17, in response to an appeal from King Hussein, British paratroops landed in Jordan.

Both these American and British decisions were dramatic indeed. To many Americans, the landing of their troops in the Lebanon would have seemed almost inconceivable only a few months before. But they had now become accustomed to thinking rather more about the Middle East, and the President's decision to go forward, in keeping with the Eisenhower Doctrine, was in general strongly supported. As for the British, Macmillan said at the time that the decision to send British paratroopers to Jordan was one of the hardest he had ever made in his life. Considering that Suez was only two years old, it was indeed playing with fire. By this time the position was in reality very different. The Americans and the British were united. The Communist hand in the Middle East was now clear for everyone to see. And the legitimate governments of both the Lebanon and Jordan had begged the West to come in.

Naturally Khrushchev was not prepared to take this lying down. His plans for following up the coup in Iraq had been seriously disrupted by the firmness of Dulles's reaction and by the bravery of President Eisenhower in making the decision to land in Lebanon. Thus plans which the Communists had been brewing for a long time and had suddenly been able to put into operation were robbed of the completeness of victory which Moscow hoped for. Accordingly, two days after the landings in Lebanon and Jordan,

Khrushchev jumped in with letters to Eisenhower, Macmillan, de Gaulle and Nehru, urging that an emergency Summit meeting should be held within three days "to take urgent measures to end the military conflict which has begun in the Middle East." He suggested that the meeting should in fact take place at Geneva on July 22.

The Western powers were not, however, prepared to be stampeded into a Summit conference of this kind, at which they would inevitably be placed on the psychological defensive. Macmillan therefore proposed on July 22 that a Summit meeting should take place in the sense that a special session of the UN Security Council should be held in New York. After twenty-four hours of intensive consultation in Washington, the Administration said it was willing to accept the Macmillan proposal "if such a meeting were generally desired." This was really further than Dulles had meant to go, and when the following day, July 23, Khrushchev accepted Macmillan's proposal with the specific suggestion of July 28, President Eisenhower declared that this date would be "too early for us." General de Gaulle had meanwhile come out with a proposal for a five-power Summit meeting in Europe, which he subsequently amplified into a suggestion that India should join the Big Four at a meeting in Geneva on August 18.

The Americans and British with varying degrees of enthusiasm adhered to the Macmillan proposal for a meeting of the UN Security Council, and Khrushchev replied with a number of angry letters to all concerned. In fact, nothing immediate happened at all, since the actual presence of the Americans in Lebanon and the British in Jordan had stabilized the situation in the Middle East itself. Consequently a few days later, on August 5, Khrushchev withdrew his agreement to a meeting at the Security Council and proposed a special session of the UN General Assembly instead. Dulles and Eisenhower agreed, and this emergency session met on August 13, after an adjournment from August 8.

Dulles had never approved of the old regime in Iraq, in spite of its pro-Western attitude—or rather indeed, one might say, because of it. But he reckoned he knew Communism when he saw it. Accordingly, he approached the grave challenge of the appeal from President Chamoun in a spirit of resolution. Only a few months before, he had been suggesting that American forces would be ashamed to have the British or French with them in any Middle East operation. Now, however, he realized that the position was changing, and he recognized that, if the Anglo-American operation were not mounted in response to the appeal of the Lebanese government and King Hussein, the failure of the West to help its friends would weaken and disillusion the remaining pro-Western forces in Saudi Arabia and the Persian Gulf states. Nevertheless, as Macmillan had put it, the decision was indeed hard. There was no assurance that intervention in the Lebanon and in Jordan might not have precisely the opposite effect to that intended. What saved this from happening was the fact that the nationalism which Nasser had been preaching for six years to the Arab world had by now begun to build up resentment at the possibility of Soviet interference, as well as that of the West. What the Arabs wanted least of all was to become the central battleground of a global war, and, in spite of the deadly risks, Dulles saw that sending the marines to Lebanon was the lesser of two evils. It was, if one may presume to say so, brinkmanship of a high order.

Khrushchev's Summit idea had at first caused dismay in Washington, where a meeting of this kind, even at the United Nations as suggested by Macmillan, was widely regarded as an almost certain road to disaster. In the press, Walter Lippmann declared that "At this time a public confrontation between Mr. Eisenhower and Mr. Khrushchev would be a ghastly spectacle"; and James Reston in *The New York Times* summed up the situation with the words "President Eisenhower has agreed to attend what he and his principal advisers profoundly and unanimously believe to be the wrong meeting at the wrong time and place on the wrong subject." American fears about having a Summit at the United Nations were understandable, since there could be little hope of confining the discussions either to the right people or to the right subjects.

On the other hand, as Khrushchev's antics at the 1960 session of the UN General Assembly were later to prove, fears that he would successfully dominate the situation to the extent of converting people to his own point of view were probably exaggerated. However, 1958 was still in the era before Khrushchev had personally invaded the holy portals of American territory at all, and the doubts of the New York police about their ability to control hostility to him had yet to be disproved. The British were therefore widely blamed for having pushed Dulles into an awkward situation, when he felt obliged to accept Macmillan's proposals for a special session of the UN Security Council "if such a meeting were generally desired." Macmillan, nevertheless, was in part excused personally, as American public opinion felt that he was under considerable pressure from the Labour Opposition.

By this time relations between Dulles and the British Foreign Secretary, Selwyn Lloyd, had become close and cordial. They were increasingly seeing things the same way, and their understanding was beginning to recreate a sense of common Anglo-American purpose. When Selwyn Lloyd had been in Washington on July 17, he and Dulles had discussed Khrushchev's general demand for a Summit meeting with considerable care, and they had agreed that the Western attitude should not be too negative. Thus, when Macmillan publicly suggested on July 27 that an emergency Summit might be held at the Security Council, Dulles himself had been in on the idea from the beginning. He was being a little disingenuous, therefore, in not more effectively repudiating some of the comment that he had been pushed rather further than he meant to go. One specific reason for his drawing back, however, was that Robert Murphy in Beirut was by now cabling optimistic reports about the possibility of withdrawing the American marines from Lebanon within a few weeks, and he hoped this would see the end of the crisis anyway. In the end the American troops were skillfully withdrawn after achieving their object, but it was not to happen as soon as Murphy had hoped.

Dulles had in fact yielded reluctantly to the idea of a Summit, in order to avoid another rift between London and Washington, but since he never wanted it, so long as American troops were in the Lebanon, he managed to stall successfully. When the General Assembly of the United Nations finally met on August 13, and had been opened by President Eisenhower, Dulles and Selwyn Lloyd both submitted written declarations undertaking that American and British troops would be withdrawn from Lebanon and Jordan respectively, either when the governments of those two countries requested this to happen, or alternatively if appropriate measures had been taken meanwhile by the United Nations to maintain peace and security. After a few more weeks both governments were in fact in a position to let the troops go, and the crisis came to an end. In Dulles's view the negotiation and supervision of this type of operation was exactly the kind of function for which the UN was best suited.

Dulles had shown his relative confidence over the Middle East crisis, and his mounting concern about Latin America, by adhering to his plan to visit Brazil on August 4 and 5 for discussions with President Kubitschek. He went because he wanted to reassure the Latin Americans that, in the atmosphere of possible meetings at the Summit, the views of the smaller nations would not be ignored; and also because he feared the effects of Latin American feeling against the United States on the voting in the UN General Assembly, where it could no longer be assumed that United States policies would get the support of the rest of the hemisphere. As Secretary of State, Dulles had been strongly urged to go to Brazil both by Vice-President Nixon and by Dr. Milton Eisenhower, the President's brother, who had recently returned from a rather disturbing visit to Central America. In Rio de Janeiro Dulles asked for and got a frank statement from Brazil, and he was particularly disconcerted to discover the alarm which Washington's trade policies were creating all through Latin America. While talking a good deal at home about the need to keep down raw material prices, the U.S. government was nevertheless pushing them up by clamping on tariffs, and thereby hitting at some of the primary commodities on which the Latin American economies depended. Dulles and the President of Brazil agreed that a meeting of the presidents of all the countries of the American continent should be convened, in order to draw up programs for the economic development of Latin America. More immediately, Dulles would meet all the Latin American ambassadors in Washington in order to prepare the ground.

On the night of August 22–23 the Nationalist-held islands off the coast of China, Quemoy and Little Quemoy, suddenly came under a heavier barrage of Communist fire from the mainland than anything they had suffered for over three years. This bombardment was kept up day and night, except for occasional lulls which were as complete as they were at first inexplicable. Five days after this process had begun, namely on August 28, the Chinese Communist radio broadcast a message to the Nationalist commander in Quemoy, calling upon him to surrender and saying that an invasion was imminent; Peking also announced that this was a first step to the liquidation of Formosa.

Thus, the moment the Middle East looked like simmering down, the Far East was brought to the boiling point; and, although the Russians and Chinese do not always work together very well as a team, it seemed that the timing was deliberate. Moreover, what was rather worse now than in the previous tension of 1954–55 was that Khrushchev had himself been in Peking at the beginning of August; and it seemed that the degree of caution which he had always previously urged on the Chinese was no longer being exercised. In a letter to President Eisenhower on September 8, indeed, he expressed his concern at the situation in the Formosa Straits and said that "an attack on the Chinese People's Republic would be an attack on the Soviet Union."

At first Dulles was not unduly worried by the crisis. By September 4, however, he felt it necessary to go and see Eisenhower at Newport, Rhode Island, where the President was on holiday, in order to compose a fresh statement about the American attitude. The Administration was in fact in a tight corner for two reasons. First, a tremendous clamor had arisen in the press, both of the United States and of its allies, demanding that America should state clearly whether it was or was not going to defend Quemoy. Secondly, as the Chinese Communists and the Russians certainly knew, since the last period of crisis over Quemoy and Matsu three years before the Nationalists had been steadily committing more and more of their limited forces to the garrisoning of these two islands. Consequently, if the islands were overrun, the military strength of the Nationalists would receive a blow out of all proportion to the significance of the territory lost, from which it would follow that the United States would inevitably be faced with a much greater burden in attempting to help defend Formosa itself.

The folly of these latter developments suddenly became generally known, and the Administration was roundly condemned on the grounds both that it should have prevented them and that, since it evidently had not done so, Chiang Kai-shek had pulled a fast one. Moreover, public opinion on both sides of the Atlantic had considerably matured since 1955 on the whole question of defending Quemoy and Matsu. By and large, the view had grown that it would be madness for the Americans to get involved themselves in the defense of these offshore islands. Nevertheless, the situation had been dramatically changed by the revelation that, if the islands were in fact lost, such a substantial proportion of the Nationalist forces would be destroyed.

For all these reasons Dulles was pressed again and again to give an answer about the American position. His real difficulty was, first, that no final decision had in fact been reached in the National Security Council, and secondly that, while he himself was less and less disposed to support American participation in the defense of the offshore islands, he still needed to make the Communists fear that such participation would take place. After his Newport meeting he accordingly made a highly equivocal statement, recalling that under the famous Formosa Resolution of 1955 the President had been authorized to use American military force as he thought fit, adding that "military dispositions have been made by the United States so that a Presidential determination, if made, would be followed by action both timely and effective." Three days later, on September 7, 1958, units of the U.S. Seventh Fleet, which at that time included no less than six aircraft carriers and a strike force of five hundred aircraft, began convoying Nationalist supply ships from Formosa to the three-mile limit off Quemoy.

As the days passed and no successful invasion of Quemoy took place, though the intermittent bombardments continued at an unprecedented level, attention became focused more and more on the American attitude rather than the situation on the spot. What was not generally known, and indeed has not been revealed until now, was that Chiang Kai-shek did not want to have American troops actually on Quemoy, since he would lose face badly if, after all he had done to reinforce the islands, his own troops had not been able to defend their highly fortified positions. At the same time he did, of course, want to have the basic backing of the United States as a deterrent to the Communists. Moreover, although Dulles was uncomfortable about the level to which the stakes had risen, as a result of the Nationalists having put so many of their forces on Quemoy, he was unable to protest effectively about it in public. This was because a promise had in fact been extracted from him by Chiang Kai-shek, at the time of the evacuation of the Tachen Islands in 1955, that American help would be forthcoming to help strengthen other outlying islands, notably Quemoy and Matsu.

Among all America's allies, however, not a voice was to be found in favor of the United States getting embroiled in any kind of war, however local, to defend the offshore islands. Criticism from within the United States was as nothing to what was being said, for instance, by the British Labour Party abroad. Thus, although the Communists did not manage to seize the offshore islands, they did succeed in isolating Dulles and the Administration once again from a large part of Western public opinion. In the circumstances Dulles handled the situation with shrewdness and ability. On September 30 he declared that the United States would favor an evacuation of the offshore islands by the Nationalist forces if a "reasonably dependable" cease-fire were arranged. By October 6 a cease-fire did in fact take place on the Communist side.

When on October 14, however, Dulles said that the mere continuation of the suspension of the bombardment did not constitute the "dependable cease-fire" to which he had referred on September 30, Peking replied by accusing American vessels of entering Chinese territorial waters and reopened the shelling. On October 21 Dulles flew to Formosa for talks with Chiang Kai-shek, after which a communiqué stated that: "Under present conditions the defense of the Quemoys and Matsu is closely related to the defense of Formosa." The word "related" implied that the United States would in fact now regard the Quemoys and Matsu as coming under the Formosa resolution, by which the President was specifically empowered to act by personal decision. The communiqué added, however, that the Nationalist government maintained "its great mission" to restore freedom to the mainland Chinese, but that this should be carried out by giving effect to Dr. Sun Yat-sen's three principles of nationalism, democracy, and social well-being, rather than by force. In effect this marked the end of the crisis and, although the shelling continued for a while, it never again reached the same intensity. In due course the situation reverted to something like normal, and it is fair to say that Dulles had once again steered his way with skill between a series of ugly precipices. Once again he had shown that his brinkmanship had not lost its cunning.

Before considering Dulles's last crisis, Khrushchev's renewed challenge over Berlin, a word should be said about the readjustment of his views on trade between the Communist countries and the rest of the world. As the Soviet economy developed, and as the economic conditions between the United States and the Soviet Union in the uncommitted world increased, Dulles had been under mounting criticism from allied businessmen and others for continuing to support as steadfastly as he did the longstanding embargo on the sale of so-called strategic goods to Russia and—a much longer list—to Communist China. By 1958 it had become obvious that the Communist countries were more and more able to manufacture for themselves many of the items on the banned list; indeed they were able to offer for sale to other countries material and equipment of a comparable nature. In addition, the Soviet economic offensive in Asia and Africa was beginning to assume major proportions, so that any conditions laid down by the United States for either trade or aid were increasingly irritating to its allies and friends. Although Dulles had been one of the toughest proponents of banning goods to Communist countries, he did at this point begin to take an active part in seeing that the lists of such goods were materially shortened.

The Berlin crisis, which began at the end of 1958 and was not to be over before Dulles died, opened on November 10 when Khrushchev made a speech in Moscow, declaring his intention of transferring control of East Berlin to the East German government. With this further change in the focal center of Communist-inspired crisis, back to Europe, there began a dangerous, and at that time novel, phase in the perennial struggle between East and West over the fate of the German capital. Khrushchev followed up his first statement with a further declaration on November 14, that he was "preparing an appropriate document on the status of Berlin." Shortly afterwards he formulated his demands in the form of a six-month ultimatum expiring on May 27, 1959, although he specificly repudiated the use of the word "ultimatum." The Soviet proposals for Berlin were formally handed to the American, British, French, and Federal German ambassadors in Moscow by the Soviet foreign minister, Gromyko, on November 27.

Khrushchev's principal demand was "that West Berlin should become a demilitarized Free City" with the United States, Britain, France, the Soviet Union and possibly the United Nations guaranteeing its status. There would be a separate agreement in which Eastern Germany would guarantee communications between West Berlin and the outside world, in return for a Western undertaking that West Berlin would no longer be used for subversive activities against Eastern Germany. Khrushchev said that, if no progress had been made on this idea by the end of six months, he would sign a separate peace treaty with Eastern Germany, adding that a Western refusal to agree to his proposals would "not stop us from executing our plans," since there would be "no other way out."

Without the presence of the Western forces in Berlin there could, of course, be no guarantee whatever that this outpost of the free world would not be absorbed into Eastern Germany and its citizens cruelly punished for resisting Communism for so long. Moreover, Khrushchev did not speak of a "free city of Berlin," as a casual observer might suppose, which would at least imply that East Berlin would be equally removed from Communist military occupation. He spoke only of a so-called "free city of West Berlin," which would leave East Berlin totally Communist and continue the anomaly of a divided city—an intolerable situation as a permanency in any case.

If the Western powers had accepted this, there can be no question that their retreat would have been taken as a signal for many other people in Western Europe to start coming to terms with the Communist empire. If, on the other hand, the West would not accept the so-called "Free City" that Khrushchev proposed, then they could presumably continue to be present in West Berlin, but only on condition that they dealt with and therefore recognized the East German regime, a preliminary objective for which the Kremlin leaders have worked month by month for many years. For the West to recognize Eastern Germany, however, inevitably implies withdrawing the full recognition which it has already given to the Federal German government in Bonn as the legitimate government of Germany. Again, to take this step would have struck a harsh blow at all that Dr. Adenauer had stood for.

All this was naturally so elementary to Dulles that it formed no more than his subconscious thought. At the same time, many people in the United States had begun criticizing him again for meeting each of the successive crises in Lebanon, Quemoy, and Berlin without any new ideas. It was said that, every time the other side took a fresh initiative, all the West could do was to reply with the same old clichés designed to maintain the status quo. On Berlin, however, there was implicit recognition of the fact that there was no room for compromise, and it was Dulles himself who made two successive observations at the end of November, which suggested that his mind, if not his resolve, was more flexible than some people thought.

On November 26, he conceded at a press conference, under the sharp probing of his audience, that the Western powers might conceivably deal with the East Germans as agents of the Soviet Union; the implication of the word "agent" was that it reserved the right to go over the heads of the East Germans, if necessary, to their superiors, the Russian government. Secondly, Dulles's critics urged him at least to consider some modification of NATO, in return for concessions by the Communists which might loosen the situation in Eastern Europe. When none of them had put up any convincing suggestion as to how this might be done, it was in a sense Dulles himself who again showed flexibility of mind in hinting that there might after all be more ways of uniting Germany than by free elections—a hint which started a brief but sharp new wave of mistrust in the mind of his old and faithful friend, Dr. Adenauer.

On December 14 Dulles flew over to Paris for the regular ministerial meeting of the Atlantic Council, although he was by now beginning to feel the pain which finally compelled him to resign as Secretary of State three months later. The Western ministers confirmed their support of the American, British, and French governments in maintaining "their position and their rights in Berlin, including the right of free access"; then, after thus reflecting the vital spirit of unity in the face of Khrushchev's challenge, they turned to the much more difficult position of NATO itself. There the alliance had become confused and weakened by the attitude adopted by General de Gaulle since he had become President of France in May, six months before.

Dulles had several intimate and lengthy talks with de Gaulle. But nothing satisfactory emerged from them. Dulles wanted two things of France, agreement for intermediate missile sites on French territory and the maintenance of stocks of atomic weapons for use with them, both the missiles and the nuclear stocks to be under American control. De Gaulle's price, however, was that France should be accepted as a nuclear power itself, with a higher and more independent position among the Western allies. De Gaulle put up his famous demand for a kind of Western triumvirate and at the same time refused to allow any part of the French Air Force to be integrated within the kind of closer Western European air command which General Norstad had requested. In all, it was an uncomfortable visit for Dulles, and he obtained little except perhaps the one vital fact that the Western allies were unanimous in rejecting Khrushchev's threat.

Although this was not Dulles's last visit to Europe, it was indeed nearly the end. On January 4, 1959, Anastas Mikoyan, the second most powerful man in Russia, arrived in Washington on an epoch-making unofficial visit. This was the first time that any Soviet figure of this caliber had set foot in the United States, and, while the visit was announced as being in the nature of a holiday in which he would also discuss trade relations, it undoubtedly provided an opportunity to test out the firmness of American opinion in backing the strong stand adopted by Dulles and Eisenhower over Berlin. On January 5, Mikoyan had a ninety-minute talk with Dulles, leaving for a tour of the United States immediately afterwards in which he addressed meetings of businessmen, industrialists, and bankers. When he returned to Washington on January 16, he had two further meetings with Dulles and was received by President Eisenhower in Dulles's presence on January 17. Mikoyan appears to have gone back to the Soviet Union convinced that the Americans meant business on Berlin, having also paved the way for Khrushchev's own famous first visit later on in the year.

Dulles, however, had one last piece of business to complete. Although he had led the resistance to Khrushchev's ultimatum with firmness and courage, he knew that he had upset Adenauer by some of the things which he had said about Germany, things so unlike his traditional stand in the past. On February 4 he flew the Atlantic for the last time on a five-day visit to London, Paris, and, above all, Bonn. His meeting with Adenauer was moving and intimate. He entirely satisfied the Chancellor that nothing had really changed between them. When they parted, Adenauer said afterwards that he knew he was seeing "his friend" Dulles for the last time. After returning to Washington on February 9, Dulles said that he had been encouraged by the "unity, understanding and resolve" which he had found, and that general agreement had been reached upon the steps to be taken if the access of the Western powers to Berlin was blocked.

That same day, February 9, it was announced from the White House that Dulles was leaving for a short period to undergo a hernia operation in the Walter Reed Military Hospital, and that his duties as Secretary of State would be assumed jointly by Christian Herter and Douglas Dillon. Three days later Dulles underwent his operation, and it was found that he was again suffering from cancer. Whether Dulles knew that it had been cancer all along, the world will probably never know, though he must have suspected it. But he definitely told Adenauer on his last journey that it was only hernia, and it seems that he believed this—because he wanted to believe it. His doctors had told him that, if he did not get cancer again within eighteen months of his first operation, he was almost certainly all right. Two years were up in November, and so he had good reason to trust that all was well. But hernia in this way, after his previous cancer, can in fact be an alarming symptom. If Dulles had known he was dying, should he have continued in the tremendous office of Secretary of State? Men who have been in power for a long time begin to think they are indispensable, and certainly Dulles felt deeply that he had to deal with Khrushchev's threat to Berlin before he might be forced to leave the scene. Moreover, as Eisenhower showed during the rest of February and March, the President was determined not to lose his most faithful friend and counsellor, until he absolutely had to.

Dulles's courage never shone more brightly than in the gathering darkness of his own death. Even if some might condemn him for holding on to power long after he was fit for it, his faith in his own experience and ability was more justified than it would have been with lesser men. The inevitable in any case could not be warded off for long. For two months Dulles fought to live, partly in the hospital and partly trying to convalesce in the warm sunshine of Florida. On April 15, 1959, however, he finally had to resign as Secretary of State. Both the President and he had postponed the decision until they had no option at all. President Eisenhower, announcing his resignation, said that Dulles had become "incapacitated for carrying on the administrative load in addition to the making of policy." Even then, the President was delaying before appointing Christian Herter officially as Dulles's successor as Secretary of State. Four days afterwards, on April 23, Eisenhower announced that he had appointed Dulles as his Special Adviser on Foreign Affairs with Cabinet rank. It was a month later, on May 24, 1959, that John Foster Dulles died in the Walter Reed Military Hospital in Washington. He was given a national funeral, and an era of history came to an end.

CHAPTER 16

The Verdict

WHAT was the truth about Dulles? Was he great, or disastrous? Or both? Or neither? Did he lead the West successfully against the Communist world? Or, having held vast power through one of the most critical periods of human history, did he miss the one vital opportunity to negotiate before America lost its nuclear supremacy and Russia became too strong? Did his famous brinkmanship really take us all to the very edge of an abyss? Or did he in fact save us from going over? And what, after all, was the effect of his presence on Anglo-American relations, on the standing of the United States with its allies, on the tightness of the whole Western alliance itself? The final answers to these questions may not be given for many years, since the bulk of Dulles's papers have not yet been opened to the historian; they are being collected and preserved in a special library at Princeton. Time in any case is needed to let passions cool. But, as the previous pages show, so much has already been written and said, that the essentials are already known, and certainly some understanding of Dulles's role in the nineteen-fifties will greatly help us to win peaceful coexistence in the nineteen-sixties.

There is no such thing as being entirely objective in national politics, since politics are always a matter of emotion, instinct, and to a lesser degree apparent self-interest. Hence, many of the judgments passed on Dulles as Secretary of State tend to be subjective, the more so because he was a man whose way of doing things stirred people almost as violently as what he did. For this reason there will certainly be no general agreement about him for a long time, at least until most of those are dead who lived through his era with him, rejoicing or suffering according to their predisposed points of view or the degree to which they felt they were directly affected by his actions. Somewhere, however, there is an objective truth in the eye of history and those without passion can already begin to discern its main outlines, if they are honest with themselves in defining what they are looking for. In this spirit, and this spirit alone, it is possible even to attempt a verdict on the political achievements of this remarkable man who stood at the center of power for six long years.

In his diplomacy as in his law, Dulles had an unusual capacity for making himself respected rather than liked. He managed on occasion to get himself disliked by Americans, distrusted by his allies, dreaded by the neutrals and denounced by the Communists all at the same time. All through his period of office, he was apt to be anathema to both the extreme Right and the not-so-extreme Left, sometimes to each together but nearly always to one or the other. He upset the complacent with his continual warnings about Communism just as he offended the progressive wishful thinker by the persistence of his methods for dealing with it. And it is this characteristic distinctiveness of his performance, as well as his own complex nature and personality, which accentuates the sense of disagreement about him.

Much of Dulles's own time and effort was spent in trying to appease the American Right, trying to carry with him as many right-wing Republicans as he could, without sacrificing his own views of letting the United States slip back towards isolationism. History may well judge that his greatest achievement was that he eased the Republican party through into the twentieth century; that he helped them to face up to the international realities of the modern world, so that American power might continuously sustain the West with the kind of leadership which, in the nature of things, could come from nowhere else. It is scarcely surprising, therefore, that Dulles is criticized most from the Left, by certain elements in the Democratic party, and above all by British and other European Socialists. Although this criticism takes many forms, the essence of it is that Dulles was too rigid to understand the way the world developed after Stalin died, that he was obsessed with military rather than political problems, that he was so much the prisoner of his own impulse to say "either/or" that he could not handle his allies. Dulles could not see, the Left argues, that neither capitalism nor perhaps Communism in its present form will triumph, in the sense that either finally swamps and eliminates the other. There is an enormous middle ground where peaceful coexistence must develop, where each side will come to terms with the other by economic competition, by diplomatic agreement, by the action of progressive world opinion, even, if you like, by a balance of power in all the senses of that term.

While the validity of much of this left-wing criticism has not been adequately appreciated in America, Dulles's difficulties with the Right have in general been very much underrated in Britain. No one could pretend that Dulles ever stood to the left of center. He was what he was by upbringing, experience, and inclination. But he certainly never shared the emotions of the diehards, the political backwoodsmen who made McCarthy possible. Dulles was too cosmopolitan, too astute, and too responsible to have anything but contempt for them, even though he felt he had to humor them and in his early days in office in 1953 he kept them very much in mind whenever he spoke in public. Dulles had thought so much about Communism before coming to power that inevitably he did not find it easy to change his main conclusions after Stalin died. He tended to go on believing too long, for instance, that inherent weaknesses in the Soviet system would lead to fundamental changes which it required only Western toughness to accelerate. But he did gradually shift his position on neutralism, partly as a result of long talks with Nehru; and in this respect, as in others, he ended by disavowing beliefs which he had started by holding as articles of faith. For him this was a radical process, and it went further than the stereotyped thinking of some of his left-wing critics normally gives him credit for.

Although Dulles may have been too optimistic about the internal weaknesses of both Russia and China, he was under no illusions about the strength and implacability of Communist determination to rule the world. And the fact that he saw that this aim had not changed by one iota, with the shift from Stalin to Khrushchev, continually nettled and sometimes exasperated those who wanted to believe otherwise. If Dulles was slow to adjust to the possibility that Communism and capitalism will have to learn to live together, since the only alternative in the nuclear age is to die together, he understood only too well that Khrushchev's smile can be far more deadly than Stalin's frown, that peaceful coexistence in Communist terms means a continual battle for total Communist victory, not the flaccid live-and-let-live of Western liberals and social democrats. Dulles was hated by the Western Left, because he made himself a standing reminder to them that Communist aims are indeed extremely unpleasant to contemplate, that appeasement and neo-Communism is no answer to them, and that day by day, week by week, month by month, and year by year, hundreds of thousands of dedicated, hard-working people on the Communist side are laboriously and soberly engaged in trying to secure the absolute destruction of Western society and the central heritage of Western civilization.

Dulles made a mistake, however, in concluding that, because Communism is wrong-headed and politically aggressive, all those who propagate it are also morally evil. By going too far he became unrealistic, and for a long time he made it virtually impossible for himself to have any genuine understanding of neutralism. When asked in a broadcast in October, 1958, within a few months of his death, whether he saw the struggle with Soviet Communism primarily as a moral struggle or primarily as a power political struggle, he replied quite honestly: "Primarily a moral struggle." Yet a moment later he showed some confusion of thought when he added:

> There is no dispute at all between the United States and the peoples of Russia. If only the government of Russia was interested in looking after the welfare of Russia and the people of Russia, we'd have a state of nontension right away.

As far as it goes, that is true enough. But if Dulles had really regarded the problem in this light, he would have found it less difficult to accept the halfway house of coexistence than his deep Presbyterian sense of morality did in fact permit him to do. While the Left hated him, that is to say, for apparently standing so far to the Right, there was some justice in their criticism that the factors which made them hate him were also factors which made him less good in dealing with Khrushchev than he would perhaps have been with Stalin.

In the same broadcast, it was typical of Dulles to describe with some justification how he himself differentiated between his basic strategy and the varying tactics he employed to attain his main objectives. He declared:

> In basic things I admit to being rigid, standing firm and standing solid. Now, as to the mechanics with which you carry things out, your day-to-day tactics, I do not think that the charge of rigidity can be made against me. Indeed ... oftentimes I am accused not of being rigid and consistent, but of being inconsistent. So I think that when it comes down to the details, to the tactics, where there is room for flexibility, I try to show it.

Inconsistency, of course, is not necessarily the same as moving in a political sense from Left to Right or Right to Left. But, while Dulles's multitude of inconsistencies did madden many of his friends as well as his opponents, this sense of irritation was certainly not confined to any one particular group in the political spectrum. In Britain, for instance, he managed to anger both the Conservative Right for being too anti-British and the Labour Left for being too anti-Communist.

Was Dulles inflexible? The answer depends on how you look at it. Although he is widely accused of rigidity, he is almost equally condemned for having reversed practically every policy he started out with; for reverting from liberation to containment; for wooing the neutrals when he had dismissed them as immoral; for intervening militarily in the Middle East, in spite of declaring that the whole area must be kept out of the cold war; for disengaging from the mainland of Asia after "unleashing" Chiang Kai-shek; and for saying that there are other means of uniting Germany than by free elections, having stood by free elections for over four years. These and other changes surely reflect, however, an ability to learn from experience rather than a determination to stand pat for fear of losing face. If, like the Bourbons, he had learned nothing and forgotten nothing, then indeed he could have been indicted for stupidity. But whatever Dulles was he was not stupid.

The fact is that, although the relative strength and influence of the United States undoubtedly declined during the period that he was Secretary of State, from 1953 to 1959, the tide was flowing so strongly against the West through most of that time that it is to his credit that the position at the end was no worse than it was. Admittedly he made an error in trying to assert that things were better than they were. But that is politics. By and large he was highly successful in checking the spread of Communism to even further countries in a troubled period, when strong nationalist movements were everywhere breaking the old order and turning it upside down. Although the prestige of the Soviet Union increased, as did that of Communist China, no single territory fell to a Communist takeover, not even in the end Syria or Iraq; North Vietnam and North Korea were lost well before Dulles assumed his responsibilities. His success in holding on might well not have been possible without, for instance, the conclusion of peace in Korea in 1953, the commitment of American military power behind various alliances in Asia in 1954, the entry of Germany into NATO in 1955, and the American-British intervention in Lebanon and Jordan in 1958. Such negative gains are unimpressive because they are open to argument, but history will at least show that Dulles's part in all of them was a major one and in some was decisive.

Part of the controversy about Dulles's handling of foreign policy is over the question how far he shaped events and how far they shaped him. Admittedly the main pattern of East-West relations in the postwar world was established, first, by the Truman Administration's policies of economic aid and military alliance in response to the threats of the Stalin era, and, secondly, by the growth of Soviet nuclear power and Khrushchev's intensification of the Communist drive among the uncommitted. Dulles, it is sometimes argued, initiated nothing of lasting importance and made no great decisions, merely extending policies which were already in being when he succeeded to power. But if this were true, how is it that he can also be so uniquely blamed for "massive retaliation" and "brinkmanship," for "pactomania" and even "agonizing reappraisal," indeed for the whole jargon of clichés which grew up in the vernacular of Washington while he was at the Department of State?

The truth is that these words were just as much oversimplifications as the accusations against him of lack of originality, rigidity and inertia. Dulles was no more shaped by events than Acheson was. It is given to very few to influence history decisively, and Dulles cannot lay claim to the stature of a Churchill. But it is highly unlikely that the same course would have been followed if he had not been there. Some would say that it would have been better, some worse. Given the growth of military and economic power on the Communist side, however, and the surge forward of nationalism in Asia and Africa, the West would have been far more likely to lose more ground than to gain it.

Dulles justifiably believed in the priority of military strength, as a basis without which nothing could be achieved by contact with the Communist bloc. Khrushchev's conversations with British ministers, when he visited London in 1956, showed how right this was by revealing his personal fascination with the whole problem of the realities of power. Khrushchev despised Eisenhower for not exercising the power that was his, just as much as he later despised de Gaulle for trying to exercise power which he did not have. Coexistence has, indeed, only come to be the word of the hour because the Communist world revolution has come up against nuclear military resistance which it cannot overwhelm by direct attack. Dulles, however, made it plain long before he came to office that a world which did not allow for change was a world that was doomed. His immense interest in Woodrow Wilson's failure over the League of Nations in 1919, and his own heartfelt participation in the founding of the United Nations in 1945, sprang largely from a desire to provide some constitutional means whereby the status quo could be altered, legally and with the consensus of world opinion behind it. Dulles gave much thought to the twin problems of deterrence and change, and it is worth quoting at some length from his views on these two subjects. On deterrence he once said:

> There is no illusion greater or more dangerous than that Soviet intentions can be deflected by persuasion.
> "We are living," says Lenin, "not merely in a state, but in a system of states, and the existence of the Soviet Republic side by side with imperialist states for a long time is unthinkable. One or the other must triumph in the end. . . ."
> The United States maintains at great expense a powerful

military establishment.... Our military goal is, as put by George Washington and repeatedly affirmed by Dwight D. Eisenhower, to have a respectable military posture—that is a military establishment that others will treat with respect. We maintain this military establishment out of concern for the effective defense of the principles upon which peace must be based. If there are some who do not accept those principles, they must at least accept the fact that violation of them, and resort to aggression, will be bitterly costly to themselves....

The fact that we are committed to a strong military establishment does not, however, mean that military considerations ought to dominate our foreign policy. We shall fail in our search for peace, security and justice unless our policies, in reality and also in appearance, give priority to the hopes and aspirations for peace of the peoples of the world.

Then, on peaceful change he declared:

A frequent cause of war has been the effort of satisfied peoples to identify peace as a perpetuation of the status quo. Change is the law of life, of international life as well as national and personal life. If we set up barriers to all change, we make it certain that there will be violent and explosive change....

What is vital ... is to recognize that the renunciation of force under these conditions implies not the maintenance of the status quo but peaceful change. World order cannot be assured merely by the elimination of violence. There must also be processes of peaceful change whereby justice manifests itself.

If Dulles comes out of the first test with credit, in that he held back the spread of Communism when world trends were against him, how does he do on the second, the question of actual negotiation with the Soviet Union? Could he have negotiated any kind of settlement with success? In arriving at an answer, it must first of all be recognized that Dulles failed entirely to achieve by negotiation, or by any other means, the famous roll-back of Communist power which his election speeches in 1952 demanded. And in so far as the liberation, say, of only some of the peoples under Communist rule in Eastern Europe could scarcely have been achieved without negotiation—except through war—he never even looked like getting down to successful negotiation of that kind. This, however, is not quite what people mean when they accuse Dulles of having failed to negotiate. If the Right saw talks with the Russians in terms of concessions on their part, the Left thought of any such contact more in terms of a settlement involving concessions by the West.

Hardly anyone outside the United States ever took Dulles's talk about liberation seriously, and probably only relatively few Americans did. As for Dulles himself, it is hard to be certain. Some of the otherwise most interesting comment about him since his death has treated his roll-back failure as if it were a central element in the success or failure of his policies as a whole. But the truth is not nearly as definite as that. Dulles could be quite a good politician when he chose, and before the Republican Convention in 1952 he was surprisingly frank in private about the possibilities of emphasizing the liberation of Eastern Europe as a plank in the Republican platform, in order to win the support of the considerable number of voters who either came of East European stock or were themselves first-generation immigrants from the countries of Eastern Europe. When asked how he would actually carry out the liberation of their homelands, Dulles dismissed that as a problem for the future. In a sense, of course, it was—as every politician knows who has ever said more at election time than he cared to remember after he was elected. In Dulles's case there was no doubt whatever that he ardently approved of liberation as an aim even if he did not believe that it could be achieved in the foreseeable future. Indeed he substituted liberation for containment as a description of American policy, partly because he wanted to condemn Acheson anyway, but partly also because he profoundly believed that it was immoral and anti-Christian to accept as a formal right the imposition of godless Communist rule on peoples who yearned to reject it.

All this, however, is a parallel issue to that of negotiation, and failure in the latter is developed into a charge against him with a venom which does not apply to the former. Dulles was concerned in three major periods of negotiation with the Russians: the Berlin Foreign Ministers' Conference of 1954, the Geneva Summit between Heads of Government in 1955, and the long interchange of letters and Notes between Washington and Moscow in 1958, first over the Middle East and later over Berlin. In all of these the record speaks for itself. Although Dulles was responsible for the foreign policy of the dominant partner in the Western alliance, he took his general stand in common with the British, the French, and above all the Germans. Herr Willy Brandt, the last official visitor Dulles ever received in the State Department before his final retirement and death, has lately confirmed in the name of the German Social Democrats much that Adenauer stood and fought for, and it is inconceivable that Dulles should ever have repudiated this crucial German attachment to the West for the sake of a theoretical agreement with the Russians, which neither he nor any serious Sovietologist could trust. He would have been quite wrong to do so. Dulles's own attitude was well expressed in an aside to one of his staff during the Berlin Conference, when he asked, after a bit of an argument, whether this official would be satisfied if Molotov suddenly dropped everything and accepted the whole Western proposal for free elections. The surprised official replied, "Why, yes," to which Dulles retorted: "Well, that's where you and I part company—because I wouldn't. There'd be a catch in it." As indeed there would have been.

There are four main reasons why no negotiated East-West settlement was in fact possible on any question of fundamental importance during the Dulles era. The first is that it takes two to reach any agreement, and, on the Soviet side, the years immediately following Stalin's death in 1953 were a period in which the struggle for leadership was still unresolved, with the natural consequence that no one in Moscow was in a position to come to such a settlement even if he had wanted to. It was not until April, 1958, almost exactly five years after Stalin, that Khrushchev assumed complete control in the Kremlin, and by then the Soviet Union was making such strides in so many different directions that any form of standstill looked totally unattractive from the Russian point of view.

Secondly, part of the basis for these Soviet gains was the fact that the power background had altered fundamentally. Russia's nuclear capacity was beginning to balance out America's, the process being accelerated by the arrival of guided missiles and the Soviet lead in their technical development. Russia's first atom bomb was exploded in 1949, its first hydrogen bomb in 1953. In 1955 Moscow began a crash program of long-range bomber construction, and in 1957 proved the accuracy of its new intercontinental missiles by putting the first space satellite into orbit. How can anyone claim objectively that, with this tremendous rise taking place in Soviet striking power, all Dulles had to do in order to reach a settlement was to offer American concessions and, even supposing he could have got Congress to support him, reduce American military readiness?

Such an attitude would rightly have been taken as a sign of weakness, and the Soviet leaders would have pursued their ultimate objectives even harder. That these have not changed, with or without Dulles, was shown by the implacable hostility to the West, and all it stands for, in the communiqué issued by the eighty-one world Communist Parties at the end of their Moscow conference in December, 1960. The truth was that, when the Americans had total nuclear supremacy, they could not use it to force the Russians to reach a peaceful settlement, and by the time they were losing it they no longer held the initiative.

Thirdly, of course, Dulles and the other Western leaders did try. They argued at very great length and in minute detail with the Russians, first, about the central problem of Germany and then, when both sides were quite clear that progress had been nil, about disarmament. Although Dulles was always a skeptic about the chances of success, those who worked with him are unanimous in their assertion that this did not prevent him from putting some of the hardest work of his career into these negotiations. Certainly, the efforts made by the United States to achieve at least a start in the field of disarmament or arms control has had the full force of self-interest as well as idealism behind it. And Dulles made his own particular contribution in this respect, by bringing Adenauer around to acknowledge that an effective disarmament agreement would reduce tension without reducing Western resolve.

Fourthly, as has already been suggested, Dulles was always a prisoner of Washington politics. Even to this day, observers in Britain seem to blind themselves to the strength and fury of the McCarthyites. Dulles entered the State Department when they were at their height, and, although he had the full support of Eisenhower, whose towering popularity was the only force in the country which could have faced up to McCarthyism, he and the President agreed to play their hand cautiously. And bitterly disappointing as it sometimes was to feel that the White House could have done more than it did to curtail the wilder extravaganzas of McCarthyism, the general line was certainly wise.

As Secretary of State Dulles had to watch his step more carefully than anyone else, a fact of which he was well aware. Already the storm had erupted in sheet lightning round the head of Dean Acheson. Acheson was cruelly excoriated for the deaths of thousands of Americans in Korea, because it was felt that a pronouncement of his had led Stalin to think that a Communist seizure of South Korea might not meet with opposition, let alone military intervention, from the United States. The position of Dulles should never indeed be assessed without thinking of Acheson too. Acheson was crucified with a hatred so lasting that some staunch Republicans declared astonishment on hearing that he was still in the United States when President Kennedy appointed him to look into NATO problems in 1961. "We thought he'd gone to Moscow long ago," they said. Dulles's relations with Congress were never as bad as Acheson's, in spite of all the moves at various times to get him sacked. He could not possibly have been branded as a fellow-traveler or even a Communist as Acheson sometimes was—however mad that may seem. Nevertheless, Dulles took the lessons of Acheson's experience as a text from which he never departed and, quite apart from his own views about negotiation with Soviet Communism, he felt bound very closely by the limitations of domestic American politics.

Dulles had good and valid reasons, therefore, for being able to claim at the end that, in terms of roll-back or negotiation, no one else could have done any better. But, while his record comes out of these two severe tests far better than is customarily believed, on the other major issue, his relations with the rest of the Western alliance, definite failure must be added to frustration. The name of John Foster Dulles is still used by some Europeans as a synonym for American non-co-operation, and certainly for Britain his time at the State Department included the nadir of Anglo-American relations in this century. The most important need of any alliance is mutual trust, and it was just this that Dulles was peculiarly ill-fitted to promote; indeed the warring elements in his own character often inspired him to destroy trust, even where it already existed.

The proper conduct of the Western alliance on the part of the United States was succinctly summed up by Dr. Adenauer, after returning to Bonn in April, 1961, from his first rather agonizing meeting with President Kennedy in Washington. "The United States, being the most powerful country," Adenauer declared, "is the natural leader in that alliance; among free people, however, leadership does not consist in the strongest member simply notifying his partners of his wishes, but in letting them know his intentions in good time and discussing those intentions with them." Dulles got off to a bad start in his relations with Western Europe by pressing too hard for the European Defense Community, and this established a precedent from which he never fully recovered. In *War or Peace* he had written: "Disunity alone prevents Western Europe from being a great—perhaps the greatest—distinctive area of spiritual, intellectual, economic and military force." And his determination to bang European heads together provoked very sharp reactions, above all in France where Bidault protested angrily with some justification that he was doing his best, and Michel Debré, later de Gaulle's prime minister, proclaimed in the Senate that Dulles's attitude constituted "intolerable interference in internal French affairs." One can sympathize profoundly with Dulles for his exasperation with the French as well as his disappointment over the EDC, but his method of using the big stick reflected a misplaced confidence in powers which he did not possess, and it was as unsuccessful as it was unwise.

One of Dulles's weaknesses was his own extremely suspicious nature. He often found it very difficult to trust even members of his own staff, let alone his allies. Before he first assumed office, for instance, he was uncertain how his relationship with Eisenhower would really work out, and, as a reinsurance policy, he welcomed the idea of having General Bedell Smith as his Under Secretary of State; he felt that Bedell Smith, one of the most upright men in Washington, who had been Eisenhower's chief staff officer in the war and was a close friend of the President-elect, would help to keep the line to the White House open if anything went wrong. But after Dulles had approached Bedell Smith someone suggested that Bedell Smith might be disloyal, that the boot might be on the other foot, that he might in fact act more as a watchdog for the President than an apologist for the Secretary of State. Dulles was consumed with doubt and delayed a long time before confirming the appointment. To this day it is not absolutely clear what Bedell Smith's role was. But it is on record that he rendered Dulles the kind of loyal and reliable service which anyone who knew him knew he would do. Dulles almost never reversed the decisions Bedell Smith made when the Secretary of State was out of Washington, a position which was by no means the case later on with Herbert Hoover, Jr.

Internationally an atmosphere of distrust similarly pervaded the Western alliance all too often while Dulles was in power. Although his allies recognized that in him they were dealing with a man of substance, he did not always manage to give them any impression that loyalty to the alliance was of much account. Because he did not seem to trust them, they did not trust him. Even Adenauer, his faithful friend, who was more suspicious by nature than Dulles himself, had at least two periods of acute anxiety when he felt that Washington was letting him down. Dulles, it is true, rushed over to reassure him in September, 1954, and also made the last painful journey in February, 1959. But Dulles never did have enough tact, or show enough understanding of other people's points of view, to keep the alliance on a steady course in spite of these squalls. Although he had a passionate desire both to promote European unity and to bind the West solidly together against Communism, he all too frequently failed to inspire confidence in his leadership. And in this respect a great opportunity was lost, since he had many of the qualities which in a simpler man might well have rallied everyone behind him.

On the personal plane, a good many people felt that it was peculiarly baffling dealing with Dulles, since you never knew from his deadpan expression what impression you might be making on him, or sometimes whether he had even taken in what you were saying. And in the field of policy, Dulles himself was always schizophrenic about colonialism. He could never bring himself, that is, to give his soul to the Europeans, because he was always looking over his shoulder at what he imagined would be the effect on Asia and Africa. Apart from his own characteristically American feelings about colonialism, he believed that the United States would inevitably lose out to the Soviet Union if it became associated too closely with the wicked European colonial powers. He seldom seemed to allow for the possibility that his own apparent conviction of American superiority, and the behavior of some of his officials in the more primitive countries, was ironically branding the United States itself as the worst imperialist of all. And he probably would not have believed anyone who pointed out to him that in some of their former colonial territories the French and British had become a good deal more welcome and popular than Americans. Dulles, in fact, never really admitted to himself that the concept of Commonwealth was taking over from colonialism, and he appeared blind to the evolution of ideas in Britain which was bringing this about.

As has been said already in these pages, Dulles was not exactly anti-British. But he was always particularly suspicious of them, often profoundly irritated by them, and sometimes despairingly contemptuous of them. The British were apt to be the last people whose views he wished to hear. In fact nearly every British paper sent to the State Department was doubly scrutinized; it was gone through with a fine-toothed comb to discover the supposed catch in it. As a result the British themselves occasionally felt bound to resort to nondiplomatic methods for getting their views across to the Secretary of State; one was to plant them on American secret service agents in the knowledge that they would then get back to Allen Dulles, who would pass them on to his brother, who would take them at their face value. But this was hardly the spirit in which an alliance ought to work.

The fact that Dulles was often much affected by the impression made on him by individuals was unfortunately important in assessing his relations with his allies. Adenauer appealed to him as clear, courageous, and resourceful. The leaders of the French Fourth Republic struck him as slippery and unreliable. With the British he was dominated for much of the time by his friction with Eden. What he blamed the British for in general was partly that they failed to make the most of themselves. Although he never forgot, or allowed the British to forget, that the main power in the West

had long since passed to America from Britain, he still respected
British organizing ability. But he became, in consequence, more
contemptuous and disappointed when they failed to show it. He
despised them for this far more than he despised the French for
what he regarded as their natural ineptitude. He felt that the
trouble with the British was partly the weakness of individuals and
partly the lack of punch in British policy. He was especially irritated
by their constant claim to "special relations" with America. It was
not that he totally denied such a position, though his own views
were far less positive on the point than theirs were. What really
annoyed him was that he heard them talk in this way, and yet,
when he needed them, he felt that they did nothing but snap at his
heels. Thus the British attitude to China was a constant irritation
to him, the more so because he personally felt very strongly about
China, and because he considered that the British had been much
too facile in washing their hands of the Far East.

The tragedy of Dulles, however, was the extent to which he
allowed this kind of thinking to affect his handling of his allies.
Of course they were often maddening. Of course he was sometimes
justified even in his worst criticism about them. Of course he could
not help but feel that, with the power of America behind him,
he could and should try to force the pace of agreement along his
own lines. But the end result was unfortunately the proof that he
was unable to rise above his own nature. While Dulles was in
office, the Western alliance was seldom solidly united and sometimes in open disarray. Unity was naturally more difficult to
inspire as the direct threat of Soviet military action was relaxed.
But this has always been the case ever since the war, and it demanded even more of American leadership than did the anxious
days of Stalin, in which the North Atlantic Treaty had originally
been conceived and signed. It was this leadership which Dulles
failed so signally to give, and the fact that he did not succeed in
rallying the West is the one cardinal indictment against him. In
spite of his own deep thinking about Communism, his immense
output of words, his absolute determination and his razor-sharp
intellect, he somehow never managed to sustain the enthusiasm
or confidence of allied statesmen for long enough to lift the alliance

as a whole into the new dimension which America, quite as much as its allies, so badly needed.

Parallel to Dulles's failure with his allies was his failure with the neutrals. This was a special pity, in that it was so unnecessary and by no means followed from his inability to galvanize the alliance. Indeed, in so far as anticolonialism was one of the permanently nagging reasons for his never going quite all the way with the British, the French, the Belgians, or the Dutch, he ought to have won a certain amount of kudos with the neutrals. But unfortunately he managed to make the worst of both worlds by condemning the immorality of neutralism with equal vehemence. What he lost on the swings, he thus singularly did not gain on the roundabouts. Nor, looked at the other way around, did his condemnation of neutrality ever gain him the sympathy which might have been expected from some of his allies, since most of them understood and appreciated the problem and outlook of the uncommitted much better than he did; the close and cordial relations between Britain and India was the outstanding example.

As a Presbyterian elder, Dulles in his unbending way took a puritanical view of both colonialism and neutralism, and even the greater sin of Communism could not make him condone these lesser ends, at least until late on in his career. Indeed, the very depth of his feelings about the world threat of Communism made the other two seem worse, not better. He felt that the colonialist powers were unwittingly *selling the pass* to Communism, and he simply could not conceive at first how any well-informed neutrals could possibly feel as they did. On the one hand, it seemed to escape him almost entirely that orthodox Communist tactics are to infiltrate colonial territories immediately *after* they have just won their independence, and not before, counting on this moment of weakness to yield maximum success, particularly if independence has come before the territory might be ready for it, as happened in the Congo. And, on the other hand, he took a long time to understand the genuine dilemma of those neutrals, who simply believed that the safeguarding of their own newly won independence depended on their keeping clear of both the cold war blocs.

Dulles held more power in his own hands than any modern American except Franklin Roosevelt. This could never have happened under a strong President, and, while he was very fortunate in his relationship with Dwight Eisenhower, the weakness of the White House allowed the flaws in his own character to show up more than they might otherwise have done. Dulles's isolation was also accentuated by his manner of working and the absence of any close confidant at his own level. He formulated policy by writing most of the briefs himself. He used his staff to give him the facts in a junior capacity and, although he did circulate drafts within the Department, there was not much give or compromise in discussion about them. Thus, consultations of this kind tended to polish rather than to change the views he already held.

In the last analysis, however, Dulles stands or falls by the whole general concept on which these views were based, and the fact that he did not succeed in providing the actual leadership required does not invalidate the quality of his own ideas or the sincerity with which he tried to implement them. In spite of his faults he did in fact provide a rock in the river of Communism, on top of which anyone who cared to do so could climb. Moreover, in some ways, the kind of obstinate determination and utter conviction which he displayed was just what was needed in the unsettled period after Stalin died. It was no bad thing at all that American policy should be obdurate, tough, and uncompromising in that stage of the fight.

Dulles was always rightly worried by the shortness of Western memories, by what he regarded as a fundamental misunderstanding in much of the West about ultimate Communist aims, by people's willingness in fact to let their wishes father their thoughts. He abhorred the ready drift into accepting Communism as just another form of government, and the easy hope that tactical concessions by the West would change the long-term strategic intention of Soviet Communism to dominate Asia, Africa, Europe, and eventually America too. He was convinced that every Communist success only bolstered the appetite for more. At the same time, he was entirely sincere in recognizing that no peace could be kept if the two sides refused to talk with one another; and he favored patient negotiation on particular subjects, however long this might take and however disappointing the early results. The only stipulation on which he absolutely insisted was that, since truth and lies are equal as a means of achieving Communist ends, no agreement must be concluded which depended merely on the Soviet word. There must always be a built-in means of checking words by deeds.

This, then, was what John Foster Dulles stood for and fought for. And, in that he himself was slow to change, he acted as a kind of sheet anchor for Western policy. But towards the end even he was moving, just as Khrushchev was moving, towards recognizing the principle of balance on which the world of the nineteen-sixties was beginning to be built. In Dulles's era, however, none of this was yet quite settled. It began with overwhelming American power and ended with the uncertainties of the missile gap. His own strength was that he never failed to remain true to his principles as he himself saw them, and the proof that he succeeded lay in the bitter respect which his name provoked in Moscow. Dulles's positive and uncompromising faith was indeed his strongest asset, and it may be summed up in words which he himself has chosen for an inscription on the walls of the future John Foster Dulles Library of Diplomatic History at Princeton University:

> This nation of ours is not merely a self-serving society but was founded with a mission to help build a world where liberty and justice would prevail.
> Love of peace by itself has never been sufficient to deter war. There can never in the long run be real peace unless there is justice and law and the will and the capacity to use force to punish an aggressor. The task of winning peace and its necessary component, justice, is one which demands our finest effort.

Dulles might have been more appreciated if he had not lived in the age of the airplane and the telephone. Without his aircraft he could not have attempted a fraction of the personal diplomacy which was his own special hallmark. And without the telephone or telegraph or radio what he said in one place would not have been so instantaneously repeated in every other. A hundred and fifty years ago he would certainly have been regarded as a great man. His moral qualities, his toughness, his self-assurance, his energy, and his great intellectual capacity would all have constituted a complex of power and rectitude, which neither his friends nor his enemies could have denigrated. But in the modern world even these are not enough. Greatness requires at least some instinct for the feelings and aspirations of others, a humanity, a sensitivity which Dulles lacked. And while it would be wrong to deny that his constant traveling contributed to the furthering of the policies which he supported, or that the wider publicity given to his words by mass communication increased their impact, this was not quite the point. Indeed, these journeys sometimes did him harm, in conveying an unfortunate but understandable impression of aloofness and vanity, and the reports of his speeches helped the world's press to fasten onto a handful of catch phrases for which, taken out of context, they pilloried him. In spite of Dulles's laudable determination to meet those with whom he was dealing and to speak to the world at large, neither his personal presence nor his choice of words were always his strongest points. The final verdict must therefore be somewhat ironical. Although he traveled and spoke so much, his actual policies and the concepts that lay behind them deserve a higher place in the judgment of history than the methods by which he carried them out.

Index

8